A Short Guide to Writing About Psychology

THE SHORT GUIDE SERIES

Under the Editorship of
SYLVAN BARNET
MARCIA STUBBS

A Short Guide to Writing About Art, Eighth Edition
by SYLVAN BARNET

A Short Guide to Writing About Biology, Sixth Edition
by JAN A. PECHENIK

A Short Guide to Writing About Chemistry, Second Edition
by HERBERT BEALL and JOHN TRIMBUR

A Short Guide to Writing About Film, Sixth Edition
by TIMOTHY CORRIGAN

A Short Guide to Writing About History, Sixth Edition
by RICHARD MARIUS and MELVIN E. PAGE

A Short Guide to Writing About Literature, Tenth Edition
by SYLVAN BARNET and WILLIAM E. CAIN

A Short Guide to Writing About Music, Second Edition
by JONATHAN D. BELLMAN

A Short Guide to Writing About Psychology, Second Edition
by DANA S. DUNN

A Short Guide to Writing About Science
by DAVID PORUSH

A Short Guide to Writing About Social Science, Fourth Edition
by LEE J. CUBA

A Short Guide to Writing About Psychology

SECOND EDITION

DANA S. DUNN
Moravian College

PEARSON
Longman

New York   Boston   San Francisco
London   Toronto   Sydney   Tokyo   Singapore   Madrid
Mexico City   Munich   Paris   Cape Town   Hong Kong   Montreal

Senior Vice President and Publisher: Joseph Opiela
Senior Acquisitions Editor: Katherine Meisenheimer
Executive Marketing Manager: Thomas DeMarco
Production Manager: Savoula Amanatidis
Project Coordination, Text Design, and Electronic Page Makeup:
GGS Information Services, Inc.
Cover Design Manager: Nancy Danahy
Cover Images: Copyright © Stockbyte/Getty and Photodisc/Getty
Image Montage: Nancy Danahy
Senior Manufacturing Buyer: Roy Pickering, Jr.
Printer and Binder: R. R. Donnelley and Sons Company—Harrisonburg
Cover Printer: The Lehigh Press, Inc.

For permission to use copyrighted material, grateful acknowledgment is made to
the copyright holders on pp. 223–225, which are hereby made part of this
copyright page.

Library of Congress Cataloging-in-Publication Data

Dunn, Dana.
   A short guide to writing about psychology/Dana S. Dunn. — 2nd ed.
     p. cm. — (The short guide series)
   Includes bibliographical references and index.
   ISBN 0-205-52156-8
   1. Psychology—Authorship. 2. Report writing. I. Title.
   BF76.8.D86 2007
   808'.06615—dc22

                           2007014459

Please visit us at **http://www.ablongman.com**

ISBN-13: 978-0-205-52156-2
ISBN-10: 0-205-52156-8

   4 5 6 7 8 9 10—DOH—10 09 08

For Jacob Kennedy and Hannah Yvonne,
lovers of words

Contents

Preface

How people act, think, and feel is fascinating. Behavior attracts our attention. We wonder about people's intentions and about the actions of others. In fact, we can't help ourselves. In this sense, everyone is a psychologist.

Professional psychologists, however, study behavior more formally and critically than casual observers. Some formulate psychological theories about people or animals and test them in experiments. Others practice therapy, administer surveys, or do field research. Psychologists routinely share their findings, most often in writing. Whether as teachers, researchers, practitioners, or students, psychologists are writers. Indeed, the ability to convey scientific ideas in clear, concise prose is virtually a prerequisite for contributing to the discipline.

A Short Guide to Writing About Psychology, Second Edition, is designed to help undergraduate students of psychology master the whys and wherefores of writing in psychology. By reading this book, students will acomplish many goals:

- Search and read the psychological literature using library and online sources.
- Select and refine paper topics.
- Outline, draft, write, and revise papers.
- Learn to use APA style.
- Plan and execute different types of writing in psychology.
- Give and receive feedback on their writing.
- Present research findings in oral as well as written forms.
- Create tables, figures, and poster presentations.

Each chapter contains practical advice on writing, illustrative examples, and helpful checklists and flowcharts, and it concludes with active learning exercises for students to do as class assignments or on their own.

The book is timely and up-to-date. It is a brief, handy book for writing APA-style papers using the current edition of the *Publication Manual of the American Psychological Association* (APA, 2001). The book can be a main text for a course on writing in psychology. *A Short Guide to Writing About Psychology* can also be a supplementary text in other psychology courses, including research methods, various experimental or laboratory courses, and advanced topical offerings. Instructors can use the book for in-class discussion or assign it for out-of-class reading. When a course is over, the book will be a reference for writing psychology papers in the future; without practice, the details of APA style fade from memory, but they are readily retrievable herein.

NEW TO THIS EDITION

The second edition of *A Short Guide to Writing About Psychology* contains some new features designed to help students write about psychology and psychological research. Reader comments regarding the first edition led to several helpful additions to the book including:

- Comments on expressive and transactional forms of student writing.
- Additional types of student writing activities, such as letters, one-minute papers, and blogs.
- An overview of the writing process from beginning to end (see Table 4.1).
- Structured guidelines for writing an Abstract (see Table 5.1).
- Additional examples of electronic (online) citations.
- A helpful discussion on how best to use electronic media for giving PowerPoint presentations (see Table 10.4).

ACKNOWLEDGMENTS

I thank friends, colleagues, and peer reviewers who read and commented on the manuscript: Robert T. Brill, Stacey B. Zaremba, and Michelle Schmidt, all of Moravian College; Bonnie Falla and Linda LaPointe, Reference Librarians, Reeves Library; Randolph A. Smith, Ouachita Baptist University; Perilou Goddard, Northern Kentucky University; Ken Weaver, Emporia State University; David Anderson, Allegheny College; Nancy Digdon, Grant MacEwan College; Marianna Footo Linz, Marshall University; Graham E. Higgs, Columbia College; Lynn Pardie, University of Illinois at Springfield. Jackie Giaquinto offered her usual, unfailing help, and Jenn

Boberg diligently tracked down library references for me. Christine Puk-szyn, Jaime Marks, and Sarah Dougherty graciously allowed me to use their writing samples. I am grateful to Professor Joel Wingard, who sparked my interest in teaching writing some years ago. I thank my wife, editor Sarah Sacks Dunn, for her support and good humor. I also want to thank past and present students from whom I learned to teach writing. I am also grateful to the Moravian College Faculty Development and Research Committee for a 2001 summer stipend enabling me to begin this book and to the college for granting me a sabbatical leave during spring 2002 to complete it.

The Short Guide series editors, Sylvan Barnet and Marcia Stubbs, pro-vided encouragement, support, and thoughtful comments early on. The Longman editorial team, old friends and new, guided the book from con-cept to completion. I want to thank Senior Acquisitions Editor Katherine Meisenheimer, Senior Vice President and Publisher Joe Opiela, and Assis-tant Editor Rebecca Gilpin for their helpful suggestions on the second edition. Thanks to my students, Todd Bennett, Laura Sahlender, and Sarah Hopkins, for suggesting changes and improvements. I appreciate the recommended changes to the first edition offered by the following review-ers: Nancy Alvarado, California State Polytechnic University, Pomona; Perilou Goddard, Northern Kentucky University; Jean W. Hunt, University of the Cumberlands; Anne Moyer, SUNY at Stony Brook; Carrie Switzer, University of Illinois at Springfield. I complied as best I could; any errors in judgment are mine alone. Most of the work on this second edition was completed in the Outer Banks of North Carolina in August 2006. I thank my hosts, Larry and Ruth Sacks, for their hospitality.

I welcome comments from readers and instructors who use this book. The life so short, the craft so long to learn.

DANA S. DUNN
Moravian College
dunn@moravian.edu

*A Short Guide to Writing
About Psychology*

1

WRITING ABOUT PSYCHOLOGY

Nulla dies sine linea.

—Roman adage

The late B. F. Skinner (1981), a distinguished psychologist and prolific author, obeyed this ancient proverb about writing: "No day without a line." He wrote daily. Good writing is a learned skill, one taking practice, effort, and desire. To write well, you must write often. Of course, writing is neither the easiest nor the most popular activity. In the words of two good writing teachers, "The best writers struggle" (Elbow & Belanoff, 1995, p. 3). Yet I believe that anyone can become a better writer and that, in fact, everyone should strive to do so—the outcome is well worth the effort. I hope you will not struggle much, but becoming a good writer in psychology, another discipline, or in general depends upon committing time and energy to the task. There are tried-and-true ways to improve writing skills, and we will look at many of them in this book.

WRITING AS A PROCESS

Learning to write is a process, a series of actions that leads to an outcome, a personal expression of a belief, an idea, or an observation. But good writing can follow only from good thinking. A writer learning about prejudice and social intolerance (e.g., Fiske, 2002; Oskamp, 2000), for example, would pursue this interest through four distinct parts of the writing process in psychology (adapted from Reich, 2001):

- **Inquiry**—identifying a topic that is interesting and worth writing about, such as psychological research on prejudice and stereotyping.
- **Discovery**—searching the psychological literature to find scholarship on bias and intergroup conflict, taking notes and making observations about important findings.

- **Evaluation**—reading, thinking, and reacting to previous research on prejudice and discrimination, possibly conducting independent research to verify, challenge, or extend conclusions on intergroup conflict.
- **Communication**—drafting, writing, and revising a paper or a presentation on the causes and consequences of prejudice, stereotyping, and conflict.

These parts of the writing process appear to be linear, a sequence of steps, but don't be fooled. Writing is a recursive process that loops forward and back. Once you begin writing, for example, your topic may need to be refined further. A topic shift will necessitate more library research, which means more reading. Additional reading will influence your subsequent writing, and so on.

This book provides guidance for all the steps in the writing process. Most psychologists follow this overall process when writing about their research because they have already accepted and internalized beliefs that are valued by the discipline. What about students like you? Besides the academic aspects of the writing process, why should you want to write and write well?

Why Write, Anyway?

When students are asked to explain why writing is an important activity, their typical responses reflect concern with improving grades, performing well on essay exams, and the like. Writing well is portrayed as leading to tangible rewards, notably good grades, but this is a rather shortsighted goal. Why write? There are two main reasons to take pen—or more likely, word processor—to paper: self-understanding and shared understanding.

WRITING FOR SELF-UNDERSTANDING

By self-understanding, I mean that writing is an excellent way for you to really grapple with your ideas in meaningful, exciting ways. Socrates admonished his pupils, saying, "Know thyself"—a tall order for anyone to carry out, though writing is a good way to try. Writing about your beliefs, hopes, even dreams, or in a more practical vein, about the nature of some psychological effect for a project or term paper is one way to really explore your interpretation of ideas. There is no better way to truly understand a concept, argument, issue, or controversy than to write about it. Writing about almost anything forces you to think critically, to identify and define key points, problems, and questions. Your vague feelings and beliefs must be sorted through, critically examined, and then shaped into language representing what you really believe to be true. Putting things into your own words is a powerful way to understand challenging concepts, as well as a means to challenge concepts.

When you write to understand yourself, you are engaging in *expressive writing*. Expressive writing is usually a private, continuous form of writing that allows a writer to explore whatever thoughts and feelings flow from his or her stream of consciousness. The freewheeling nature of expressive writing allows writers an opportunity to create new ideas, to integrate what they already know with what they are thinking about, reading, or currently discussing.

Sometimes, of course, reaching understanding about something—a complex theory or some surprising fact, for instance—takes time. Writing about something you do not understand or are unsure about can help you to reach some tentative conclusions about it. Graham Wallas (1926, p. 106) put it best when he repeated an overheard remark, "How do I know what I think until I see what I say?" Saying something in writing is a form of *doing*, of making sense out of our thoughts and experiences by putting them on paper. Many psychologists who write agree with this assessment, and more than a few developed insights into behavior by writing about it first. Some even claim that personal difficulties, anxieties, and traumas can be constructively dealt with through writing (Pennebaker, 1997; Pennebaker & Graybeal, 2001; see also Lepore & Smyth, 2002). Self-understanding, then, is very much a goal of writing.

A Simple Exercise

If you want to really appreciate the fact that writing is a form of self-understanding and a good way to learn, try the following simple exercise (adapted from Scott, Koch, Scott, & Garrison, 1999). Rewrite your notes from a class, but don't copy them verbatim. Instead, put the ideas, especially any abstract concepts and accompanying definitions, into your own words. Ideally, select a tough class, one where the course material is demanding and your notes are lengthy. As you rewrite the notes, add in transitional information—connecting phrases such as *and, but, however, because of, in order that*—to develop and supplement the examples drawn from lectures and discussions (Scott et al., 1999). Your reward for this extra work will be coherent narratives that "fill in the blanks" or expand on ideas that, though mentioned in class, were not always adequately captured in your notes. Chances are good that the course material will become clearer and more memorable to you due to the combined verbal processes of thinking, reading, and writing entailed in reworking the notes. If such rewriting becomes an active routine, I guarantee that you will learn, recall, and apply course material more readily than if you just passively review your original notes.

WRITING FOR SHARED UNDERSTANDING

Besides wanting to understand ourselves, we all have a need to be understood by others. When we write for others in order to share our views on some issue or idea, we are performing *transactional writing*—writing that establishes a transaction, a relationship between the writer and the reader. Writers write to persuade, to teach, to explore, to argue or to debate a question, or to propose an explanation, among other purposes. Readers, too, approach transactional writing with a purpose, usually to learn something new, and they often respond to it. Their responses take the form of classroom discussion, public letters to the editor, or the crafting of their own position papers or the writing of books.

Transactional writing is important for psychology and would-be psychologists: Our ideas lead nowhere if they are isolated from the reactions of others. Writing is a formalized way of seeking shared understanding from other people; they may not always agree with us, but their comments, criticisms, suggestions, and arguments can refine our own thinking and writing. As a student of psychology, your observations about behavior matter as much as those of professional psychologists, but only if you are capable of communicating them effectively to others. If you want to be understood by your professors as well as your peers, being able to write down your ideas in a straightforward manner matters a great deal. When you offer a novel interpretation of some behavior, you must be able to clearly explain how and why your claims should matter to others.

One more thing: Seeking shared understanding involves identifying and addressing an audience. To whom are you writing? Many students will answer, "to the instructor, the person grading me." This answer is reasonable, but not entirely true. Ideally you are writing to and for anyone interested in behavior, including those who are not yet aware that psychology is a rich and interesting field. If you try to write only for your instructor, you will probably end up speaking in code by relying on psychology's professional jargon. Shared understanding is inhibited when too much technical language (e.g., "dissonant cognitions" instead of "conflicted thoughts") is used. Jargon is often necessary for scientific writing (Bem, 2000), but you must always strive for clarity by defining any terminology in your own words.

I hope you will learn that writing about psychology is important for another reason besides disclosing insights about mind and behavior. Being able to write well is an end in itself, an ability that will serve you well whatever you do in the future.

FORMS OF WRITING IN PSYCHOLOGY

When psychologists write, their work appears in one of several common forms. **Empirical reports,** which are based on observation and experimentation, are the most typical form of writing. Such reports describe the theory, methodology, results, and implications of original research. A perceptual psychologist could describe and demonstrate the conditions under which people are susceptible to a particular visual illusion. When you read an article in a psychology journal, chances are very good that it describes some empirical study.

Eventually, all the empirical research concerning a psychological question is evaluated, extended, or revised. **Literature reviews** thematically organize existing empirical studies and identify important themes and results within the psychological literature, and highlight what is known about the topic and what questions remain to be answered. A personality psychologist could review the extensive literature on self-esteem and its consequences for psychosocial well-being. A particular type of review paper, a **meta-analysis**, uses an advanced statistical technique to summarize the effects of independent studies examining the same psychological phenomenon.

Occasionally a psychologist will write a theory paper instead of a review. **Theory papers** discuss the origins of and advances in some topical area of research while offering a new way of thinking about or interpreting a behavior of interest (i.e., a new theory for explaining self-esteem). Whereas reviews condense knowledge, theoretical papers present fresh perspectives and frameworks.

Not all writing in psychology concerns theory development or summary reviews of empirical studies. Some psychologists also write about innovations in the methodologies used to examine psychological phenomena. In order to adequately study some behavior, for example, researchers must be trained in appropriate techniques. New procedures for tackling research problems are written up as **methodological papers**. For example, such a paper might describe a new, simple way to randomly assign research participants to multiple conditions in a memory paradigm. Some professionals also write **case studies**—thorough, detailed histories of individual lives or the experiences of organizations. These studies are meant to illustrate problems, turning points, or changes encountered by a person or group. Case studies are often dramatic, illustrating unusual psychological effects or behaviors. A clinical psychologist could describe the therapeutic experience of a client experiencing the early onset of Alzheimer's disease, for example. Unlike the majority of empirical studies, however, case studies do not aspire to documenting shared effects or common trends in behavior. Instead, they focus on the unique, not the general.

Student Papers

What about student papers in psychology? Students are often asked to conduct experiments or other types of empirical investigations. Following data collection and analysis, a research report is written (see page 82 in Chapter 5). **Research reports** compare obtained results with those described in published research. Writing research reports enables students to interpret their findings in light of existing studies. To examine how perceived stress alters the frequency of recalled dreams, student researchers might compare the sleep habits of college students with those of working adults. **Lab reports** are usually shorter versions of research reports. Finally, advanced students might conduct independent research, writing very long and detailed research reports commonly known as **honors theses**.

Research reports are not the only form of student writing in psychology. Students also write literature reviews, **term papers** that impose a coherent structure on collections of previously published articles (see page 117 in Chapter 5). Data gathered by other researchers are examined critically in light of a student's own thesis or an organizing theme assigned by an instructor. Term papers are often expository, designed to explain what is known about a topic (e.g., the effects of divorce and remarriage on the social development of young children). Shorter pieces of writing designed to put forth a point of view on a psychological topic, challenge conventional wisdom, or debate issues are variously referred to as **position** or **reaction papers**. Reaction papers require a student to make a persuasive argument, one designed to convince readers to think about and possibly accept a novel position (e.g., day care has beneficial effects on the intellectual development of children from low-income families). Other methods are available for students to react to what they learn. Describing your understanding of a complex or controversial issue to a peer by writing a **letter** is a fine way to get a sense of your feelings about it. By their nature, letters compel us to simplify issues for others by stating them in plain terms. Some students find they can identify key ideas by writing a **one-minute paper** at the end of class (Cross & Angelo, 1988). One-minute papers are usually assigned by instructors who use the last few minutes of a class to assess student learning via focused prompts—for example, What is the most important thing you learned in today's discussion? What issue are you still uncertain of following today's class? (see Cuseo, 2005, for other prompts). Finally, the Internet spawned what we know as **blogs**, the short name for **weblogs**, which are personal, online journals written by people who intentionally share their thoughts and feelings with users on the Internet. Students use blogs to keep friends and acquaintances up to date on their lives and experiences. Some academics, including psychologists, use blogs to discuss research issues. Writing in **daily journals** is another way for students to reflect on what they learn in a class and to apply it to their own experiences. Theory papers (see page 118 in Chapter 5), as well as methodological writings and case studies, are sometimes assigned to students as well.

INTRODUCING APA STYLE

Many psychologists and students of the discipline write their papers using a style promoted by the American Psychological Association (APA). This style—commonly referred to as "APA style"—is described in the *Publication Manual of the American Psychological Association* (APA, 2001). APA-style papers rely on a standard organization, one prescribing where and how particular information should be placed for maximum benefit to readers. If you have ever read an article in a psychology journal, chances are it was written in APA style. Not all psychology papers are written using APA style, but the style is so commonplace in the discipline that any student of psychology should be familiar with it.

APA style will be presented throughout this book. You may already be familiar with some other popular styles for writing, such as Modern Language Association (MLA) style (Gibaldi, 2003) or that promoted by the University of Chicago Press (2003). Similar to these other approaches, APA style is simply another means to organize and present research. Originally developed in 1928, APA style now enjoys widespread use by researchers, writers, editors, publishers, and students in and outside of psychology. Besides the psychological community, APA style is often the

WRITER'S GUIDEPOST 1.1
Save Everything That Goes into Writing a Paper

Considerable time and effort goes into any piece of writing. Besides the finished work, most writers are left with false starts, including discarded opening sentences, unused references, extraneous paragraphs, notes scribbled on scraps of paper, even full-blown and detailed outlines. Often, a few good but forgotten ideas are a part of the stack of papers that led up to the final draft.

I believe that you should save at least some, possibly all, of the materials that went into your paper. Why? In the first place, some instructors like to see all the "routes," including any dead ends, that you took in writing a paper. Portfolios are perfect for filing away the extra stuff. In any case, many writing instructors want to see evidence portraying the development of your ideas. Better writers usually have a sizable stack of leftover materials, whereas the weaker ones just have a single draft, maybe a forlorn outline. Writing is work, after all, so it isn't too difficult to pick out the hard workers from the rest of the pack.

Second, it is often the case that unused material can be recycled for another purpose. The sentence that did not make it into one paper may be perfect for another; the same goes for those unused references or neglected paragraphs you worked on so hard. Save them because they may come in handy later. I regularly find a use for "leftover" material. You can, too. Remember, effective recycling is also a creative process.

choice for writing in business, criminology, economics, nursing, social work, and sociology (APA, 2001).

PLANNING YOUR WRITING: TIMING IS EVERYTHING

Writing almost anything requires a degree of planning. You can plan your writing whether you have a little or a lot of available time. Let's consider how to effectively use available time for answering a test question or writing a paper.

Answering a Test Question

The **essay question** is one form of writing encountered by virtually all students of psychology. Essay questions, which appear on timed tests, are "open ended," meaning that you must create an answer based upon your own opinions and what you know about a topic. Here is an example of a short essay question, one requiring a definition and brief description:

What is "working memory"?

Essay questions requiring longer answers contain more than one question or require responses with multiple parts. Here is an example:

Freud's theory of psychosexual development and personality hinges on the importance of the so-called Oedipal conflict. Describe this conflict and comment on whether it is consciously perceived. Is the nature of the conflict the same for boys and girls? Why or why not?

This question requires more than just defining a term or two. A theory must be explained and supported by examples, and a distinction between the possible experiences of boys and girls must be established.

Students often tackle an essay question by reading it quickly and then immediately writing down whatever comes to mind. A quality answer is sacrificed in the rush to get something, anything, down on paper. Without a plan, students tend to write too much and miss the main point of an essay question.

How should you go about answering an essay question in a planned but timely manner? Here are some steps to follow:

1. Put down your pencil and read the essay question.
2. Take a few minutes to think about what the question is specifically asking you to do. Should you provide facts, opinions, or both?
3. Take another minute, pick up your pencil, and jot down a brief outline of your answer to the question somewhere on the exam (see page 58 in Chapter 4 for advice on writing outlines). What are the main points you want to make? Use supporting material from class lectures, discussions, and readings, and whenever possible, provide concrete examples to illustrate your points.
4. Begin to write now. Follow your outline and write legibly. You will not get credit for a great answer that is unreadable.
5. Reread the question and your answer: Did you address every point raised by the question? If not, revise your answer.
6. Don't overwrite. Most teachers prefer a well-thought-out answer that gets to the heart of a question.

Table 1.1. A Timeline for Writing Papers in Psychology

Date paper assigned: _____

Activity	Time Estimate (hours, days)	Date Completed
1. Identify a topic (page 13, Chapter 2)	_____	_____
2. Do library research (page 20, Chapter 2)	_____	_____
3. Do background reading (page 39, Chapter 3)	_____	_____
4. Design study and collect data	_____	_____
5. Write first draft of paper (Chapters 4 and 5)	_____	_____
- Draft the Results section (page 98, Chapter 5; Chapter 6)	_____	_____
- Create tables or figures (Chapter 8)	_____	_____
6. Format references (page 141, Chapter 7)	_____	_____
7. Proofread draft (page 178, Chapter 9)	_____	_____
8. Seek instructor/peer feedback (Chapter 3)	_____	_____
9. Revise draft (Chapters 4 and 5)	_____	_____
10. Proofread revised draft (page 181, Chapter 9)	_____	_____

OTHER ACTIVITIES

_____	_____	_____
_____	_____	_____

Submission date for final paper draft:

_____

Optional: Present paper (see pages 186–199 in Chapter 10)

Source: Adapted from Dana S. Dunn, The Practical Researcher: A Student Guide to Conducting Psychological Research, Table 1.3, p. 24, McGraw-Hill, 1999. Copyright © 1999 by Dana Dunn. Reprinted with permission of The McGraw-Hill Companies, Inc.

Writing a Paper

Papers take more time to write than do answers to essay questions, but writing a psychology paper involves more than just making time for writing. You must take into account the time needed for library work and for doing an experiment, as well as for drafting, writing, and revising your paper. There is much to do, so you must know at the start how much time you have to complete everything. Organization is essential for bigger writing projects; doing them well involves planning specific activities and allotting the time needed to complete them.

A Basic Timeline

Table 1.1 (opposite page) illustrates a basic timeline you can use for writing any paper. The basic activities involved in doing most writing projects in psychology are noted in the table's first column. You can always skip any activity that is not relevant for the paper you are writing. Where appropriate, the table references, discussions, and tips provided elsewhere in this book (e.g., guidance regarding topic selection—activity 1—is found on page 13 in Chapter 2). Activity 5 also has subsections appropriate for writing APA-style empirical papers. Any additional activities unique to your writing project can be added in under "Other Activities."

To use Table 1.1 effectively, begin by jotting down the date a paper is assigned (see the top of the table) and then the due date for the final paper (see the last entry line in the table). Mentally working backward from the due date, how much time do you have to write the paper? By parceling out the available time, you will need to estimate how much time each activity will take, recording these educated guesses in the second column of Table 1.1. Will your proposed schedule work or are changes necessary to meet the deadline? Adjusting a writing schedule is normal; some activities go more quickly than anticipated, others drag on. Finally, the third column in Table 1.1 provides a place to write down the date that each activity was accomplished so that you can monitor your progress.

WRITING HABITS

As we close this first chapter, there is one more thing to consider in your development as a writer: Where will you write? I recommend picking someplace that is quiet, a place where you can work for uninterrupted periods of time. Try to make it a place where all you do is write—do your studying and socializing elsewhere. It should be well lit, comfortable but not plush, and entirely free of distractions (no radio, stereo, television, or phone). For instance, I usually write at home with my back to a window so that my attention is not drawn to pretty scenery or any people walking by. We already know that Skinner the behaviorist wrote each day. He did so very early in the morning in the basement office of his Cambridge home. Novelist Stephen King recently wrote a book at a small desk adjacent to his laundry room (King, 2000). Ernest Hemingway composed no more than three pages a day, and he did so while standing. William Faulkner wrote the novel *The Sound and the Fury* while tending a turbine engine. He claimed that the low, constant humming helped him think. Quirks aside, the message is clear: Pick a place to write that works for you.

Besides selecting the right spot to write, some rituals usually have to be observed once you are there. Some writers sharpen pencils, draft exclusively on legal pads, or work at the same time (and for a fixed period) each and every day. My ritual is simple: I prefer to write in the morning, so I invariably have a cup of strong coffee within reach. Do whatever you need to do to be comfortable and to get started writing. As you establish a routine in your chosen space, you will find that getting started writing becomes easier and easier.

One more thing: Good writers write all the time. Frequency—how often you take pen to paper or crank up your word processor—matters as much or perhaps more than where you write. In fact, shorter but more frequent writing sessions are likely to lead to greater productivity when it comes to creating prose. The more often you write, the easier writing will become for you. Make writing a daily habit. Remember: No day without a line.

EXERCISES

1. Using your own words, rewrite notes from a recent class. Add transitional phrases to develop and supplement class examples of important concepts.
2. Locate a quiet place for daily writing. While working there, write a one-paragraph description of your usual writing habits. Write a second paragraph describing the habits you want to develop.
3. Determine whether how often you write improves your fluency. After each of your classes, spend 15 minutes writing about what you learned and what you still want to know about that day's topic. Assess your prose production after a week or so of this drill.

2

SEARCHING THE PSYCHOLOGICAL LITERATURE

Psychology is a vast discipline. What will you write about? Selecting a research topic in psychology is an important step in your development as a writer. You must choose and research a topic before your writing can begin in earnest. Unless an instructor assigns a topic, you are probably free to pursue almost anything that interests you. How will you choose a topic worthy of being written up in a paper? How will you find useful information about your topic?

SELECTING A RESEARCH TOPIC

You must begin at the beginning and select something that fascinates you. Sometimes the choice is easy or obvious; other times you will need some inspiration. Proven sources for research paper topics include the following:

- **Coursework.** Past or present courses are a great source of topic ideas. Look at a course syllabus or glance through a textbook's table of contents: What did you most enjoy reading about? What was challenging or puzzling to you? What topic are you looking forward to learning about? What issues have received insufficient research attention?
- **Your instructor.** Course instructors are excellent sources of paper ideas. Approach your instructor, asking if he or she can recommend some important questions from one of psychology's subfields.
- **Happenstance.** What is currently happening in your life or on your campus that might well serve as a paper topic? Are there any local or national controversies that could be refined into a paper topic or that have a pronounced psychological component? One teacher–researcher recommends taking a walk around your campus to observe behavior as it happens (Martin, 1996). What sorts

13

of questions occur to you while observing others? Can one of these idle speculations be converted into a paper topic?

- **Classic research.** One pedagogical tradition involves having students conceptually replicate a classic piece of research. The term *conceptual replication* refers to repeating all the steps in an original study while making some changes, adding a twist to the effort in order to ask a new question. Identify some classic experiments within a subfield and consider how the original hypothesis could be altered to ask something different about behavior.

- **Extending existing research.** The psychological literature is full of current research that can be taken in new directions. Go to the periodicals section of your library and glance through the tables of contents of a few psychology journals. What articles attract your attention? Read the abstracts from these articles. How can you extend their current findings?

- **Paradoxes.** What psychological events contradict your expectations or beliefs about how things should be? Can you identify any daily experiences that defy expectations or lead to surprising conclusions? Harvard University social psychologist Daniel Wegner (1989), for example, based a research program on the ironic persistence of unwanted thoughts. He empirically investigated a story told about the Russian author Leo Tolstoy. Tolstoy challenged his brother to actively try to *not* think of a white bear (try this simple thought experiment yourself). The lad could not do so, and he repeatedly experienced "white bear thoughts" while actively trying not to think of the bears (to not think about something, of course, you must first think about it). Attempts at such mental control inevitably backfire, an irony that highlights the information-processing limitations people possess. There are no doubt many as yet unstudied paradoxes in our thought and behavior—can you think of any that might make a reasonable research project?

- **Yourself.** You are a great source of ideas. What have you been thinking about lately? Each day, many thoughts occur to you as questions, and quite a few deal with your own behavior ("Why did I do that, anyway?") or the actions of others ("Why does Phil always get so boisterous in crowds?"). What are your current fears, hopes, and dreams, for instance, and could any of them be developed into a paper topic?

Some other suggestions for identifying paper topics are provided in Table 2.1.

Table 2.1. Other Sources for Developing Paper Topics in Psychology

1. Attend a psychology colloquium, listening carefully to the speaker for things you find intriguing, disbelieve, do not understand, or want to learn more about.

2. Hold a brainstorming session with peers to generate a list of possible topics.

3. Try freewriting as a way to identify possible paper topics (see page 56 in Chapter 4).

4. Search for specialized Internet Listserv mailing lists or chatrooms where you can "lurk" in order to find popular as well as contested issues in your area of interest.

5. Look through reference works dealing with psychology and the social sciences (see Tables 2.3 and 2.4).

6. Interview a psychologist about his or her research and teaching interests.

7. Look over review questions in a psychology textbook.

8. Go to a library's psychology section and see if any titles intrigue you.

9. Examine *PsycCRITIQUES*, the searchable database of book reviews from *Contemporary Psychology—the APA Review of Books*.

10. Search the References sections of articles, books, or textbooks for interesting titles or topics.

11. Review a book's subject index to locate keywords or terms suggesting possible topics.

12. Examine the published proceedings from the most recent APA or APS conventions.

13. Locate and read the blogs of some psychologists for ideas.

14. Examine newspaper headlines for current events or controversies that might be recycled into paper topics.

Maintaining a Research Notebook

As you mull over possible topics, I have one very helpful suggestion for you: *Obtain a research notebook*. Carry this notebook with you at all times so that you can jot down research or writing ideas as they come to you. Keep it by your bedside. As soon as you think of a possible topic, write it in your notebook. A research notebook contains the following:

- Topic ideas and observations
- Questions about your topic
- Findings from the psychological literature

- Your search history of terms (i.e., to avoid wasting time revisiting found references and Web sites)
- Reactions to and comments about research findings
- Miscellaneous musings on writing and psychology

You can turn your research notebook into a **dialectical notebook** by writing your entries concerning readings, class notes, or passing ideas onto right-hand pages only. Later, after some reflection, you can reread the "right-side" entries and jot down your reactions to them on the blank left-side pages. A dialectical process is a careful analysis of reasoning regarding a topic based on a critical discussion, one that often involves highlighting the conflicts that lie between opposing points of view. In essence, by recording your reactions to your earlier thoughts on the left-hand pages, you are engaging in an analytical discussion with yourself. These "self-discussion" reactions can be a great source of paper topics based on your insights into human behavior (Dunn, in preparation).

Some students prefer to maintain a research notebook in a computer file (Hult, 1996), a less portable option unless you have a laptop, a PDA (Personal Digital Assistant), or computer access in the library. Whichever notebook option you choose, be sure to date *all* your entries in order to track the evolution of your thinking about a topic (Thaiss & Sanford, 2000). When you refine the topic further, take notes on the process of narrowing it down into a manageable scope. What changes will you introduce to the original idea? How did the original idea change, develop, or mature over time?

A research notebook will prove invaluable, too, for doing library research. It will serve as a convenient repository for your reactions to readings and an accurate record of source names, call numbers, and the like. But we are getting ahead of ourselves—let's get back to the process of narrowing down a research topic, an activity that will go much more smoothly if you rely on a research notebook.

Narrowing Your Focus

Once you identify a general topical area for your paper, you will need to narrow your focus into a specific question or a small set of questions. There are two parts to this process. The first is identifying the topical question you will research in the psychological literature. Your goal is to locate prior research pertaining to the topic, to read it, and to determine what results will prove useful for your paper. The second part of the process—translating your topic into an empirically testable question or hypothesis—is beyond the scope of this book. There are a variety of sources available that can help you achieve this second goal once the first is underway (e.g., Dunn, 1999; Martin, 1996; Rosnow & Rosenthal, 1996; Shaughnessy & Zechmeister, 1997).

One way to narrow a topic is to summarize it using a phrase or sentence. When a topic is *too broad*, it can be summarized in only a few words (e.g., "short-term memory"). An entire area of the memory literature from cognitive psychology is devoted to short-term memory studies, so further refinement of the topic is needed. To write a reasonable paper, some aspect of short-term memory research must be identified. Ideally, the first pass at narrowing a topic will result in a descriptive sentence, one containing a bit more depth and detail than a broad phrase. Here are three examples of possible paper topics following this winnowing process:

- Current perspectives on short-term memory capacity differ concerning how much information can be retained and in what form it is stored.
- There is an ongoing debate concerning whether short-term memory and working memory are actually the same or distinct parts of memory.
- Perhaps short-term memory or working memory is actually a part of, rather than separate from, long-term memory.

In each case, a descriptive sentence indicates that the scope of the originally broad topic is now more focused.

A second strategy for narrowing a topic involves naming it and then completing some sentence "prompts" (Booth, Colomb, & Williams, 1995).[1] To name a topic, describe it in a sentence by filling in the blank stems of prompts like these:

I am interested in studying _____.

I am working on _____.

I am going to conduct research on _____.

I am fascinated by _____.

I believe that a change in _____ causes a change in _____.

By finishing any of these prompts, you begin to identify a research problem worth investigating. The sentences based on these prompts can

---

[1]Adapted material from Booth, Colomb, and Williams, *The Craft of Research*, pp. 43–44, The University of Chicago Press, 1995. © 1995 by The University of Chicago. All rights reserved. Reprinted with permission.

be written down in your research notebook. If these prompts seem too open-ended, try a more structured approach by filling in the blanks in this sentence stem (Booth et al., 1995, p. 43):

> I am interested in studying _____ because I
>   want to find out who/what/when/where/whether/why/how
>   _____.

Answering the additional stem by addressing who, what, when, and so on specifies the motivation for your interest. Responding to this second question type also develops questions about your intended topic. What makes a particular psychological issue worth researching? What, precisely, do you want to know?

Once the question begins to take shape, go to the library to begin searching for journal articles, books, and book chapters that are relevant to it. As you read and take notes on the literature (see page 45 in Chapter 3) and begin to understand the real nature of your question, you should develop a rationale for the research. Identifying this foundation is important once your research is underway because your readers will benefit from your deeper understanding of the topic. You can return to this prompt later to see how your rationale is unfolding (from Booth et al., 1995, p. 44):

> I am studying _____ in order to find out
>   how/why/what _____.

Ideally, you will eventually write a topic, question, and rationale similar to these in your research notebook:

Topic: I am studying how information is stored in long-term memory.

Question: I am studying how information is stored in long-term memory because I want to learn about the relative effectiveness of different rehearsal strategies.

Rationale: I am studying how information is stored in long-term memory in order to create an experiment designed to promote effective learning of new information.

We have moved from a broad topic to a narrow question, one that culminates in the rationale for a specific experiment. We can now add a fourth sentence prompt, one highlighting the topic's significance (Booth et al., 1995):

Significance: I am studying how information is stored in long-term memory so that I can demonstrate how research results have practical applications to everyday life.

Any topic and research question can be examined on a variety of levels. Such depth usually indicates that the chosen topic is a good one and that all levels will be represented in your writing.

PROCESS OVERVIEW: SEARCHING THE PSYCHOLOGICAL LITERATURE

Once you have a research topic and a focused question, develop a plan for searching for related, published research. Most search plans include six basic stages, which are summarized in Table 2.2. I will provide a brief overview of the stages here and then spend the remainder of the chapter discussing them.

The first thing you need to do is go to your institution's library (see stage 1 in Table 2.2) to look up your topic in a general reference book dealing with psychology (see stage 2). Such books are usually found in the reference area of the library. With some search terms in hand, you can look through your library's online catalog for any books pertaining to your topic (see stage 3), which is then followed by a computerized literature

---

Table 2.2. Searching the Psychological Literature in Stages

Stage 1—Go to the library.

Stage 2—Find entries about your topic in general references in psychology (see Table 2.3). Read and make note of any key terms from the entries. Examine the bibliography of each entry for useful citations. Consult other social science resources (see Table 2.4).

Stage 3—Search the library's online catalog, making certain to consult the *Library of Congress Subject Headings*. Repeat stage 3 until your search is exhausted.

Stage 4—Employ retained index terms in either a computerized search using a database in psychology (e.g., PsycINFO). Repeat stage 4 until a sufficient number of appropriate references are located.

Stage 5—Search other sources, including any available databases (online and CD-ROM) and the Internet. Additional local sources (e.g., textbooks) should also be consulted. Repeat stage 5 until this search is exhausted.

Stage 6—Collect all references (i.e., obtain copies of articles, check out books), read, and take notes (see Chapter 3) in preparation for (any) empirical work and the writing of a research paper. If necessary, go back to stage 1 and begin again.

---

search or one done manually (see stage 4). Once books, chapters, and journal articles are found in stages 3 and 4, you proceed to stage 5 where additional searching for sources in the library, on CD-ROMs, or on the Internet occurs. Stage 6 involves tracking down all the references you find, then reading and taking notes on them as you begin to design your research project and to write a paper about it.

DOING LIBRARY RESEARCH

The purpose of library research is to locate as much up-to-date information about a topic as you can. Academic libraries—those found primarily on college or university campuses—contain books, journals and other periodicals, reference works, electronic databases, print indexes, encyclopedias and dictionaries, government documents, and special collections of materials. Your institution's library, for example, is apt to maintain a collection of books and journals that support the social and behavioral sciences, including the psychology major. In this section, we discuss research tools available in the library and how to use them in a literature search. Keep in mind that we are following the search stages outlined in Table 2.2.

A Brief Guide to Reference Works in Psychology

The best place to start a library search is with background material pertaining to a topic. Unless you are already familiar with your research topic, a general source is better than a specific one. Go to the reference area of your institution's library. Once there, locate the general psychological references and look up the topic in one or more of them. Table 2.3 is a listing of some common reference works in psychology that are routinely found in academic libraries. Keep in mind that your institution may have others worth consulting; space is provided at the bottom of Table 2.3 for you to record additional resources.

Once you look through the psychological references shown in Table 2.3, check some other social–behavioral science resources often found in reference areas to make sure you are not missing anything related to your topic. Several of these additional sources are identified in Table 2.4. If you identify others, make note of them for future reference by writing their names at the bottom of Table 2.4.

There is one cardinal rule for working with reference sources in the reference area of your library: Befriend a reference librarian. Reference

WRITER'S GUIDEPOST 2.1
Sources as Resources

There are three basic kinds of sources found and used in literature searches:

- **Primary sources**—The "raw," or original, materials used in writing psychology papers constitute primary sources, and they come in two types. Any data you collect in an experiment or other empirical investigation, as well as your findings, can be considered a primary source. An APA-style paper you write describing your hypothesis, empirical investigation, and results is also a primary source. Within the psychological literature, journal articles, books, book chapters, or other empirical reports are also primary sources when they are written by investigator–authors who actually conducted the research.

- **Secondary sources**—In psychology, secondary sources are usually commentaries or reviews that incorporate primary sources for some purpose, such as extending a theory in a new direction or placing it within a novel framework. Articles found in journals such as *Psychological Review* or *Psychological Bulletin* are secondary sources, as are chapters in books such as the *Annual Review of Psychology*. Books that seek to organize the literature and that are written for a professional audience are usually secondary sources as well.

- **Tertiary sources**—A tertiary source is usually based on information drawn from secondary sources, and it is written for a popular or lay audience of readers. The goal of a tertiary source is to share but not evaluate information, so most publications falling within this category simply restate what is already known. Psychological topics appearing in encyclopedias, dictionaries, or handbooks are usually tertiary sources. In general, tertiary sources are *not* used in APA-style papers.

librarians are trained to perform effective searches of the literature pertaining to virtually any topic you can name. These professionals are experts who can quickly and efficiently help you locate information to build a quality paper, but best of all, they love to answer difficult questions!

Table 2.3. Some Useful Reference Works in Psychology

Benner, D. G. (Ed.). (1985). *Baker encyclopedia of psychology*. Grand Rapids, MI: Baker Book House.

Bruno, F. J. (1988). *Dictionary of key words in psychology*. London: Routledge & Kegan Paul.

Chaplin, J. P. (1985). *Dictionary of psychology* (2nd ed.). New York: Dell.

Corsini, R. J. (Ed.). (2001). *The Corsini encyclopedia of psychology and human behavior* (3rd ed.). New York: Wiley. (4 volumes).

Eysenck, H. J., Arnold, W., & Meili, R. (Eds.). (1979). *Encyclopedia of psychology*. New York: The Seabury Press.

Goldenson, R. M. (1970). *Encyclopedia of human behavior*. New York: Doubleday. (2 volumes).

Gregory, R. L. (Ed.). (1987). *The Oxford companion to the mind*. New York: Oxford University Press.

Harré, R., & Lamb, R. (Eds.). (1983). *Encyclopedic dictionary of psychology*. Oxford: Basil Blackwell.

Kazdin, A. (Ed.). (2000). *Encyclopedia of psychology*. Washington, DC: American Psychological Association. (8 volumes).

Magill, F. N. (Ed.). (1993). *Survey of social science: Psychology series*. Pasadena, CA: Salem Press. (6 volumes).

Ramachandran, V. S. (Ed.). (1994). *Encyclopedia of human behavior*. San Diego, CA: Academic Press. (4 volumes).

Reed, J. G., & Baxter, P. M. (1992). *Library use: A handbook for psychology* (2nd ed.). Washington, DC: American Psychological Association.

Wolman, B. B. (Ed.). (1977). *International encyclopedia of psychiatry, psychology, psychoanalysis, and neurology*. New York: Van Nostrand Reinhold Company. (12 volumes).

Wolman, B. B. (Ed.). (1989). *Dictionary of behavioral science* (2nd ed.). New York: Van Nostrand Reinhold Company.

OTHER REFERENCES AVAILABLE IN YOUR LIBRARY:

_____

_____

_____

Table 2.4. Other Abstract and Index References

BIOSIS—Indexes the life sciences and biomedical research around the world. Allows users to access abstracts, journals, and books, as well as information about scientific meetings and patents.

Current Contents—A weekly publication listing the tables of contents for many recently published scientific journals. An online database is available, allowing users to search by key terms, author names, and article or journal titles.

Educational Resources Information Center (ERIC)—Indexes journal articles and an array of unpublished resources covering education, evaluation research, teaching, testing, counseling, and developmental issues. ERIC is available online and on microfiche.

MEDLINE/PubMed—An online service containing references and abstracts from 4,500 biomedical journals. Links to additional scientific sites and resources are available.

Social Science Citation Index (SSCI)—A published and online index of the research literature found in the social–behavioral sciences and related disciplines.

Social Sciences Index (SSI)—An index of major journals in psychology and the social–behavioral sciences, including anthropology, law and criminology, and political science, among many others. SSI is available in print and online.

Social Work Abstracts—A publication (with quarterly CD-ROM version) containing abstracts drawn from published research in counseling issues and social work.

Sociological Abstracts—Printed and online versions contain abstracts from journals in sociology and related fields of study, including social psychology, education, demography, and race relations.

OTHER USEFUL REFERENCES YOU IDENTIFY:

_____

_____

_____

Reference librarians cannot offer you their expertise, however, unless you consult them directly. Some students are too bashful to ask for help; others assume they can find what they need on their own. I never consider doing any serious search of the psychological literature without asking one of my college's reference librarians for assistance. They have saved me from making foolish mistakes or missing good references on many occasions. Your school's reference specialists can do the same for you, *but you must ask for their assistance*. Better yet, make an appointment so that a librarian can show you all the psychological references found in your school's library.

Using Online Catalogs

Beyond reference works, the other main library resource is the **online catalog**—an electronic database that allows users to search a library's entire contents either on-site or from a remote location. Such searches can be initiated by using book titles, author names, keywords, and subject headings (searching by combinations of the latter two are also possible). In addition to books, a library's periodical holdings, government documents, and any special collections are often accessible through the online catalog. If you are not already familiar with the scope of your institution's online catalog, find out when bibliographic instruction is offered and sign up. Naturally, approaching a librarian and asking for assistance is a quicker solution.

When searching the online catalog for books related to your topic (stage 3 in Table 2.2), begin by locating any books by researchers whose names you already know. Following a search by author names, try searching by book titles, then by keywords. Online catalogs are often hooked up to printers, enabling you to print out author names and book titles as you find them. You should then identify relevant subject headings by looking up your topic in the *Library of Congress Subject Headings* (*LCSH*; Library of Congress, 2005), a five-volume guidebook often stationed adjacent to the online catalog. The *LCSH* enables you to locate a topic alphabetically and then find more specific or related search terms. Any subject headings you do find can be entered into the online catalog.

When locating a book using the online catalog, the information on the computer screen is very similar to that found on traditional card catalog entries. The book's title and author will appear, as will the work's **call number**, a series of letters and numbers determined by the Library of Congress. The call number denotes the book's location in the library's stacks. The online screen for a book will also show the date of publication, the publisher's name, and the city where the latter is located. Subject keywords indicating how the book is cataloged are also there. Most online catalogs also provide a description of the book, including its physical dimensions, number of pages, and whether any illustrations or indexes are included.

Once you print out all the book titles and call numbers you find, head to the stacks and determine what works should be checked out for use in your paper. Locating a given book is easy because a unique call number is printed at the bottom of its spine. Books are grouped and shelved in the library according to their call numbers. One other important note: Most online catalogs will let you know if a book is shelved and available, or if it is checked out. Save yourself some frustration by checking a book's status before going to the stacks to retrieve it.

Psychology Online: Using Databases

Students strongly approve of learning to use electronic information resources for their research and writing (Schultz & Salomon, 1990; see also Cameron & Hart, 1992; Joswick, 1994). You will, too. A thorough and quick search of the psychological literature can be achieved using computerized databases (see stage 4 in Table 2.2). Chief among these is *PsycINFO*. This database contains up-to-date citations and abstracts from journals, books, and book chapters in psychology, as well as in education, nursing, psychiatry, and sociology. PsycINFO, which is updated monthly, is an online database, meaning that it is accessible through an Internet connection. The PsycINFO database comprises psychological works dating from 1887 up to the present. If your institution has a connection to PsycINFO, it is probably available over the campus network. Some workstations with database access are set up so that users can read and then print out available abstracts and citation information; others have a helpful feature indicating whether your library has an identified periodical in its collection.

CONSIDERING A TUTORIAL BEFORE SEARCHING

Searching PsycINFO is easy because the instructions are user friendly and the software is extremely flexible. To save time and effort in the long run, though, consider making an appointment with a reference librarian for a tutorial before accessing the database (Joswick, 1994). I recommend this because studies demonstrate that between 30% and 50% of all users of electronic databases miss relevant materials (Sewell & Teitelbaum, 1986; see also Kirby & Miller, 1985; Nash & Wilson, 1991). PsycINFO is searchable using subject headings, author names, and keywords or phrases. Obviously, any of the keywords and search headings found in the earlier stages of your literature search should be used here.

I will warn you that PsycINFO is so efficient it is easy to be overwhelmed by the number of citations even one keyword or subject heading can uncover. PsycINFO covers the whole world, so you may want to limit your search to English publications (a feature allows users to look by a specified language). On occasion, however, you may come up with too few or even no references. Do not conclude that there is no litera-ture on your topic; rather, assume that you are not yet using the right search terms. As you gain experience with the database, you will learn to properly broaden or narrow your search.

BASIC SEARCHING USING PsycINFO

As a database, PsycINFO is accessible through most college and uni-versity libraries. Although readily available, different campuses rely on different software platforms to support the database. Thus, instructions for access and use on one campus can be quite different on another. As always, the best advice is to visit your institution's library and to speak to a reference librarian for guidance about learning to use the database.

Once you are in the PsycINFO database, the best way to begin to search for research material is by entering subject terms related to your topic. Subject terms are often the key words found in research publications on a topic. Some subject terms can be found in text books, for example, or in any of the sources or reference works referred to earlier in this chapter (see Tables 2.1, 2.3, and 2.4). Alternatively, PsycINFO has a feature allowing a user to ask for possible search terms. For example, I decided to locate possible search terms for the word *stress*, so I typed in that word, clicked on a box marked "Sug-gested Subject Terms," and then clicked "enter." A second later the screen was filled with a list of 20 search terms related to stress (e.g., occupational stress, chronic stress, financial strain), any one of which can then be entered into the PsycINFO database to narrow the search for relevant sources.

I decided to search for publications on *social stress*, so I clicked on the advanced search function in PsycINFO, typed the subject term into the search box, selected "Subjects" as a search field (an optional step), and clicked the "search" button. A moment later, my search revealed over 1200 citations related to the subject of *social stress*. Nat-urally, that's far too many citations to look through, so some further winnowing is needed. Fortunately, additional features in PsycINFO allow a user to narrow the search still further (e.g., social stress and major depression), including selecting only peer reviewed journals, fo-cusing on year(s) of publication, and so on. PsycINFO is very flexible and user friendly. In a short period of time, you will narrow in on only those references relevant to your research topic. Once you do, PsycINFO allows you to examine detailed citations containing Abstracts or other short source summaries, as well as helpful bibliographic information (e.g., journal name, volume number, year of publication) that will help you locate or order copies. Once you become familiar with PsycINFO, you will be able to search the psychological literature with ease (for further ideas on searching electronic databases, see McCarthy & Pusateri, 2006).

SEARCHING THE INTERNET

The worlds of education and research in psychology changed forever when we entered the Internet age. The word *Internet* refers to a world-wide network of interconnected computers. This network began as an experiment in information sharing between a small group of universities, and it has blossomed into today's "information superhighway." Virtually anything you want to know is only a few key taps and "mouse-clicks" away. Thus, what information you search for and how you search for it becomes a very important consideration in your research and writing.

Searching the Internet for information is relatively easy because of various **search engines**—advanced software designed to search and locate organized Web sites or the mere occurrence of particular words and phrases entered by a user. There are hundreds of millions of Web sites housed in computers around the world; so much information, so little time to sort through it all. A process-of-elimination approach—that is, eliminating irrelevant information while retaining useful information—drives many information searches on the Internet. To find what you need, you must follow some basic rules of navigation or risk frustration and the loss of valuable research time.

To navigate the Internet using the graphical interfaces (the images that remain more or less constant on computer screens), users must type in a URL (uniform resource locator). A URL is the unique address for a given Web site. Once typed into an address bar, the address quickly takes you to the specified site. The components of a typical URL are shown in Figure 2.1. If an incorrect address is entered, you will be unable to go to a given Web site. It is often important, too, to take notice of whether the components of a URL contain capital letters. In general, capitalization or some correct mix of upper- and lowercase letters is required for the path to a document or the file name of the document.

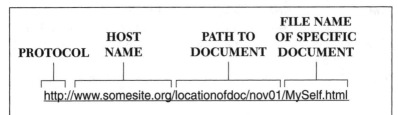

Protocol—Specifies the method by which your Internet software exchanges information with a site (usually not sensitive to capitalization).
Host name—Names the server where the files of interest are stored, often the name of an organization or an individual's home page (usually not sensitive to capitalization).
Path to document and file name of specific document—Leads a user to some specific document of interest (often sensitive to capitalization so that specific combinations of upper- and/or lowercase letters may need to be used).

Figure 2.1. Components in a typical URL.

When relying on the Internet for writing, follow these two guidelines (APA, 2001, p. 269):

- When citing Internet addresses, be accurate so that interested readers can visit them.
- When using Internet materials, reference specific documents, not just home pages or Web sites (see Figure 2.1). Reader effort to locate materials should be minimal.

Search and Metasearch

Imagine that you type in the URL for a search engine (a list of popular search engines is provided at the top of Table 2.5), and then enter the word *psychology* into the area designated for initiating a search. What would you find? You would find entirely too much information, as I did after conceiving this simple demonstration. My search engine immediately identified six subcategories (organized collections of sites covering links to cognitive psychology, social psychology, etc.) and 187,000,000 individual Web sites (as of this writing) featuring the word *psychology* in some way. An important, if obvious, conclusion is that specific search terms yield more useful information than broad ones. No one with a paper to write is going to visit even a fraction of those Web sites! To improve your research efficiency, begin searching by specific terms within a category.

A second alternative is to rely on a metasearch engine, a search engine that hunts through other search engines and organized catalogs of Web sites for you. Metasearch engines enable a user to conduct systematic, specialized information searches using deliberately narrow terms. Such searches are sometimes successful (Barker, 2001). Some popular metasearch engines and their URLs are shown in Table 2.5.

Table 2.5. Some Search Engines and Important Internet Sites in Psychology

SOME POPULAR SEARCH ENGINES

Altavista—*www.altavista.com*	Microsoft Network—*www.search.msn.com*
AOL—*www.search.aol.com*	Netscape—*www.search.netscape.com*
Excite—*www.excite.com*	Web Crawler—*www.webcrawler.com*
Google—*www.google.com*	Yahoo!—*www.yahoo.com*
Lycos—*www.lycos.com*	

SOME METASEARCH ENGINES

Copernic—*www.copernic.com*	Ixquick—*www.ixquick.com*
Dogpile—*www.dogpile.com*	Metacrawler—*www.metacrawler.com*

IMPORTANT INTERNET SITES IN PSYCHOLOGY

American Psychological Association—*www.apa.org*

American Psychological Association's search engine—*www.psychcrawler.com*

Association for Psychological Science—*www.psychologicalscience.org*

HELPFUL INTERNET ADDRESSES YOU FIND:

_____	_____
_____	_____
_____	_____
_____	_____

Note: All of the above URLs are preceded by "http://".

There are countless helpful Web sites devoted to psychology or particular areas of the field—far too many for me to discuss in this chapter. A few good sites are noted at the bottom of Table 2.5. Space is provided for you to record the URLs of any good sites that you find as you research a topic or write about it.

Other Internet Resources

Besides search engines and specialized Web sites, there are three other basic Internet resources for writers: online journals, electronic mailing lists, and e-mail.

ONLINE JOURNALS

Increasingly, online journals are appearing in a variety of academic disciplines, including psychology. An online, academic journal generally operates like a printed journal, except that its contents are always "virtual," accessible only on the Internet rather than in a bound, physical periodical. Although the reputation of online journals is rising, writers must still be careful when it comes to using online articles as sources of ideas or supporting citations. Wise writers determine whether a given online journal is as rigorous as many printed journals. Are all electronic submissions subject to peer review? Most submissions probably are, but if the site you are using does not require this, find a different online journal. Is there an editorial board and if so, are its members recognized experts in psychology? This concern can be quickly addressed by examining the journal's Web site. A more worrisome concern is the security of online publications (Pechenik, 2001). Can readers and writers be certain that virtual papers contain original data that have not been tampered with (before or after virtual publication) or that submissions will always be retained in some permanent (and permanently accessible) research archive? Web-savvy editors can probably offer some guarantees about these issues, but again, you must be confident about a source before using it.

Many printed psychological journals are now available online as well, which can be a real help to student writers who do not have access to a printed copy of a journal. If your library does not subscribe to a particular journal, see if it is accessible online.

ELECTRONIC MAILING LISTS

Discussions of psychological issues often take place on the Internet in Listserv[2] electronic mailing lists. Each of these lists is a discussion group devoted to some topic. There are electronic discussions going on all the time concerning almost any topic you can imagine. To take part in a discussion or to just read others' thoughts ("lurking" in Internet parlance), you need only subscribe to the list. After you join an electronic list, messages from other subscribers will appear in (and sometimes fill up) your e-mail box. You can participate in the electronic discussion by either responding to a message or posting one of your own. These lists can be a good way to learn more about issues currently being debated within a subfield. Alternatively, if you have a specific question about a topic or source, you can post a message and generally receive thoughtful responses and suggestions rather quickly.

E-MAIL

A final, useful Internet resource is electronic mail, or e-mail. Writers rely on e-mail to directly contact sources for specific information or materials, such as copies of unpublished or "in press" articles. As an instructor, I do not encourage my students to e-mail psychologists unless there is no other way to have their particular question(s) answered. There may be some issue that a researcher raised in an article by referring to an as-yet-unpublished study, for example. To obtain information about this non-public material, a student must contact the author. To obtain the e-mail address of a psychologist, check the author notes of publications or go to his or her institution's home page. Most colleges and universities maintain directories where faculty e-mail addresses or personal home pages are found. To make sure your question is worth an e-mail, ask your instructor for advice.

Using the Internet: Caveat Emptor

The Latin phrase *caveat emptor* can be translated as "Let the buyer beware." In other words, before you commit to making a purchase, be sure you are doing the right thing. After the fact, the responsibility for the choice and any accompanying errors lies with you alone. The same warning must be issued about relying on the Internet for research. The Internet is a formidable tool; the world is literally at your fingertips. You can

---

[2]Listserv is a registered trademark of Eric Thomas of France Individual.

find scholarship in psychology in seconds, so that traditional library research can (almost) seem to be a thing of the past, a happily lost bit of drudgery. Don't believe it. The Internet is a great timesaving tool, but there is no substitute for reading and carefully evaluating the sources you use. Part of your education as a writer in psychology involves learning to determine whether a source is valid. Remember to be critical by asking yourself the following sorts of questions:

How do I know this source is true, valid, and reliable?

Was this research material subject to any form of peer review?

Was the research found on the Internet previously published somewhere? If not, why not? If so, does the report on the Internet match the original publication?

Chapters 3 and 6 also provide additional advice when it comes to determining the quality or usefulness of a reference in psychology.

Here are some guidelines for using the Internet when writing psychology papers:

1. **The Internet is not the only research tool.** Use the Internet only *after* you search an online catalog, PsycINFO, and other sources.

2. **Search with a purpose.** Search intentionally, using specific terms or author names—do not surf mindlessly, hoping to hit on some "mother lode" of psychological information.

3. **Be a time miser.** Restrict the amount of time you commit to searching the Internet, and then stick to it. After completing a basic search of the psychological literature in the library (see guideline 1 above), I would allow myself no more than 1 hour on the Internet. It is simply too easy to waste valuable writing time browsing through cyberspace.

4. **Never believe everything you read or encounter on the Internet.** Be a skeptical and critical cyber consumer. Remember: There is no Internet fact checker to verify the accuracy of what's out there. You are on your own, so be careful about what sort of information you decide to use.

5. **Choose Internet sites carefully.** Stick with those that are clearly sponsored by national, professional organizations in psychology or those maintained by active professionals in the discipline.

6. **Beware: Things change rapidly.** Internet sites come and go without warning or fanfare. Anytime you decide to use a site in your writing, verify that it is still active.

7. **Be selective; the Internet is not.** Searches are usually based on "word searches," not term or index searches (cf., metasearches), which means that any incidence of a word or phrase appearing anywhere in the Internet is fair game (recall the search for *psychology*). Most search engines offer advice on how to refine a search, and you should rely on it before proceeding.

8. **Avoid Internet addiction.** Too many students become overly dependent on the Internet. Generations of undergraduates researched and wrote quality papers before the advent of the Internet, a gentle reminder to keep this helpful tool in perspective.

KEEPING TRACK OF REFERENCES

One of the essential tasks that all writers face is keeping careful track of the references they use. Scholarly guidelines demand that all ideas drawn from the work of others be properly credited (see Chapters 3 and 6). Beyond this academic concern is a more practical one. If you do not keep accurate records of the articles or books you consult, you may not be able to locate a particular source again. Professional guidelines dictate that if you cannot accurately credit a source, then you have no business using it. Besides, any sources you draw from the psychological literature are not just for you; they are also for your readers, who may want to consult the sources for their own purposes. If readers cannot locate works you cite because the bibliographic information you provide is either sparse or wrong, you will be demonstrating an ethical lapse (APA, 2001) and showing poor judgment. Learn this important lesson now and benefit from it in the future: Log your references.

Logging References in a Working Bibliography

There are numerous ways to keep track of your references. You could always tote along your research notebook to record information about worthwhile references. Any entries should be dated, of course.

A more traditional approach involves developing and maintaining a working **bibliography**. A bibliography lists article and book references about a subject or written by some author. As you research your topic and collect references, you are creating a working bibliography for your paper. To save time, it is a good idea to accurately record bibliographic information about a helpful source the first time you encounter it. Once you begin to write your paper, you need only consult your working bibliography to track something down.

There are three basic ways to keep a working bibliography:

1. Record complete citations in your research notebook, alphabetizing them later when the paper is written.
2. Keep a working, alphabetized bibliography in a computer file. Various software programs will do this for you.
3. Maintain a stack of alphabetized notecards (i.e., lined index cards) of complete citations.

Whichever approach you choose is up to you. Just be sure to get in the habit of logging your references. An alternative approach for the standard working

WRITER'S GUIDEPOST   2.2
Citation Triage: A Quick Determination Regarding Reference Relevance

The term *triage* refers to a medical sorting process that determines whether further treatment will be given and to whom. Writers and researchers have to make similar decisions about the viability of their references—which ones will be kept, which discarded. Once you skim or read a reference and decide to keep it, *make a photocopy of its first page* and place it somewhere safe (Scott et al., 1999; see also, Booth et al., 1995). Why? There is nothing worse than losing track of a reference and then trying to find it again. Further, there is little more annoying than working on the last stages of writing a paper, only to find that you lack some of the details for a citation soon to appear in the References section of your paper.

A carefully filed and photocopied first page will usually incorporate all the details you need for citing a reference. If not, then before filing it away, you can quickly write down the missing information on the photocopy. I promise you that this simple bookkeeping action will save valuable time and prevent unintended trips back to the library and its labyrinth of (now reshelved) books and journals. Why not get it right and get what you need the first time?

(continued)

Here are some key bibliographic details you need from research sources that pass your triage test:

- Author(s) name(s), including first and middle initials
- Editor(s) name(s), including first and middle initials
- Title of source (including any subtitle)
- Edition number of a book
- Complete journal title (no abbreviations)
- Volume number for journal or reference book
- Issue number for journal
- Publisher for book or book chapter
- Place of publication for book or book chapter
- Year of publication
- All page numbers, especially for journal articles and book chapters
- Date and site of presentation, poster session, speech, colloquia, etc.
- Call numbers of library books

bibliography is described in Writer's Guidepost 2.2. The basic information that should be recorded about any citation is also highlighted there.

EXERCISES

1. In your research notebook, write a sentence describing each of three possible topic ideas. Alternatively, use the sentence stem strategy to identify possible topics. Narrow each topic as necessary.
2. Select a topic and perform a literature search using the resources at your disposal. Begin a working bibliography by listing five references in your research notebook.
3. Go to the library and locate an example of a primary, secondary, and tertiary source pertaining to your topic.

4. Enter a topic in psychology into an Internet search engine and examine the first five "hits" you receive. How similar are these Web
sites to one another? Does the information pertaining to the topic
seem reliable or contradictory? What cues make you reach either
conclusion?

3

READING
THE PSYCHOLOGICAL
LITERATURE

Reading is the equivalent to thinking with someone else's head instead of one's own.

—Arthur Schopenhauer (1788–1860)

Reading is seeing the world through the eyes and mind of another person, a vicarious way to learn, to know, and to connect. Reading is exciting, challenging, even pleasurable, an essential activity that helps writers develop into experts. Reading is a precursor to writing—good writers are voracious readers. To write well, learn to read well by evaluating and sifting through arguments, theories, and research findings. The more you read, the more you will have to say in your writing. Reading helps you learn many new words and concepts, expanding your vocabulary and your knowledge of psychology, respectively, in the process. Eventually some of these words and ideas will influence your thinking and writing. Finally, reading exposes you to different styles of writing, enabling you to learn from and perhaps occasionally emulate various scholars and researchers working in psychology.

In this chapter I provide advice about reading the psychological literature and about evaluating references in order to decide whether they make good additions to a paper. I also offer advice on note taking and avoiding plagiarism. Before tackling these topics, however, I will focus on an important issue affecting reading and writing in psychology: the primacy of scientific journals.

THE SCIENTIFIC PECKING ORDER: WHY JOURNALS ARE FIRST

It is a fact of life for psychologists that the bulk of the research done in the discipline is published in psychology journals. A **journal** is a professional periodical, a topical, bound publication that usually appears every month or so. Journals contain APA-style research reports. There are hundreds of psychology journals covering a wide variety of content areas (for a sampling, see the appendix). Two decided strengths of journals are their sheer number and the diversity of their content, scope, and purpose. Chances are that there is a journal out there somewhere dealing with almost any topic you can think of, in or out of psychology.

Some journals are judged as being of a higher quality than others due to their scientific rigor, the status of the authors who publish there, and other relevant academic criteria. Quality journals are subject to peer review, meaning that authors submit their work to an editor, knowing that it will be read and evaluated by other professionals who will critically comment on its scientific merit. These peers, along with the journal's editor, control whether the work will be accepted and appear in print. Another mark of quality journals is a relatively high rejection rate (often 80% or higher); only a small number of articles are accepted for publication, which is evidence of their meritorious standing.

Why else do journals have a special place in psychology? These scientific periodicals are both **timely** and **time bound**. Journals are published on a regular schedule, which means that the research presented in them is relatively up-to-date. I use the word *relatively* because most journals have a publication lag, so that once a paper is accepted for publication, it may be several months, perhaps even a year, before it appears in print. Researcher–authors have often moved far beyond the issues and findings covered by these "in press" works. Still, research appearing in a journal is relatively current, and currency is a key for interested researchers who want to keep up with the latest developments in psychology. Timeliness is a decided virtue of journals, casting them as generally superior sources of new material when compared to the "permanence" of books.

The time-bound nature of journals, though, presents an important caveat. Whenever you rely on a journal article for information, you must verify that it accurately represents current understanding of a topic. Subsequent research by the same or other authors may supersede the findings of a particular article. Related advances, too, are not necessarily published in the same journal. You have to look around to keep up with new research.

Finally, journals address specific questions, presenting the available research in a similar format. An article may review theory or present empirical data, but it will do so by addressing a specific, substantive question dealing with some aspect of human behavior. For all these reasons, journals serve as the coin of the scientific realm of psychology.

HOW TO READ AND EVALUATE THE LITERATURE

Like writing, reading should be done in a quiet place, with a purpose and without distractions. When you read a novel or a mystery, the purpose is pleasure or recreation. It is fun to vicariously experience the thoughts of others. Solving a criminal puzzle and determining "whodunit" is a compelling and satisfying activity, as is reading an adventure, a drama, or a funny tale about everyday life.

Reading the psychological literature poses another agenda besides seeking enjoyment or personal edification. Your mission is to expand knowledge by working with existing knowledge. You are actively looking for answers to questions, so you must locate information related to your ideas and arguments. Whatever you find must be read and evaluated, though only some of it will end up in your paper. Your purpose in reading is analytical, skeptical, and integrative: What can be used from what is already known? Is the research factual, rigorous, and reliable? Does available research help or hinder your assumptions? What information changes what you already know?

Answering these questions requires you to recognize quality sources in psychology. The ability to separate scientific wheat from chaff is based partly on experience, of course, and partly on following sound guidelines for reading. The guidelines provided here are not divinely inspired, but they can help you identify useful sources in the literature:

- **Professional, not popular.** Rely on materials written for psychologists by fellow experts rather than publications aimed at general audiences. The *Journal of Social and Clinical Psychology* is a better source for studies of stress and coping than magazines like *Psychology Today* and *Time*.
- **Focused on questions you are trying to answer.** If you are interested in the emotional attachment between infants and mothers, avoid general works on human development or specific papers dealing with father-child bonds or sibling relationships.

- **Empirical.** Empirical works are based on scientific investigation and subject to independent verification. In general, the best research is experimental, though rigorous observational, correlational, and qualitative studies are also useful.
- **Primary.** A primary source describes the results of original research conducted and written up by the same psychologist (see Writer's Guidepost 2.1 on page 21).
- **Frequently cited by other psychologists.** A good rule-of-thumb for judging the merit of a scholarly work is the impact and influence it has on other researchers. A piece of research that is used by other researchers is a good bet.
- **Recent.** Timeliness is important in the development of scholarship, and newer evidence can change established knowledge.
- **Available.** An article or book is useful only if you can obtain a copy.

A checklist based on these criteria is provided in Table 3.1.

How to Read a Journal Article

Journal articles offer a window into the inner workings of . . . psychology. They document how . . . psychologists formulate hypotheses, design empirical studies, analyze the observations they collect, and interpret their results. Journal articles also serve an invaluable archival function: They contain the full store of common and cumulative knowledge. (Jordan & Zanna, 1999, p. 461)

Table 3.1. A Quick Checklist for Evaluating Whether to Use a Source

Answer *Yes* or *No* to each question:

1. _____ Is the source professional rather than popular?
2. _____ Is the source focused on your research questions?
3. _____ Is the source empirical?
4. _____ Is it a primary source?
5. _____ Unless the source was recently published, is it cited frequently in the literature? By psychologists? If not, then by whom?
6. _____ Is the source recent?
7. _____ Is the source available?

If you answer *yes* **fewer than five times**, reconsider using the source in your writing.

Reading journal articles is not a passive activity. With experience, learning to read a journal article is not difficult, but such fact-filled, tightly reasoned text takes getting used to (that they are helping you learn to write research reports will make them seem less formidable).

Writers are readers who rely on particular guidelines as they study written materials, including these:[1]

- **Reading cannot be rushed, and many works will need to be read more than once.** Reading something, anything, takes time, especially when the material is technical. Allow yourself enough time for reading. Don't rush or you will miss details and recall little information later. Be aware that many sources will need to be reread several times.

- **A dictionary must always be close at hand.** No one knows all the words there are to know in any language. Whatever your age and experience, there are still words you have not encountered. Whenever you come across an unfamiliar word (e.g., *encomium, supernumerary*), stop and look it up (do so with these two examples, right now).

- **Readers must be healthy skeptics.** Healthy skepticism is the willingness to thoroughly but carefully evaluate the claims presented in any work in psychology. A healthy skeptic examines conclusions before accepting them: Is this hypothesis the right one? Are results interpreted appropriately? Does the theory make sense?

- **Write as you read.** Take notes, jot down pithy quotes, and if the book or article belongs to you, underline, circle, and record your reactions in the margins. You will learn much more by writing while you read than if you just read something straight through.

- **Interpretation is open ended.** Your opinion matters. Authors do not have any definitive or "right" answers to a psychological question. As readers, we are free to question answers, even to substitute our own. Divergent points of view are to be encouraged, not squelched.

ACTIVELY QUESTIONING WHAT YOU READ

What about the specific practice of reading a journal article? How should such reading be accomplished? It should be done in a critical, evaluative fashion: Ask questions and look for answers. While reading

[1]From *Concepts to Completion: Writing Well in the Social Sciences,* 1st ed., by Williams/Brydon-Miller. © 1997. Reprinted with permission of Wadsworth, a division of Thomson Learning: www.thomsonrights.com. Fax 800-730-2215.

each section of a journal article, ask yourself the corresponding questions presented here:

- **Title and Abstract.** What does the title tell you about the research? Does the Abstract provide sufficient information about the hypothesis, research design, results, and implications? What else do you need to know?
- **Introduction.** What question is being studied? Why is it being researched? What specific innovations does this study provide that previous efforts lack? What answers do the investigators hope to obtain?
- **Method.** Who were the research participants? Students? Older adults? White rats (*rattus Norvegicus*)? What is the nature of the study's operationalization—the translation of a research hypothesis into an empirically testable question? Did the operationalization make sense? What independent variables were manipulated? What dependent (outcome) variables were measured? Were all instructions, questionnaires, or surveys clear?
- **Results.** What evidence is there that any manipulations and measures were effective? Was the main hypothesis supported? What were the main findings? Were they explained in coherent, behavioral terms?
- **Discussion.** How does the research add to what we know about the topic? Did the study answer any questions? What are they? Does it lead to new questions? Which ones? What are the practical and the theoretical implications of the research? What's next?

These same questions can help you write and revise your papers. Other questions worth asking while reading empirical research are provided in Table 3.2.

Skimming: Doing a Quick Prereading

> I took a speed-reading course and read *War and Peace* in twenty minutes. It involves Russia.
>
> —Woody Allen

Sometimes writers need to get a quick, reliable sense of what a study is all about, but there is no time for a close reading. Such prereading or "skimming" is not a race; it must be done thoughtfully. Skimming written material to look for key issues and ideas is a "first pass" to get a sense of whether it's relevant to your work. You can read the material more thoroughly when you are drafting your paper.

Table 3.2. Other Critical Questions to Ask When Reading Journal Articles

- Does the introduction's literature review provide sufficient context for the research question? Are any key terms defined?

- Is there a control group? If not, is the absence explained? Does the explanation make sense?

- Is the Method section detailed enough so that anyone could replicate the study? What details were missing?

- Were the participants sampled, selected, and/or randomly assigned to groups? Do the participants represent some larger population? Does the study's sample size appear to be large enough?

- Can you understand the written description of any results, even if you are unfamiliar with the statistical analyses that were used to obtain them? Do any accompanying tables and/or figures help or hinder your understanding?

- Are the implications of the work convincing or do they stretch the research's credibility?

- How could this research be improved? What specific changes would you recommend?

Source: Adapted from Dana S. Dunn, The Practical Researcher: A Student Guide to Conducting Psychological Research, *Table 4.12, p. 127, McGraw-Hill, 1999. Copyright © 1999 by The McGraw-Hill Companies, Inc. Reprinted with permission of The McGraw-Hill Companies, Inc.*

SKIMMING A RESEARCH ARTICLE

Here is a five-step process for skimming a research article (adapted from Booth, Colomb, & Williams, 1995, pp. 82–84).[2] Remember to jot down notes as you skim any work.

Step 1: Get a sense of the whole work. To obtain a quick sense of an empirical article:

- Read the Abstract.
- Is the article a recent publication or an older work?
- What is the quality of the journal? What sorts of articles appear there? Are submissions subject to peer review?
- Do you know anything about the author? Is the author a recognized expert on the paper's topic or in psychology?

[2]Adapted material from Booth, Colomb, and Williams, *The Craft of Research,* pp. 82–84, The University of Chicago Press, 1995. © 1995 by The University of Chicago. All rights reserved. Reprinted with permission.

- Look at the headings (they comprise the outline) within each of the main sections of the paper.
- Skim the References section to locate familiar and new citations.

Step 2: Identify the main argument. Read the last few paragraphs of the introduction to locate the hypothesis. Once you know the study's main question, turn to the Discussion to see how well it was supported and whether there are implications for future work. If details in the Discussion are hard to locate quickly, skim the Results.

Step 3: Locate supporting points. If the hypothesis and findings are clear, you can decide whether the article should be kept for further reading. If you are still unsure, repeat step 2. Alternatively, identify areas within each section that specifically support points the author(s) wants to make. The presence of transitional phrases (e.g., "First, . . .", "Second, . . .", "Finally, . . .") will lead you to the supporting points. Skim the accompanying text to assess the value each point contributes to the overall argument.

Step 4: Scan for key themes. Look over the article for any key themes or concepts (especially unfamiliar ones) related to the research. Check to see if any of these key themes appeared in articles or other sources that you previously discarded. If so, you may want to look at them one more time.

Step 5: Skim paragraphs as needed. The first four steps should give you a good sense of the article. If you still feel uncertain about the work's scope, skim each paragraph in the text to find its main idea.

SKIMMING A BOOK

A five-step process of skimming can be adapted for reading a book (Booth et al., 1995). Treat each book chapter like an article and apply steps 2 through 4 above. In lieu of step 1, try this:

- Quickly skim the book's Preface.
- Check the Table of Contents for overview, summary, and/or concluding chapters.
- Look at individual chapters and the headings therein (the latter form an outline); read any (brief) chapter summaries.
- Glance at the References section, taking note of the currency of citations as well as the cited authors.
- Skim the Index for terms and topics that are frequently cited in the book.

One more issue to keep in mind while reading: No piece of research is perfect or comprehensive. There are always some unanswered questions, something more that you would like to know. As the late statistician Jacob Cohen (1990, p. 1311) wrote:

> A successful piece of research doesn't conclusively settle an issue, it just makes some theoretical proposition to some degree more likely.

Inevitably, there is always more to know.

TAKING NOTES ON WHAT YOU READ

Note taking is an important skill. Your goal is to briefly summarize the main points of what you read into a few sentences, assimilating the ideas into your thinking about the topic. Unless there is a particular reason to record a specific quote, always use your own words. There are two reasons for doing so: avoiding plagiarism (which is discussed in detail below) and actively thinking about ideas in order to make them your "own," to integrate them with other information you already possess. Passive forms of note taking, such as copying material or highlighting text with a marker, will not help you remember what you read. You might just as well carry original sources around with you, consulting them as needed. Note taking should free your mind and focus your writing.

Using Notecards

Taking notes on notecards, lined or unlined 3-by-5 inch index cards, is a venerable tradition. In our age of laptop computers and palm-sized personal data gadgets, relying on notecards can seem to be a decidedly dated activity. In spite of these technological great-leaps-forward, notecards remain a convenient and portable way to take notes for research papers. The chief advantage of the notecard system is that it forces you to neatly and briefly record the most important ideas from a reading. Only a few focused sentences can be written on a notecard, assuming that essential bibliographic information is also recorded there (see Writer's Guidepost 2.2 on page 35).

The content of a typical notecard can include a brief quotation; key terms and definitions; short summaries of findings, theories, or hypotheses; questions about the reading, which can be used to develop a paper's thesis; or your evaluation of an article or book ("controversial ideas but overly technical writing"). The top few lines of a card contain the bibliographic source information. Beneath this information lie the actual notes about the source. Some researchers (including me) prefer to write a one-word designation in the bottom left corner of a notecard, such as "summary" when a card outlines the scope of a work or "quote" when an exact quotation is lifted from a source. You then have a quick way to determine a card's contents when writing. Finally, as long as you keep them together, it is routine to maintain several notecards about the same reference.

Using a Research Notebook

In lieu of note cards, many writers keep a small notebook containing the same information. Your research notebook (see page 15 in Chapter 2) can serve this purpose. One advantage is that a notebook's binding usually prevents precious pages from getting lost, unlike loose notecards. Some students use a two-page system for taking notes on sources and drafting their papers. Open your notebook so that two pages, a left and right page, are blank. Write notes about a source on the left page, just as you would record comments on a notecard. Later, when reviewing the notes, jot down your thoughts and reactions to them on the right-hand page. (This option is somewhat different than the dialectical notebook option on page 16 in Chapter 2.)

Table 3.3 contains some note-taking tips that can promote research efficiency as well as rigor.

RECOGNIZING AND PREVENTING PLAGIARISM

One of the worst sins a writer can commit is to plagiarize, to copy verbatim the words and ideas of another person, passing them off as his or her own. Deliberately plagiarizing someone else's work is like lying, cheating, or stealing—damage is done to another so as to personally benefit the plagiarist. Plagiarism is a form of robbery. The theft just happens to be of words, ideas, even a style of writing, rather than of material goods. Plagiarism occurs anytime a person intentionally takes another person's words and uses them without proper attribution—that is, naming the actual author as the source and identifying his or her words as a quotation. Deliberate plagiarism is wrong because the plagiarist is intentionally copying a source to get ahead, to avoid doing work, to appear expert on some topic, or for some other misguided reason.

In contrast, unintentional plagiarists also copy the words of others, but they do so without realizing it. An accidental plagiarist might copy

Table 3.3. Note Taking 101: Some Suggestions for Taking Better Notes

- Take notes using blue or blue-black ink. Colored inks are hard on the eyes and tend to fade more quickly.

- Take notes using the form of your handwriting—printing or cursive—that is more legible to you.

- Instead of taking notes on an entire book, record your reactions to the last or summary chapter, the place where authors usually revisit main themes and tie up any loose, conceptual ends.

- When a book is a source, always take notes on the preface, the place where most authors explain their intentions as well as how their work differs from existing research.

- Avoid notes taken from a book's foreword, which are usually not very useful. In many books, a friend of the author has written the foreword, so the content is apt to offer praise rather than criticism or any serious evaluation of the book's contents.

- To save time while searching through journals, just read an article's Abstract during a first pass. Take notes on a study's hypothesis, method, findings, and implications from this short summary. Refer back to these notes later, when you prepare to read the article in depth.

- Never take notes when you are tired or sleepy; they will be illegible, incoherent, and possibly wrong.

Source: Adapted from Dana S. Dunn, The Practical Researcher: A Student Guide to Conducting Psychological Research, *Box Feature 4.1, p. 134, McGraw-Hill, 1999. Copyright © 1999 by Dana Dunn. Reprinted with permission of The McGraw-Hill Companies, Inc.*

ideas directly from a source, plan to cite the source, but then get side-tracked, subsequently forgetting to use quotation marks, a date, or the page numbers from which the information was taken. While reviewing the notes a week or so after copying them, the words look and sound pretty good, well worth adding to a developing paper. Too bad the writer does not realize that sloppy note taking, coupled with a memory lapse, leads right to intellectual theft. More than anything else, such unintentional plagiarism is embarrassing for the writer (Booth et al., 1995). Is accidental plagiarism a form of lying, cheating, and stealing? Yes. The "writer" is guilty of borrowing words and phrases from somebody else; the accidental nature of the plagiarism is beside the point. In academic

WRITER'S GUIDEPOST   3.1
Ways to Avoid Plagiarism

How can you avoid plagiarizing what someone else wrote? There's an easy way to avoid copying words and phrases written by someone else:

- Read the text you intend to summarize.
- Put the text away.
- Draft a summary in your own words.

Students often struggle to write summaries. They feel compelled to compare continually their writing against the original, and what they have to say never sounds as good or seems quite right. To combat this problem and the larger issue of plagiarism, ask yourself the following questions before you draft a summary. Write down some quick answers to these questions, which will help to shape the summary and prompt you to remember details.

1. What is the text about?
2. What is the main idea in the text?
3. Is some position, assertion, or hypothesis stated? If so, what is it?
4. Do you agree with the position, assertion, or hypothesis?
5. Is any supporting evidence provided? What, specifically?
6. Did anything surprise you in the text?
7. What questions do you still have?

Armed with your answers to these questions, you can now start to draft a summary with less fear of committing plagiarism.

circles, intentional and unintentional plagiarists are perceived and treated the same way.

A Plagiarism-Awareness Exercise

Completing the short exercise that follows will demonstrate how to quickly recognize plagiarism and avoid committing it (Prohaska, 2001). Please take out a pencil and paper before reading any further. Ready? Imagine that three students enrolled in a personality class—let's call them Moe, Larry, and Curly—each wrote an essay on psychoanalytic theory. All three students relied on the same source for their work. Here is a selection from that source (Berger, 1988, p. 32):[3]

> The first comprehensive view of human behavior, psychoanalytic theory, interprets human development in terms of unconscious drives and motives. These unconscious impulses are viewed as influencing every aspect of a person's thinking and behavior, from the crucial choices of a lifetime, including whom and what to love or hate, to the smallest details of daily life, including the manner of dress, choice of food, what we say and how we say it, what we daydream about, and how we reason—in fact, the entire gamut of our personal preferences, dislikes, and idiosyncrasies.

Now, take a look at Table 3.4. The three paragraphs shown there were drawn from the students' essays. Read each essay excerpt in Table 3.4 and then answer the question accompanying it. Write your answers to the three questions on your piece of paper. Here is an important hint: This is *not* a trick of any sort—Moe and Larry committed plagiarism. How do you know this is true?

What did you write? Are Moe and Larry plagiarists? It would be difficult to conclude otherwise: Passing off *most* of someone else's words as your own is still plagiarism. Moe obviously copied the material directly from the book (compare his excerpt in Table 3.4 with the original shown above). Larry's work is only marginally better than Moe's, though it still constitutes unabashed plagiarism. Unlike Moe, Larry included a few new words and phrases (e.g., "I feel," "they," "your") into the (directly copied) excerpt, though such minor changes fail to mask the stolen phrases and ideas. Larry's few innovations did not substantially alter the passage from Berger (1988), which is virtually intact in his essay. The fact that Larry cited the original author changes nothing (though it does make it easier for his instructor to locate the plagiarized passages).

What about the excerpt from Curly's essay? Curly read Berger (1988) and cited the work, but did *not* plagiarize it. Instead, Curly **paraphrased** what he read. He restated and revised the main ideas from Berger's work using different words. The text's original meaning is preserved but the summary is Curly's own. (For detailed guidance regarding quoting and paraphrasing, see page 134 in Chapter 7.) Writing like Curly's

---

[3]I am grateful to the author for permission to use her work in this example.

Table 3.4. An Exercise in Exorcising Plagiarism

MOE WROTE THIS:

Psychoanalytic theory interprets human development in terms of unconscious drives and motives. These unconscious impulses are viewed as influencing every aspect of a person's thinking and behavior, from the crucial choices of a lifetime, including whom and what to love or hate, to the smallest details of daily life, including the manner of dress, choice of food, what we say and how we say it, what we daydream about, and how we reason—in fact, the entire gamut of our personal preferences, dislikes, and idiosyncrasies.

Question 1: Explain why you think Moe did or did not commit plagiarism.

LARRY WROTE THIS:

I feel that psychoanalytic theory interprets human development in terms of unconscious drives and motives. In this theory, unconscious impulses are viewed as influencing every aspect of a person's thinking and behavior. They influence the crucial choices of a lifetime, including whom and what to love or hate. They influence the smallest details of daily life, including the manner of dress, choice of food. They influence what you say and how you say it, what you daydream about, and how you reason—in fact, the entire gamut of your personal preferences, dislikes, and idiosyncrasies (Berger, 1988).

Question 2: Explain why you think Larry did or did not commit plagiarism.

CURLY WROTE THIS:

According to Berger (1988), psychoanalytic theory stresses the importance of unconscious drives and motives. According to this theory, all of our thinking and behavior is affected by unconscious impulses. No aspect of our lives—our choices of our mates, our favorite foods, even the types of cars we choose to drive and the careers we decide to pursue—is immune from unconscious influences.

Question 3: Explain why you think Curly did or did not commit plagiarism.

Source: Adapted from Prohaska (2001). Adapted with permission from K.S. Berger, The Developing Person Through the Lifespan, *Second Edition, p. 32. Copyright © 1988. Reprinted by permission from Worth Publishers.*

summary is the sort of paraphrasing you should aspire to because the spirit of the source's tone, scope, and message is maintained. The issue here is a clear one: Claiming the words of another as your own is wrong.

Some suggestions for deciding when to quote or paraphrase appear in Table 3.5.

One More Word of Advice

Preventing plagiarism requires you, the writer, to take careful notes. When you copy a quotation, surround the sentence or block quote (i.e., a "block" of text, usually three or more sentences) with quotation marks

---

Table 3.5. To Quote or to Paraphrase? That Is the Question

Quotations should be used:

- To represent an author-researcher as an expert on a topic.

- When the content of a quotation is being used to give direction to a paper.

- Because original words, phrases, and ideas matter to readers. Direct quotations can be vivid, memorable, or colorful, even powerful or moving (e.g., "Ask not what your country can do for you; ask what you can do for your country."–President John F. Kennedy's Inaugural Address, January 20, 1961).

- Whenever there is a theoretical or empirical dispute or disagreement involving the terms or arguments found within a quotation.

- If particular words and phrases proved to be important for previous researchers, who have both cited and reacted to them.

- To draw attention to how a researcher creates and presents a particular argument regarding a hypothesis, fact, or observation.

- Infrequently. If you use a quotation, choose it carefully.

Paraphrasing should be used:

- To summarize something—a statement, an idea, a theory, some research findings—in a general way.

- When the focus is on content rather than on a specific comment or lengthy quotation from a source.

- To present ideas in a simpler, more straightforward manner than was true for the original source.

- Whenever only a portion, not all, of the points presented in the original are being examined.

(i.e., " ") on a notecard or the page in a notebook, and record the source's bibliographic information in the same place. (Be sure to add the page number[s] where the quote can be found in the original reference.) Write the word *quote* or *quotation* where it is clearly visible on the card.

EXERCISES

1. Go to the periodical section of your library and examine several recent issues of a psychology journal. Select an article and practice skimming, or prereading, it using the directions provided in this chapter.
2. Read the article. While you read, write down your reactions to it in your research notebook. Try to answer the questions found in Table 3.2.
3. Take notes on two of the sources you intend to use in your paper. Use notecards for one and then try the two-page system for the other. Which method do you prefer? Use your preferred method for taking notes on your remaining sources.
4. Select another article you intend to use in your paper. Read it and then put it away. In your research notebook, write a one-paragraph summary of the article using the prompts shown in Writer's Guidepost 3.1.
5. Locate a journal article that you find impossible to read or to understand. What makes it incomprehensible to you? Is its unintelligibility the fault of the author or something about the research area or topic? Describe what you would do to make this article more intelligible for future readers.

4

GETTING STARTED: WRITING

Wait.

—Franz Kafka (1883–1924)

Kafka posted the word *Wait* over his writing desk as a silent suggestion to himself, an encouragement to think things through before beginning work on any short story or novel (Boice, 1994). When Kafka waited, he used the time wisely, preparing himself for the actual work of writing. Waiting entails essential writing processes like thinking, outlining, drafting, revising, editing, and proofreading (Boice, 1994). Waiting involves crucial activities that refine and enhance any piece of writing.

Some students embrace Kafka's recommendation wholeheartedly on their own, following it much too literally: they wait too long to begin papers, staying up all night writing the day before an assignment is due. Consequently, their efforts are ill conceived, rushed, sloppy, and poorly organized. Still, some students claim that they work best under pressure, that inspiration for their writing requires 11th-hour cramming and jamming coupled with perspiration, sleep deprivation, and frequent jolts of caffeine. This form of waiting is procrastinating until the last minute, not creatively working things through in the spirit of Kafka.

I want you to adopt the attitude of waiting in the same way that Kafka did and that other successful writers do. The main goal of adopting a writer's perspective on waiting is to avoid procrastination and the "binge" writing that often results from it. Writing instructors label any marathon, forced session of writing **bingeing**. Bingeing is writing under pressure. College students are notorious for bingeing in their writing. A deadline suddenly looms large, leading to false or forced inspiration and a rushed, if "finished," paper.

There are several reasons why bingeing is apt to occur:[1]

- Motivation to write is low or absent altogether.
- A due date is distant.

[1]Adapted from *How Writers Journey to Comfort and Fluency,* by Robert Boice. Copyright © 1994 by Robert Boice. All rights reserved. Reproduced with permission of Greenwood Publishing Group, Inc., Westport, CT.

- A due date is suddenly here and now (i.e., forgotten, overlooked, or ignored due to procrastination).
- A writer is upset or distracted by other responsibilities, such as work due in other courses.
- A large block of time is frittered away.

The precursors of bingeing are common and probably familiar to you. Most of us have engaged in binge writing at one time or another. The problem is that some of us rely on binge writing all the time, now in college and soon in a career. Bingeing is counterproductive, causing a mania of "accelerated thought and poor judgment," exhausting the writer and leading to mediocre work (Boice, 1994, p. 4).

There is an easy way to combat bingeing: Write in short bursts (e.g., 15 to 30 minutes in length) rather than for hours at a time (Boice, 1994). Small but steady progress on a writing assignment usually leads to quicker completion and better work than any last-minute push. Imagine how nice it would be to have a paper completed a day or two *before* a due date—as we will see, such things are entirely possible.

To avoid the twin perils of bingeing and procrastination, embrace the writing practices presented in this chapter. An overview of the writing process involving these practices is provided in Table 4.1. As shown in the table, there are five stages to the writing process: (1) planning to write, (2) outlining, (3) drafting, (4) revising, and (5) seeking feedback. Depending on the nature of the writing being done, each stage can contain a variety of activities. Some are noted in the table. Review this material now and plan to revisit it later, once you begin to write your paper in earnest.

Table 4.1. An Overview of the Writing Process

Stage 1: Planning to write

- Use expressive prewriting (e.g., freewriting, focused freewriting) to identify or explore a topic.

Stage 2: Outlining

- Use transactional structuring and organizing of ideas.
- Identify a thesis statement.
- Select a writing style (e.g., APA style, MLA style).

Stage 3: Drafting

- "Flesh out" the outline.
- Create a "trick draft" or another rough draft.

Table 4.1. (*continued*)

Stage 4: Revising

• Rethink what is already written.

• Restructure paragraphs or pages as needed.

• Proofread the new draft for superficial errors (grammar, punctuation, spelling).

Stage 5: Seeking feedback

• Share the revision with peers or professionals.

• Create the next draft based on the feedback.

GETTING STARTED: PREWRITING ACTIVITIES

Most writers admit that getting started is the hardest thing. Confronting a blank page or an empty computer screen is daunting. How will it be filled with words that say anything?

A few paragraphs ago I argued that waiting is a virtue in writing, but now I am going to appear to contradict myself for a moment. One of the best things you can do is to begin writing before you feel completely ready to do so (Boice, 1994). Waiting involves planning writing activities or reviewing what's already been written. Starting a bit before you are completely ready allows you to make use of the fruits of waiting while also making writing a reassuring, familiar activity. You need only write in short bursts, and initial results do not have to be perfect. Your writing topic may be sketchy—that's okay. It's better to be a little loose and unsure to start than to be overly tight and constrained. The goal is for your writing to become second nature. Professional writers attest that making writing a regular habit ensures that they can write when they want to and with confidence. Beginning to write before you are completely ready or very familiar with your topic can actually help you connect ideas and locate a focus in your writing (Boice, 1994).

How should you get started? Starting to write involves *pre*-writing, that is, doing some warm-up exercises before writing. Two forms of prewriting are *freewriting* and *outlining*. Both techniques share a common goal: generating words quickly so that your paper begins to take shape.

Freewriting

Freewriting is a broad term referring to private, continuous writing about whatever comes to a person's mind (e.g., Elbow & Belanoff, 1995; Williams & Brydon-Miller, 1997). Freewriting is a nonstop form of writing. A pen or pencil is literally put to paper and never lifted for 10 minutes or so. During that time, the writing is not only free from stopping, it is also free from the editorial niceties we impose on ourselves (they come later). When freewriting, never stop to consider verb tense, spelling, grammar, punctuation, neatness of handwriting, or whether the scribbled ideas say anything. Freewriting can also be done via computer—what we might call "freetyping"—and it's helpful to turn off the screen, thereby avoiding online editing until time is up (see "invisible writing" in Elbow & Belanoff, 1995, p. 13). Learn to generate words, to write quickly and comfortably, turning off both internal and external editors for a while in order to see where your thoughts lead.

As long as you honestly present thoughts and feelings on paper, there is no right or wrong way to do freewriting. When you become stuck, unsure what to say next, simply write about being stuck or how annoying it is to be at a loss for words. The good news, however, is that during bouts of freewriting, most people do not find themselves "speechless" for long.

The results of this written, mental free fall can be very interesting and quite productive. Once the words come, subsequent reviews of the freewriting reveal that people usually have something to say. Not all the freewriting that fills your first pages is useful, of course, but a few stray sentences or phrases are frequently salvageable. Alternatively, some line of reasoning or an observation will be worth exploring further in an essay or paper. Again, the point is to get used to writing, to become comfortable with spouting words and phrases, to conjure up a few ideas for a paper or other writing.

Here is a sample of freewriting done by one of my students, Jaime Marks:

> I just met with my research group and we spent an hour discussing our various aspects of the project. Unfortunately, it seemed that no matter what aspect we discussed all of it had somewhat disheartening news. I am amazed, fascinated, and humbled at the extent to which children today are being faced with such difficult decisions. And we wonder why there is so much dysfunction today I wonder how some kids manage to succeed with some much against them . . . financial worries lack of parental support, etc. I wonder what it

must feel like to be a teacher and see children come in day in and day out with so much distress.

FREEWRITING EXERCISE 1: ARE YOU EXPERIENCED?

Freewriting is hard to appreciate, let alone understand, without some experience. First-timers think it sounds silly, even gimmicky, or that it is a waste of time. Why not take a few minutes now to try freewriting? Get out some paper and something to write with, or sit down in front of a computer. If you have a timer or clock handy, use it. *Start writing now and do not stop until 10 or so minutes have passed. Don't censor your thoughts. Just write about whatever comes to mind.*

How did you do in your first try at freewriting? How much writing did you generate? Most students surprise themselves by filling a page or two with little difficulty. The lesson here is that producing words is not that difficult. Hold onto your first piece of freewriting because you may use it later. If you can, try one more 10-minute freewriting trial in the next day or so: Is it easier the second time? What did you write about?

FOCUSED FREEWRITING

When freewriting is used to explore some topic, to develop an idea for a paper, or for another specific reason, it is labeled **focused freewriting**. Focused freewriting is different from the basic type only in its emphasis on exploring *one* thing. Focused freewriting "harnesses the 'freewriting muscle'—the muscle that enables you to allow the words to go down on paper quickly without planning or worrying about quality—for the sake of exploring one subject" (Elbow & Belanoff, 1995, pp. 12–13). In lieu of writing about whatever comes to mind, you write nonstop for brief periods by focusing on one thing while looking for meaning related to it (Hacker, 1991).

When writing a psychology paper, focused freewriting can help you complete various tasks:

- Generate a topic for the paper.
- Explore possible hypotheses.
- Create a rough draft of a given section of an APA-style paper.
- Develop experimental methods and procedures.
- Identify concrete examples to support or illustrate a theory.
- Interpret and apply results.
- Reflect on research findings, identifying implications and future directions.
- Overcome the hurdle of getting started writing.

Focused freewriting is then polished through revision (a topic introduced later in this chapter). Gradually, bits and pieces of freewriting can be cut and pasted together (by moving text through word processing or literally by rearranging and taping scraps of printouts and handwritten papers together; see Bem, 2000; see also, Writer's Guidepost 1.1). The advantage of selectively using focused freewriting is that the paper moves forward, developing and growing, before more traditional writing begins.

In this sample of focused freewriting, Ms. Marks tries to identify a paper topic:

> I am racking my brain and can't seem to come up with anything that will work. I think that I have finally come up on something, mostly because it is something that has affected me personally. As my grandmother slowly declines in health from Alzheimer's disease, I am fascinated and saddened by the whole thing . . . what about with Alzheimer's in a situation where are not necessarily coherent? How do family members deal with the situation? I am interested in studying depression among these patients, if they are aware of how much they are declining . . .

FREEWRITING EXERCISE 2: GET SPECIFIC

Again, take 10 minutes or so, only this time write while thinking about one thing. Here are a few suggested prompts to get you started:

- Discuss the intended topic of your paper. Why is the topic interesting? What does it reveal about behavior?
- Describe everyday behavioral examples illustrating a theory or hypothesis. How can you be sure that these examples fit?
- Discuss the area of psychology that interests you most.
- Describe some behavior you witnessed that made you stop, think, and wonder.

Hold onto this freewriting so that you can use it in the future. Write in your research notebook or start keeping a journal, a place to maintain such personal, exploratory writing (see Hacker, 1991).

Outlining

Whereas freewriting is freewheeling, outlining is structured, even constrained. An **outline** is a detailed guide for your writing, the architecture, or "bones," of your work. Once an outline is established, you have a map for writing, one that can be fleshed out by freewriting and focused freewriting.

An outline identifies some formal claim, a thesis statement or hypothesis, being made in a piece of writing. The thesis statement is then supported by one or more main ideas, evidence introduced in a logical, orderly way that clarifies a writer's argument for readers. Each main idea is in turn bolstered by secondary details (e.g., facts, data, citations). The different levels within an outline force a writer to make choices about which points are most important and which are less so, while considering the order of their presentation—what makes sense, and where? Working from an outline allows a writer to move things around, to be flexible, to try different ways of raising issues before committing to one way.

A basic outline looks like this:

Thesis statement

  I. Main idea one
    A. Secondary detail
      1. facts, data, citations
      2. facts, data, citations
    B. Secondary detail
      1. facts, data, citations
      2. facts, data, citations
  II. Main idea two
       Etc.

Imagine you are describing the layout of your home: How would you outline it? There could be a hierarchical order to the rooms and their furnishings:

My Home

Living Room

    easy chair

    floor lamp

    sofa

    coffee table

Dining Room

    table and chairs

    sideboard

The level of detail provided in your outline influences how well people can visualize and understand your home's layout. In the same way, the structure of a paper's outline will affect whether readers understand what you have to say.

OUTLINING AN APA-STYLE PAPER

The writing style encouraged by the American Psychological Association was introduced in Chapter 1. The strength of APA style is the basic outline it provides for writers. The outline shown in Table 4.2 is what we might call "bare bones" because it lacks specific psychological content (for now). Any paper presenting the results of an experiment or other investigation will follow the basic outline of required main sections shown in Table 4.2.

Table 4.3 is a focused and extended version of Table 4.2. Beyond the required APA-style sections, Table 4.3 includes a plan for "secondary details"—the facts, data, and citations pertaining to an actual research project. What you see in Table 4.3 is an outline based on a student's research paper, the text of which appears in Chapter 5 (see pages 105–114). Only the body of the paper is outlined in Table 4.3. The remaining sections do not need, nor would they benefit from, outlining (cf., Table 4.2). Naturally,

---

Table 4.2. The Main Sections in an APA-Style Empirical Paper

Title page: Title, name(s), and affiliations of authors—*always* appears on page 1.

Abstract page: Brief summary of contents—*always* appears on page 2.

Introduction: Describes research problem, purpose of study, and any hypothesis(es)—*always* begins on page 3.

Method: Characterizes participants or sample, presents any equipment and step-by-step procedures used to conduct research.

Results: Explains all analyses and presents any results obtained.

Discussion: Reviews and interprets key findings, considers their implications for future research.

References: Provides an alphabetical list of all sources discussed or cited in the manuscript.

Appendix: Supporting materials that cannot be found elsewhere (e.g., stimulus materials used in the research) are added here, but only when absolutely necessary.

Author Note: Short paragraph discloses author correspondence information to readers, and other details deemed pertinent.

Tables and Figures: Summarize numerical information or visually presents data in graphed forms.

Table 4.3. Sample Outline for an APA-Style Empirical Paper

I. Introduction

    1. Overview of the research area

       a. Effectiveness of teaching strategies for group and individual learning

    2. Specific problem/question being explored

       a. Processes presumed to lead to memory retention and superior recall in groups versus individuals

    3. Review of the literature

       a. Examples: Mueller & Fleming, 2001; Brodbeck & Greitung, 2000; Clark et al., 2000

    4. Hypothesis (including any independent and dependent variables) and brief description of methods

       a. Does group study lead to better recall of information compared to pair or individual preparation?

       b. IV: Group, pair, or individual study

       c. DV: Recall quiz based on common reading

II. Method

    1. Participants (e.g., how many, sex, source)

       a. 20 (5 male, 15 female) college students; ages 17 to 28 (average = 20); convenience sample

    2. Description of any apparatus, special measures (e.g., personality inventories), etc.

       a. Short story; multiple-choice quiz

    3. Detailed description of procedure from start to finish of research

       a. Three participant conditions (group, pair, individual) read and studied a short story

       b. Later completed a recall quiz

       c. Informed consent obtained

III. Results

    1. Conceptual review of hypothesis

       a. Learning in a group was predicted to be superior to study in pairs or individually.

    2. Review of main results, including all statistical analyses and, when necessary, accompanying rationale.

       a. No significant differences were found ($p < .05$); group study was not superior to other two forms of learning.

Table 4.3. (*continued*)

    3. Review of any secondary findings

        a. None

IV. Discussion

    1. What do the results mean? Do the results support the hypothesis?

        a. Results did not support the hypothesis but remain unclear due to small sample and low statistical power; conclusions await further research.

    2. Problems with study, if any

        a. Selected reading may have been too easy; create more demanding DV

    3. What's next?

        a. Improve methodology and replicate research; consider possible role for participant frustration during learning

Note: This outline is based on the sample APA-style student paper presented in chapter 5 (see pages 105–114). The italicized print identifies specific content from that research paper. Please note that only the four main sections of an APA-style paper are shown here (cf., Table 4.2).

even finer levels of detail can be added to this or any outline. Outlines are meant to be flexible, growing or shrinking as needed.

USING OUTLINES

Outlines should remain apparent in finished work. The outline of any good paper should be discernible simply by jotting down section headings and subheadings. The main sections in APA-style papers (see Table 4.2) stand out, of course, but within each one, subheadings also represent parts of the outline (see Table 4.3). As an exercise in recognizing outlines, why not recreate the outline for one of the articles you are using for your research paper? Doing so can give you insights about what might work in your own outlines.

Table 4.4 includes additional suggestions for creating and refining paper outlines. Improving your outline will improve your paper, and it will encourage you to undertake the next step: Writing a rough draft.

Table 4.4. Suggestions for Organizing and Refining Outlines

- Remember that there is no perfect outline.

- Choose the outline style you prefer—simple or detailed. Relying on Roman numerals and uppercase letters to organize section headings and main points is a convention. If listing or numbering things is easier for you, then try that instead.

- Before creating a structured outline like the one shown in Table 4.2, jot down as many random ideas, thoughts, and facts belonging in the eventual paper as you can. Once you are done, rewrite this collection of phrases into complete sentences for the outline (see Howard & Barton, 1986).

- Make sure that all main points are summarized in no more than one or two sentences. Supporting details can be added underneath these points or saved for the actual paper.

- Determine the order of an outline's main points, making sure they flow logically from one another. Remove or relocate ideas that hinder this flow.

- Try to turn each main point into a paragraph. If a main point is too complex, revise it into more than one point (paragraph) within the outline.

- Use behavioral examples to illustrate main ideas in an outline.

- Include key studies to support the main points in your outline. Write down the author names and publication dates in the outline. The complete citation will be added to the references during the first draft.

- Refer back to the outline for guidance, but do not be afraid to revise it as you go along. Some writers suggest that outline revision should wait until an initial rough draft is completed. Others suggest that alterations to an outline should be ongoing. Choose the approach that works best for you.

- If you get stuck while writing a section (e.g., the Discussion), do some focused freewriting first, using the results to craft a detailed outline for this part of the paper. Outlines need not cover entire papers.

- Check your software. Some word processors have outline functions.

WRITING A FIRST DRAFT

The first-draft stupidity of great writers is a shocking and comforting thing to see. What one learns from studying successive drafts is that the writer did not know what he meant to say until he said it.

John Gardner

Freewriting and outlining can start a paper, but what comes next? The next step involves creating a complete rough draft. In a first draft, information is "roughly" where it should be, but the writer knows that revision will be needed. Rough drafts are "quick and dirty," designed to give the writer a sense of the whole paper, what works and what doesn't (e.g., Booth, Colomb, & Williams 1995; Hubbuch, 1985). The purpose is not to have every sentence perfect, every idea and definition clear. Rough drafts are a beginning, not an end.

Trick Drafts: Starting with the Roughest Draft

Even when a detailed outline is available, it can be hard to begin writing. Years ago I came up with a simple way to get started. My approach is guaranteed to give you the sense that progress is being made, that the writing is manageable, and that there is no reason to feel overwhelmed. I label the first, rough draft I write a "trick draft" because I literally trick myself into producing it (Dunn, 2001). It does not contain much detail, but when I am finished I feel that something is accomplished so that my next round of writing will be profitable.

Here's how to write a trick draft: Sit down in front of a computer and call up your favorite word-processing program. Type in your outline and insert **page breaks** (i.e., skipping from one page to the top of the next one) between each of the main sections shown in your outline. Naturally, secondary details and supporting information are entered on the same page as a main idea. In a few minutes, your outline has expanded to several pages. You need only begin to turn the main ideas and accompanying text into coherent paragraphs for the paper to take shape.

Table 4.5 contains simple directions for creating a trick draft of an APA-style research paper. You can adapt them as needed for other types of papers. If you follow the instructions in Table 4.5, your rough draft of an APA-style paper will have eight pages at the outset, a fact that will make working on the paper less threatening. As you expand the paper with your writing, of course, the section headings in its body will no longer appear at the top of every page. I have used this simple trick many times because any long piece of writing seems much less intimidating when you frame it out this way.

Table 4.5. Steps for Creating a "Trick Draft" of an APA-Style Paper

1. Open a new file using a word-processing program. Format the paper for double spacing.

2. Go to the middle of the blank page. Type out a working title for the paper (if you don't have one, just write "Title"). Double-space and center your name below the title, and then type your institution's name two spaces below your own. You now have page 1, the Title page. *Insert a page break.*

3. At the top and center of page 2, type "Abstract." *Insert a page break.*

4. At the top of page 3 (the first page of the introduction), center and type the same title that appears on page 1. *Insert a page break.*

5. At the top of page 4, go to the center and type "Method." *Insert a page break.*

6. At the top of page 5, go to the center and type "Results." *Insert a page break.*

7. At the top of page 6, go to the center and type "Discussion." *Insert a page break.*

8. At the top of page 7, go to the center and type "References." *Insert a page break.*

9. At the top of page 8, go to the center and type "Author Note."

10. Save this eight-page paper onto a disk or into a file. Print out a copy. *Here's the trick:* You are starting with eight pages before adding freewriting materials, points from your outline, or text for your rough draft.

Writing a Hypothesis and Composing Paragraphs

Drafting a paper also involves writing a thesis or hypothesis statement and composing paragraphs. The word *thesis* is used in the humanities, whereas the social and natural sciences rely on the word *hypothesis*. Psychologists write about hypotheses, the questions that are tested within experiments. A hypothesis is used to investigate a researcher's theory, and as such, it is the focal point of most psychology papers.

Ideally, a hypothesis is presented in a specific sentence or two:

Early physical maturation is predicted to lead to better emotional adjustment in adolescent boys than in girls.

Consider the difference between the clarity present in this sample hypothesis (i.e., early maturity is easier on males than females) and these two general variations:

During adolescence, physical maturation has different effects on the emotional adjustment of boys and girls.

> Emotional adjustment to physical maturation in adolescence varies for boys and girls.

Stick with a specific hypothesis. Unless "physical maturation" and "emotional adjustment" were previously defined, concrete descriptions of these variables would accompany the hypothesis.

Throughout any paper, however, a hypothesis is recalled in similar, not necessarily the same, words each time. Redundant phrases are boring. Referring back to the adolescence example:

> Early bloomer boys were expected to adjust to the emotional consequences of puberty more easily than girls.

> Girls whose physical maturity occurred later were found to manage the emotional rigors of adolescence better than their male counterparts.

A writer must never stray from a topic, so keeping the hypothesis in mind at all stages of the writing process is important. As a reminder, keep a scrap of paper containing the completed sentence, "My hypothesis is . . ." in front of you while you write (Silverman, Hughes, & Wienbroer, 2002). Post it on your computer monitor or prop it up on your desk. Keep it available when revising your paper as well.

Just as a hypothesis makes one strong point, so do each of the paragraphs found in a paper. Paragraphs lead readers point by point through a researcher's ideas and the arguments mustered to support them. Paragraph structure is basic: The point of a paragraph is made in its opening sentence, and those that follow explain the issue, making it more precise. The transition to a new idea is marked by a new paragraph.

A straightforward paragraph contains the following:[2]

- A sentence containing a main point
- A sentence defining general words, if any, found in the main point
- One or more examples illustrating the main point (with applicable citations)
- An explanation for why each example supports the main point
- A summary sentence

---

[2]Adapted from Jay Silverman, Elaine Hughes, and Diana Roberts Wienbroer, *Rules of Thumb: A Guide for Writers,* 5th edition, pp. 69 & 71, Mcgraw-Hill, 2002. Copyright © 2002 by Jay Silverman, Elaine Hughes, and Diana Roberts Wienbroer. Reprinted with permission of The McGraw-Hill Companies, Inc.

Variations to this basic formula are fine as long as any resulting paragraph remains a coherent unit connected to other paragraphs, as well as to the larger paper.

The danger novices encounter when crafting paragraphs is writing too much or too little. Paragraphs should be less than 10 sentences long (half this number is better still), but novice writers often cram as much information as possible into a single paragraph. No doubt you know from personal experience how boring it is to read unbroken text that goes on and on. Paragraphs are natural mental breaks for writers and readers. If there are fewer than two or three paragraphs on a page, then your paragraphs are too long.

Long paragraphs can be split where a logical break occurs (adapted from Silverman et al., 2002, p. 69):

- Some new idea or topic is introduced.
- A detailed or supporting example is presented.
- A theory, experiment, or study is described.
- A clear transition from one topic to another is apparent.

Very short paragraphs are just as problematic, particularly because too many of them imply a writer knows little about a topic or is a disjointed thinker. With few exceptions, no paragraph should be shorter than three sentences in length. If you are confronted with a paragraph that is one or two sentences long, you are either saying too little (beef it up) or the point being made is unnecessary to your argument (drop it altogether). A short paragraph can often be rescued by adding a specific example illustrating its main point. Alternatively, two short paragraphs can be combined into a longer one, or a short paragraph can be merged into a larger, more detailed paragraph.

A Recommended Order for Drafting APA-Style Papers

No paper needs to be drafted linearly. By "linear," I mean that you do not have to write a paper straight through from title page to tables and figures, with the Abstract, introduction, and so on in between (see Table 4.2). A linear approach is more useful for writing research proposals, which have a title page, an Abstract and introduction, a proposed Method and an anticipated Results section, and References, all of which are written *before* any data are collected (see pages 115–116 in Chapter 5).

Instead of writing a linear research paper, I recommend that you jump around a bit by writing some later sections before getting to the earlier ones. Remember, APA style is flexible, so there is no requirement that you write any paper from start to finish. Let me explain exactly what I mean: Table 4.6 shows an alternative approach to linear writing, one that works from the inside of the paper outward. Instead of starting with the title page, begin in the middle of the paper by writing what is most straightforward and familiar to you—the study's Method section (see step 1). Ideally, a Method section should be written right after the final procedure is determined and data collection is underway. Writing up the

Table 4.6. A Nonlinear Checklist for Drafting and Writing an Empirical Paper

_____ 1. Draft the *Method*

_____ 2. Draft the *Results*

    _____ Go back to step 1 for revising and editing

_____ 3. Draft the *Introduction*

    _____ When any reference is used, add it to the *References*

    _____ Go back to steps 1 and 2 for revising and editing

_____ 4. Draft the *Discussion*

    _____ Go back to steps 1 through 3 for revising and editing

_____ 5. Draft the *Abstract*

    _____ Create the *Title page*

    _____ Write the *Author Note*

    _____ Create any *tables* and/or *figures*

    _____ Match citations with contents of the *References*

    _____ Add *Appendix* (if needed)

    _____ Go back to steps 1 through 4 for revising and editing

_____ 6. Obtain peer feedback on rough draft of manuscript

    _____ Revise the manuscript based on peer review

    _____ Go back to steps 1 through 5 for final revising and editing

_____ 7. Submit the final draft

Source: Adapted from Dana S. Dunn, The Practical Researcher: A Student Guide to Conducting Psychological Research, *Table 3.6, p. 98, McGraw-Hill, 1999. Copyright © 1999 by Dana Dunn. Reprinted with permission of The McGraw-Hill Companies, Inc.*

research procedure then ensures that all the details are still fresh in the researcher's memory.

After the Method section is drafted, the next natural thing to write is the Results section (see step 2). Good writers have their findings firmly in mind because the Results affect how the rest of the paper is written. Remember, you are reporting research conducted to answer a focused question, not writing a long history of what led you to do the work or the inevitable switchbacks and sidetracks encountered along the way (Bem, 1987, 2000). Once these first two steps in Table 4.6 are accomplished, the drafts of both sections should be revised as needed.

Writing an introduction to the APA-style paper—step 3—follows the first round of revision. As the introduction takes shape, so does the References section of the paper. Once a draft of the introduction is complete, a review of the first three steps in Table 4.6 is performed and any necessary revising continues. Following the introduction, a draft of the Discussion section is written, followed by more revision (see step 4). Only in step 5 does the front and back of the APA-style paper begin to take shape. Step 6 involves sharing a complete rough draft of the paper with peers, who can provide fresh eyes and perspectives on the work (guidance on giving and receiving feedback is provided at the end of this chapter). Their comments, in turn, are incorporated into the paper during a last round of revising and editing. Submitting the final draft of the paper occurs in step 7.

WRITING SUBSEQUENT DRAFTS

Turning a first into a second draft is not difficult as long as you focus on the intended *audience*—the individual or group who will read your work. Your responsibility is to present your research in clear, unambiguous prose. To do so, you need to take your audience into account.

Three Issues to Consider

There are three main issues to consider when writing for an audience interested in psychology: tone, audience knowledge, and persuasion.[3] Let's tackle each in turn.

[3]Adapted from Jay Silverman, Elaine Hughes, and Diana Roberts Wienbroer, *Rules of Thumb: A Guide for Writers,* 5th edition, p. 59, McGraw-Hill, 2002. Copyright © 2002 by Jay Silverman, Elaine Hughes, and Diana Roberts Wienbroer. Reprinted with permission of The McGraw-Hill Companies, Inc.

TONE

What tone, style, attitude, or voice (see pages 170–171 in Chapter 9) for expressing ideas will you adopt in your writing? Psychologists usually write rather formally, focusing on their topics, not themselves. Many researchers focus on facts, theories, findings, even speculation, over personal experience. As a result, they often write in the third person, introducing distance and ambiguity:

> The experimenters then collected the surveys and administered the manipulation check.

Was the writer one of the experimenters? Who knows? Revising the sentence with a first-person pronoun clarifies things greatly:

> We then collected the surveys and administered the manipulation check.

Ambiguity is diminished and the sentence speeds along.

Some instructors encourage students to be dispassionate in their writing, as if complete emotional distance renders observations more objective or "professional." I disagree. I want you to write passionately about your subject while still maintaining an expert stance, one devoid of bias or personal agendas. The true fact is that no one wants to read writing that isn't lively—overreliance on the third person is incredibly dull—and how well you write about research is as important as the research itself (e.g., Sternberg, 1993). Use first-person pronouns (e.g., *I, me, mine*), just do so selectively and for a purpose (e.g., to illustrate a psychological theory through a personal example).

This book is written in an intentionally informal tone. The reason is simple: I need to keep your attention while giving practical advice about writing. A less formal tone is not an invitation for sloppy or lazy writing, however. You should never use slang (e.g., "ain't," "cuz") unless it appears in a direct quote. Avoid flowery or exuberant writing (e.g., "Psychology is so interesting! I love learning about what makes people tick!") as well as sarcasm, inappropriate humor, or an emphasis on personal experience over empirical knowledge.

AUDIENCE KNOWLEDGE

When writing, always think about what your readers *already* know and what you want them to know. Overly basic information does not need to be mentioned; with few exceptions, for example, there is little need for you to define *psychology* in a paper. On the other hand, unfamiliar or novel terms (e.g., Latin square design, confounding) must be concretely explained, preferably in the context of an example. Assume that your readers are curious and that it is your responsibility to educate them further.

PERSUASION

Science is fundamentally a human enterprise, and it involves persuading others that findings fit hypotheses. Although you are not selling anything but your ideas, you still must write convincingly or risk alienating your audience. Solid, persuasive research papers open on a strong note, drawing readers into the work. These articles always contain numerous examples describing existing research to support observation or speculation. Professional readers, including your instructor, tend to evaluate arguments in light of the psychological literature, which you must know and use (see Chapter 2). Peers are generally more interested in how well you anticipate and address those questions that occur to them as they read your work.

Finally, as a writer, a budding psychologist, you have the responsibility to act as both a teacher and a professional. Your writing is meant to inform, to teach your readers about some psychological topic or phenomenon. You have the same scientific responsibility that any researcher has: You must tell the truth about behavior and to the best of your ability.

Suggestions for Further Improvement

Here are a few more suggestions to improve subsequent drafts of a paper:

- Try what prolific writer-researcher Christopher Peterson (1996) calls the **spew method**, a close relative of freewriting. Though lacking an attractive name, the description is a directive to fill up a first draft with whatever words, sentences, and paragraphs come to you while writing. Do no rewriting or revising until the first draft is complete—let a bit of chaos precede order.
- Always print out the most recent draft of a paper so that you can write all over it before beginning the next draft. Unless you are very familiar with composing and editing on a word processor, working on a hard copy and typing changes in later usually yields better results.
- Double-space (some authors recommend triple spacing; see Parrott, 1999) drafts so there is ample room between sentences for jotting down ideas, making changes, and adding new sentences or paragraphs. Ditto for margins—keep them to a width of at least 1 inch.
- Stay away from a thesaurus. Good writers use everyday language to good effect.

- Be a pack rat: Hold onto all hard-copy drafts of papers. Some instructors like to see how a project developed from conception to completion. You might also decide to recycle or salvage some dropped idea from an earlier draft, something you cannot do once hard copies are discarded.
- Add complete references to the Reference section as you go from draft to draft. Waiting until the end to track them down is time consuming, tedious, and risky (see Chapter 7).
- As you write a draft, ask yourself questions: What's missing? What have I forgotten? If I were a reader, what would I want to know that is not here? What parts of the draft are too long or too short? Which ones are boring?

How Many Drafts?

How many drafts of a paper will you need to produce? I must answer, "It all depends." This answer is not entirely satisfying, but it is honest. The topic, your instructor's expectations, and your writing experience, effort, and skill all have an influence on how many drafts you need to produce before a polished version is achieved. I believe in erring on the side of too many drafts rather than too few. It is certainly the case that shorter papers (e.g., 5 to 10 pages) probably require fewer drafts than longer ones (e.g., 15 to 20 pages). But again, it all depends.

We will turn to revising and seeking feedback on complete drafts shortly, but there is one thing a writer can do to assess the quality of a draft early on: *Read it out loud from start to finish.* There is no better way to catch grammatical errors, awkward phrasing, or boring sections than to *hear* what you wrote. Language should have a nice cadence to it, not a ponderous or choppy flow. Long sentences are as dull to hear as they are to read. Hearing your words, too, can identify bad ideas and unsupported or missing examples. Try it. Brave souls, of course, will read their work to a live audience. That's fine, though you may want to save their goodwill for later, when you ask them to read and comment directly on your draft.

A final drafting strategy—the **reverse outline**—merits mention (Peterson, 1996). The goal is to extract an outline from the existing rough draft. Review this reverse outline to identify missing information, mislaid paragraphs, or areas of the manuscript that do not contribute to the whole. Drafting is often easier when you reexamine the larger structure present in a paper.

WRITER'S GUIDEPOST   4.1
Myths About Writers and Writing

Myths about writers and how writing *should be done* abound. Try not to believe them. Below are a few of these common "untruths." Given what you have learned in this book about writing, can you see why these myths are troublesome?

1. Good writers generate perfect manuscripts in a single draft.
2. Good writers do not write until they are in the right mood.
3. Good writers require large, uninterrupted blocks of time in order to be creative.
4. Good writers write only when they have an original, creative concept.
5. Good writers do not share their writing until it is done.
6. Good writers are naturally creative—they were not taught to write well.

Some writing myths that I have heard over the years:

1. Writing is easy. Everyone knows how to do it.
2. Grammar and punctuation are arbitrary conventions.
3. After my first-year writing course, I won't need to worry about writing ever again.
4. Scientific writing isn't creative.
5. Psychology students do not need to be good writers.

Source: Adapted from Boice (1990, p. 15). Adapted with permission.

REVISING: TOP TO BOTTOM EVERY TIME

Experienced writers make comprehensive revisions in their writing first and deal with minor details later. To their detriment, novice writers do just the opposite (Hayes & Flower, 1986). When you begin revising a paper, start globally and focus less on making superficial changes. Revising your writing involves these three steps:[4]

[4]Adapted from Peter Elbow and Pat Belanoff, *A Community of Writers: A Workshop Course in Writing*, 2nd ed., McGraw-Hill, Inc., 1995. Copyright © 1999 by Peter Elbow and Pat Belanoff. Reprinted with permission of The McGraw-Hill Companies, Inc.

1. **Rethinking**—Editing sentences and paragraphs to improve clarity or meaning; tightening up text so that it says what you want it to say; making the presentation of ideas effective and memorable.
2. **Restructuring**—Reworking the internal structure of a paper. Remember, outlines can change.
3. **Proofreading**—Proofreading a paper to catch spelling, grammar, and punctuation errors; omitting needless words (Strunk & White, 1972); verifying that the final text adheres to APA-formatting requirements.

We will consider the first two types of revision here. Directions for proofreading and formatting are found in Chapter 9.

I revise at the start of every writing session. I review what I wrote during the last session, starting at the beginning of whatever I'm writing. When I finish revising, I pick up writing wherever I left off last time. There are two reasons for revising a previous session's writing when sitting down to work. First, ideas tend to come fast and furiously when people write, especially with word processors. A review at the start of a session allows you to verify that your intentions are well represented in the text. Second, revising from the top allows you to slip back into the mindset of your paper. Knowledge and creativity get a jump-start, and you are writing before you know it.

You can also edit from a hard copy or printout of what you are writing, rather than doing so on a computer screen. When editing on a screen, you can see only a few paragraphs at a time. Working from a hard copy, however, allows you to see the whole paper at once. Spreading it out in front of you makes it easier to think about shifting paragraphs, writing new sentences over or between existing ones, crossing things out, even moving whole pages. Once you revise the paper from top to bottom, then you can make the changes permanent with your word processor.

Table 4.7 is a checklist identifying some issues to consider when revising an empirical paper.

Revisiting a Draft

Once a complete draft exists, step away from it for a day or two. An incubation period will help you see your work in a new light, possibly triggering connections you missed on the first pass (Peterson, 1996; Poincaré, 1913). After a good night's sleep or attending to other matters, you can return to your draft refreshed, ready to see things with a new perspective.

Table 4.7. A Checklist for Revising an Empirical Paper

INTRODUCTION

_____ Are the study's purpose and importance clearly identified?

_____ Is the hypothesis stated concretely and concisely?

_____ Are the variables included within the hypothesis defined?

_____ Is the hypothesis supported by existing research, observation, and/or examples?

_____ Does the hypothesis appear before some brief overview of the study's methodology, itself a lead into the Method?

METHOD

_____ Have the participants been characterized as specifically as possible (how many males, females; average age; source or population; whether they received compensation; how many withdrew or were dropped from the study, and why)?

_____ Is the procedure detailed enough so that readers can replicate the study?

_____ Are key instructions delivered to participants reported verbatim?

RESULTS

_____ Is the hypothesis repeated at the start of the Results?

_____ Is the logic provided for choosing a particular statistical test to analyze the data and test the hypothesis?

_____ Are all results explained in words as well as statistics (see Chapter 6)?

_____ Have any numbers, statistical symbols, and Greek letters appearing in the paper been verified against the original data analyses (see Chapter 6)?

_____ Are any tables and figures both referred to and explained in the text (see Chapter 8)?

DISCUSSION

_____ Is the study's hypothesis conceptually revisited?

_____ Are issues raised in the introduction and Results echoed in the Discussion?

_____ Are there alternative explanations for any findings? If so, are they explored?

_____ Were any of the obtained results unexpected or counter to the hypothesis? If so, are possible explanations entertained?

Table 4.7. (*continued*)

_____ Are any shortcomings of the research identified and explained?

_____ Are any implications or practical applications of the findings discussed?

_____ Is a direction for future investigations noted?

_____ Is the ending to the paper interesting, not dull?

REFERENCES

_____ Do the citations in the paper match those in the References?

_____ Are all references formatted according to APA style (see Chapter 7)?

GENERAL ISSUES

_____ Can each of the main sections be read independently from the others?

_____ Has the paper been proofread for grammar, punctuation, and spelling errors (see Chapter 9)?

_____ Have you made certain that no one- or two-sentence paragraphs remain?

_____ Are there enough descriptive subheadings? Would changing subheadings clarify the outline for readers?

_____ Is the paper formatted properly (e.g., for APA style; see Table 4.2)?

_____ Do tables and figures conform to APA style (see Chapter 8)?

I routinely make changes when revisiting my writing. I see things I missed or neglected to mention the first time around. Problem areas, issues I struggled with as I wrote, often seem less forbidding the next day. With a little time and some mental distance, some writers find that their "problem" is no longer really a problem, that what they said the first time is actually fine (Peterson, 1996). This is not wholesale encouragement to be satisfied with a last draft, just encouragement to revisit something with fresh eyes.

Ideally, revisiting should be done one last time, before the final draft of your paper is submitted to your instructor. Let at least 24 hours (48 is even better) pass before you take a last pass at your paper. As you revisit the paper, think about how your instructor or peers would read it. What would they like, what would they miss, what changes would they recommend? Distance and "perspective taking" can identify final changes to tighten up the paper. Once you make changes based on revisiting the paper, why not actually ask your instructor or peers to read and comment on it?

SEEKING FEEDBACK

Sharing paper drafts is common among psychologists. Indeed, most investigators ask colleagues for feedback on their empirical papers before submitting them for review and publication. Why? Additional feedback allows researchers another opportunity to improve their research summaries. Generally, a "new set of eyes" will identify strengths or weaknesses in papers that writers miss because they are too close to the work.

Writing workshops have revolutionized the teaching of writing. Students now regularly and actively seek feedback on their writing before submitting it for grading (e.g., Elbow & Belanoff, 1995). Perhaps you participated in a writing course containing a workshop component where students shared drafts with one another. Student researchers in psychology can also benefit from reader comments (Dunn, 1994).

Professor, Peer, or Writing Center?

You probably have three choices for a reader: your instructor, a peer in your class, or a tutor in the campus writing center. Due to the obvious conflicts of interest, I would avoid asking close friends, romantic interests, and family members for help. Many instructors welcome the opportunity to read their students' rough drafts. Approach your instructor during office hours to see if this is a possibility. Alternatively, ask a fellow student from your class or a trusted peer to read your paper. Be sure to select someone who realizes that you want honest criticism on, not undue praise for, your work. Finally, many colleges and universities now run writing centers that are staffed with tutors trained to comment on student papers. All you need to do is call ahead for an appointment, show up on time, explain the assignment, and share your draft.

How to (Graciously) Receive Feedback

Everyone likes praise, no one likes criticism. It is very easy to be defensive about your writing, but you must try not to be. Remember, readers genuinely want to help, and your responsibility is to listen carefully to what they say (i.e., do not shoot the proverbial messenger). I remind my students that if a peer has difficulty understanding parts of a paper, it is a virtual certainty that I will, too—and I am the one doing the grading. So pay close attention to how your reader reacts to your paper, take some notes, and make appropriate corrections in the next draft. Remembering this simple rule will help you: *Readers are always right.*

What feedback do you want from a reader? Keep in mind that your reviewer is not a proofreader; correcting surface errors in the text is your job (see Chapter 9). Instead, you are after guidance regarding the clarity of your arguments; comments on the paper's flow; an indication of what information is missing; and a sense of which parts of the paper work better than others. Invite a reader to make comments right on the draft.

When a reader finishes the draft, ask for specific reactions to it. Table 4.8 lists questions to ask a reader in order to get some discussion going. Listen carefully to the assessment, taking notes all the while. If you are not certain what a comment means, politely ask the reader to explain it to you.

Table 4.8. Questions to Ask Readers Who Reviewed a Psychology Paper

1. What is the main point of this paper?

2. What were your reactions to the study? Did it make sense to you?

3. Do you recall the hypothesis? How was it tested?

4. Was the logic behind the research methods clear? Is the detail sufficient for someone to redo the research from start to finish?

5. What were the results? Do the results support the paper's conclusion?

6. Were any parts of the paper difficult to understand? Did anything seem to be missing or need to be discussed in greater detail?

7. Do you think any sections of the paper could be condensed? Which ones?

8. Do there seem to be enough references?

9. Can you offer any other suggestions to improve this paper?

One more thing: You are not required to follow a reader's recommendations (except, perhaps, when the reader is your instructor). If you really don't agree with the comments, then don't use them (i.e., "It is still your paper"; Williams & Brydon-Miller, 1997, p. 103). Be respectful of the comments and grateful that someone took time to comment on your work, however. Always thank your reader and offer to read a draft of whatever paper he or she is working on.

How to (Graciously) Give Feedback

Giving feedback does not mean exacting revenge on a critic. Provide a peer with helpful, respectful feedback in the way that you would like to receive it (i.e., follow the "golden rule" of writing workshops). Remember that reading and commenting on other people's writing can improve your own prose; sometimes it is easier to identify problems in someone else's work rather than in your own. Perhaps the experience will help you be less likely to make similar mistakes in your own writing. You might even pick up some style tips or writing techniques by reading the peer work.

Table 4.9 asks some questions that you, as a reader, should think about while reviewing a peer paper. (Assessing your own draft with these

---

Table 4.9. Questions for Readers to Think About While Reviewing a Psychology Paper

1. Does the introduction provide sufficient depth and detail about the topic?

2. Does the hypothesis make sense to you? Do any supporting examples illustrate it well?

3. Is the method section easy to follow? Are any important details missing that would make replication difficult?

4. Are the findings clear? How well do they fit the hypothesis? If necessary, does the author acknowledge that the results do not match the predicted relationship(s)?

5. Does the paper adhere to APA style?

6. Does the discussion place the results in context? Does it offer any implications or applications? Is the paper's conclusion interesting or dull?

7. Are the transitions from paragraph to paragraph clear and logical?

8. What concrete suggestions can you offer to improve this draft?

---

questions is also a good idea.) Answers to the questions in Table 4.9 can structure the feedback you give to a peer. Try to give the most concrete feedback you can, and always find something positive to say.

EXERCISES

1. Do some freewriting in your research notebook for 10 minutes. Take a break and then do focused freewriting about your paper topic for 10 minutes.
2. Imagine you have 10 minutes to describe a research topic to someone. Create an outline of the important issues concerning your topic and write it in your research notebook.
3. In your research notebook, write a sentence summarizing a hypothesis. Write a paragraph describing a theory, independent and dependent variables, and an example to support your hypothesis.
4. In your notebook, write three short summaries of a published research finding for different audiences: (a) your instructor, (b) a classmate, and (c) someone who has never had a course in psychology.
5. Create a reverse outline from a paper you have already drafted.
6. Swap rough drafts of a paper with a peer. Offer constructive criticism to one another using the guidelines for giving and receiving feedback.

5

WRITING APA-STYLE PAPERS: CONTENT AND GUIDANCE

> You have conducted a study and analyzed the data. Now it is time to write.
> To publish. To tell the world what you have learned.
>
> —Daryl J. Bem (2000, p. 3).

You are ready to tackle the deeper issues associated with writing in psychology. This chapter focuses on the specific content within each section of the APA-style research paper. I provide guidelines spelled out in the *Publication Manual* (APA, 2001) and writing tips that I learned as both a teacher and a writer. The sections in this chapter are ready references for you when you sit down to write an APA-style paper. The emphasis here is on writing empirical papers, but guidance for preparing other types of APA-style papers is also presented.

BENEFITS OF APA STYLE

APA-style manuscripts are designed to convey research about behavior to psychologists, the wider scientific community, and interested readers. To do so, such manuscripts rely on a standard organization that prescribes where and how particular information is placed for maximum benefit to readers. APA style governs all aspects of writing in psychology, from punctuation to pagination, from organization to the ways that references are arranged. Standardization provides several benefits:

- **Consistency:** A uniform style enables readers to anticipate where particular information can be found within most publications. In turn, writers know how to prepare written work in order to meet readers' expectations.

- **Clarity:** A common writing style promotes clear reporting of research hypotheses, methods, and findings.

- **Brevity:** Scientific research is explained through concise but focused narratives.

- **Recursion:** Important ideas recur throughout any piece of psychological writing. Thus, the main sections of any APA-style paper can be read independently of the others because each reviews the same key themes as the others, though in different amounts of detail.

Collectively, these four benefits lead to one more:

- **Accuracy:** Any summary of scientific research must be as error-free as possible.

When writers make the most of these benefits, they ensure that any educated person can pick up an APA-style manuscript and make some sense out of it. APA-style writing is meant to be educational, so it should be accessible to readers in and outside the field of psychology.

Bem's Hourglass Model for Empirical Writings

Four sections represent the "heart" of the text in an APA-style paper: the introduction, Method, Results, and Discussion (see Tables 4.2 and 4.3). Social psychologist and gifted writer Daryl Bem suggests that, conceptually, the heart of an empirical publication is like an hourglass (Bem, 1987, 2000; see also, Bem, 1995). It begins broadly, narrows as statements in the Method section become more specific and increasingly focused, and then broadens once again with the Results and their implications in the Discussion (see Figure 5.1).

Keep Bem's hourglass model in mind as you begin to outline, draft, and then write APA-style papers. The shape metaphor—broad, then specific, then broad again—will help you hit the right level of detail in your writing.

WRITING THE EMPIRICAL, OR RESEARCH, PAPER IN APA STYLE

Title

The rule of thumb for writing a title is simple: Don't be boring—capture the reader's attention (Sternberg, 2000a). This rule is not an invitation to make up silly or controversial titles, of course, but it is a warning not to rely on hackneyed phrases or worn-out formulas. Too many papers are variations on the theme of "The Effects of Independent Variable Y on Dependent Variable X" (fill in your favorite X and Y), or "An Experiment on . . . ," or "A Study of . . . ." There is nothing inherently wrong with

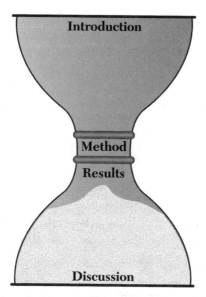

Figure 5.1 The hourglass model of APA-style empirical papers.

Source: From Dana S. Dunn, The Practical Researcher: A Student Guide to Conducting Psychological Research, *Figure 3.1, p. 80, McGraw-Hill, 1999. Copyright © 1999 by Dana Dunn. Reprinted with permission of The McGraw-Hill Companies, Inc.*

such titles, but there is nothing very engaging about them either. Readers scan titles quickly, so that any that do not pique curiosity are passed over in favor of those that sound promising.

I took a quick look through some journals to identify good titles. Here are a few:

The Role of Retrieval Structures in Memorizing Music (Williamon & Valentine, 2002)

Approach Versus Avoidance: Different Types of Commitment in Intimate Relationships (Frank & Brandstatter, 2002)

Very Happy People (Diener & Seligman, 2002)

Looking Back in Time: Self-Concept Change Affects Visual Perspective in Autobiographical Memory (Libby & Eibach, 2002)

Confidence, Not Consistency, Characterizes Flashbulb Memories (Talarico & Rubin, 2003)

How Do I Love Thee? Let Me Count the Words: The Social Effects of Expressive Writing (Slatcher & Pennebaker, 2006)

Expect the Unexpected: Ability, Attitude, and Responsiveness to
Hypnosis (Benham, Woody, Wilson, & Nash, 2006)

Go to the periodicals section of your library and take a look at journals
dealing with the content area of your paper topic (see the appendix for a
listing of some appropriate journals). Don't directly copy a title, of
course, but consider emulating the style or spirit of a good title.

What makes for a good title? A good title follows certain patterns:

- Precisely and concisely reveals the purpose of a paper
- Includes keywords highlighting theories and independent and/or
  dependent variables
- Identifies important relationships among variables (i.e., cause and
  effect, measurement, confounding, reinterpretation of effects)
- Relies on keywords so that searches of databases (e.g., PsycINFO)
  will appropriately identify a paper's relevance

APA-style titles are required to be relatively brief, ideally somewhere between 10 and 12 words. Titles that are too short do not provide enough
information. Long ones bore readers or risk muddling a study's true purpose with superfluous information.

WRITING A TITLE

The title is one of the last things to write for an APA-style paper. You
should never jot one down until you have a firm grasp of a project and its
findings. Sit down with a piece of paper or a blank computer screen and
then write down everything you think belongs in the title. The next step is
editing out excess words and phrases, especially offenders like "A study of"
or "An investigation of" or "The effects of" and so on. What you want is a
combination of words that accurately conveys the purpose of the research.

Once excess words are gone, what's left? Does the title now begin
with a word highlighting the important point made by your research
(Szuchman, 2002)? Move words around in the title so that it begins on a
strong note. Thus,

The Effects of Spatial Reasoning on Pattern Recognition in Children

becomes more focused as

Spatial Reasoning Affects Pattern Recognition in Children

Try writing several variations on the same title before committing to one:

Children's Pattern Recognition: Effects of Spatial Reasoning

Spatial Reasoning Affects Children's Pattern Recognition

There It Is Again: Spatial Reasoning Affects Children's Pattern Recognition

Thinking Spatially Promotes Pattern Recognition in Children

Spatial Thinking in Children Helps Them to Recognize Patterns

QUICK SUMMARY FOR WRITING A TITLE AND TITLE PAGE

- A title is generally no more than 10 to 12 words in length.
- A title appears centered in the upper half of page 1 (see chapter 9 for formatting guidelines).
- Avoid using redundant phrases (e.g., "The Effects of," "An Experiment on," "A Study Concerning").
- Do not use abbreviations in titles (e.g., instead of LTM, use the three words "Long-Term Memory").
- The author's name and professional affiliation (college, university, or other organization) appear double-spaced and centered beneath the title.
- A title page is shown in the sample research paper (see page 105).
- More information about writing titles can be found in section 1.06 of the *Publication Manual* (APA, 2001).

Abstract

Where titles capture reader interest, Abstracts sustain it. An Abstract is the "make-or-break" portion of the APA-style paper, the place where authors must make convincing cases for why anyone should bother reading their work. An Abstract must appeal to people already familiar with a topic as well as to neophyte browsers who might become interested in it. Writing a good Abstract is not easy, and it should be one of the last things you do when writing an APA-style paper (see Table 4.6 on p. 68). Never write an Abstract until you have finished writing a solid draft of your paper. You must know the relevant literature, your hypothesis and methodology, and the results inside and out before you attempt to write this encapsulated summary.

APA style requires that an Abstract is written as a short, unindented paragraph of between 100 and 120 words (those for theory or review papers are 75 to 100 words in length). The *Publication Manual* (APA, 2001) advocates that Abstracts should be factual, autonomous, succinct and focused, and easy to understand.

The following issues are raised in an Abstract:

- The problem being examined
- The study's main hypothesis (many papers have more than one—by no means can all of them be included in an Abstract)
- A method summary making note of any materials and/or apparatus, the participants (e.g., how many, their sex and age) or animal subjects (their genus and species must be indicated), research design, and the study's procedure
- Concise description of the main finding(s)
- Any future directions

Here is an example of a clear Abstract from the journal *Developmental Psychology*. The research examined how infants interpret the looking behavior of adults. Notice how the authors, Brooks and Meltzoff (2002, p. 958), managed to concisely describe two experiments while still covering the essential issues:

Two studies assessed the gaze following of 12-, 14-, and 18-month-old infants. The experimental manipulation was whether an adult could see the targets. In Experiment 1, the adult turned to targets with either open or closed eyes. Infants at all ages looked at the adult's target more in the open- versus closed-eyes condition. In Experiment 2, an inanimate occluder, a blindfold, was compared with a headband control. Infants 14- and 18-months-old looked more at the adult's target in the headband condition. Infants were not simply responding to adult head turning, which was controlled, but were sensitive to the status of the adult's eyes. In the 2nd year, infants interpreted adult looking as object-directed—an act connecting the gazer and the object.

WRITING AN ABSTRACT

To begin drafting an Abstract, write a summary sentence capturing the essence of each of the paper's main sections: the introduction (i.e., topic area or literature, hypothesis), Method (i.e., brief description of who participated, what they did procedurally), Results (i.e., what did participants do and did it confirm the hypothesis), and Discussion (i.e., what does it mean for what is already known, what implications does it hold for the topic). In a first draft, be concrete rather than conceptual or theoretical. Writing a single summary sentence (or two at most) for each of these main sections is not easy, but you must do so before considering additional details.

Alternatively, do some focused freewriting about your project paper, making certain to describe the study's background, hypothesis, methodology, and the findings, as well as their implications. Doing so using a word processor ensures that you can track the number of words you are using, move phrases around, and keep the Abstract to a manageable length.

Table 5.1 provides instructions for a structured approach to writing an Abstract. Frame the task this way: If you have a maximum of 120 words, you have around 10 sentences with a limit of 12 words in each available to describe what you did, what you found, and why you are writing this brief summary. By following this approach, you can draft a brief Abstract without omitting essential information. Keep in mind that the guidelines and limits noted in Table 5.1 will not work for every study, but they will help you draft something quickly that can then be refined and revised to fit the needs of your paper.

Table 5.1. A Structured Approach for Writing an APA Style Abstract

- **Background and/or purpose** (1 sentence): Describe why you conducted the study and why it is important.

- **Hypothesis** (1 sentence): Disclose the main hypothesis and variables (readers can locate secondary hypotheses and variables in the body of the paper).

- **Sample** (1 sentence): Indicate the number, sex, and age range of participants, and how they were recruited.

- **Design** (1 sentence): Explain the research design using appropriate terms (e.g., *two-group between-subject design; random assignment*).

- **Method and measures** (2 sentences): Describe the manipulation of the independent variable, presence of a control condition, and measurement of the dependent variable.

- **Results** (2–3 sentences): Focus on how results relate to the main hypothesis. If anticipated effects were not found, consider describing any interesting results that were found.

- **Conclusions** (1–2 sentences): Indicate the broader implications of the research. If possible, provide the casual reader with a "take home message."

Source: Adapted from a course handout created by Lori J. Toedter (2006).

QUICK SUMMARY FOR WRITING AN ABSTRACT

- An experimental Abstract is 120 words or less.
- A theoretical or review Abstract is 75 to 100 words in length.
- An Abstract is *never* indented like a paragraph.
- An Abstract appears on page 2 of any APA-style manuscript.
- An Abstract is shown in the sample research paper (see page 106).
- More information about writing Abstracts can be found in section 1.07 of the *Publication Manual* (APA, 2001).

Introduction

The goal of an introduction is to provide readers with a focused review of literature relevant to the question being examined by a paper. There is more to a good introduction, though, than providing context for a research problem. Introductions provide writers with an opportunity to let readers really understand the scientific reasoning behind psychological questions. Introductions allow you to make sense out of and to extend the psychological literature.

An introduction covers five issues:

1. Review of existing scholarship concerning a topic: *What is already known?*
2. Statement of purpose: *Why is this study being conducted?*
3. Theoretical implications: *How can results from this study extend what we already know?*
4. Description and definition of variables: *What variables are being measured and manipulated?*
5. Clear presentation of a hypothesis and supporting rationale: *What question is being tested? Why?*

WRITING AN INTRODUCTION

When covering these issues in an introduction, you must be clear and straightforward, not forced. Thus, it is better to indicate why a research topic is interesting at the outset of a paper (e.g., "For some, romance takes time to develop; for others it happens suddenly, even unexpectedly. What factors lead to romance sooner rather than later?") than it is to simply, even awkwardly, name the topic (e.g., "The purpose of this study is to examine factors influencing the onset of romantic attraction"). The latter approach is acceptable, but it is not great writing and it certainly does not qualify as interesting reading.

Grab the reader's attention in your opening paragraph. Consider this powerful example, which reminds readers of a great tragedy while simultaneously encouraging them to consider one of its psychological dimensions (from Lickel, Schmader, & Hamilton, 2003):

> On April 20, 1999, a tragedy struck Littleton, Colorado. Two students, Eric Harris and Dylan Klebold, entered their high school and brutally killed 12 of their classmates and a teacher. The two young men then committed suicide in the school library, where many of their victims were slain. In the days that followed, news coverage of the event gripped the United States and evoked intense discussion in the public at large. Who was, in fact, ultimately to blame for this horrible incident? It was unambiguous that Eric Harris and Dylan Klebold carried out the actions that resulted in the deaths of their victims. Nonetheless, in the minds of many, blame for the incident was not confined to the young men but extended to parents, friends, and others with whom the killers were associated. Instances such as this, in which blame is extended beyond those who committed a blameworthy event, can be described as instances of collective responsibility (Fineberg, 1970; May, 1987). The goal of the present research was to understand how people make judgments of collective responsibility in everyday life by focusing specifically on the factors that predicted how lay people judged collective responsibility for the killings at Columbine High School.

The bulk of an introduction is the literature review, a careful, reasonably thorough discussion of existing research directly pertaining to the study being conducted. Take careful note of the phrase "reasonably thorough": Your responsibility does not entail describing or citing every publication dealing with the issues raised in your paper. A literature review is not a history lesson. Only prior studies that directly deal with the current work should be cited and discussed. When these studies are reviewed, only their main findings, conclusions, relevant methods, measures, or techniques should be presented. Details, such as the number of participants, where and when the research was performed, and so on, are avoided. Readers who want details can track down a citation using your References section.

When reviewing prior research, focus on results and their relation to your ideas, not the names of investigators. Make the research the subject

WRITER'S GUIDEPOST   **5.1**
Opening Gambits for the Introduction

A good opening paragraph in an introduction attracts readers' interest, encouraging them to continue reading a paper. Kendall, Silk, and Chu (2000) offer some strategies for beginning that key paragraph on a strong note. Try opening with the following:

1. **An everyday experience.** Compare your research topic to a common event or everyday occurrence that readers will recognize (e.g., "Few professionals today do not experience a stressful imbalance between their work and home life").

2. **Absence of research.** When little research concerning a topic or question has been done, making a case for the need for research is usually not difficult (e.g., "Consciousness is shared by all sentient beings, yet we know little about its qualities or its nature").

3. **A rhetorical question.** Rhetorical questions make issues more personal. They direct readers to examine their own thoughts and feelings about a topic (e.g., "What is the nature of love?").

4. **A compelling fact or statistic.** Begin by presenting some unusually surprising piece of information relating to the paper's topic (e.g., "Where academic ability is concerned, most students rate themselves as above average—an interesting, if implausible, possibility").

5. **A metaphor or an analogy.** Use of analogy or metaphor can create a likeness between things or ideas that appear to be different, prompting readers to focus on the broad nature of a topic (e.g., "Psychologist William James believed that human consciousness flowed just like a river, continuous, ever-changing, yet always somewhat the same").

6. **Some history.** Once in a while, placing a research question within a historical context is appropriate, especially when the goal is to characterize how inquiry about a topic changed over time (e.g., "During the heydey of American behaviorism, interest in the psychology of the self went underground").

Source: From Kendall, Silk, and Chu (2000, p. 43). Reprinted with permission.

of your sentences, not the author-researchers. When reading first drafts of student papers, I routinely come across sentences like this one:

> In 1984, Robert Sternberg and Susan Grajek, psychologists at Yale University, published a paper in the *Journal of Personality and Social Psychology* wherein they examined the structural nature of love.

Actually, Sternberg and Grajek's work—not the researchers themselves, their home institution, or the journal where they published their findings—should be the focus of the sentence:

> Exploring the nature of love required a test of three alternative structural models (Sternberg & Grajek, 1984).

Author names and publication dates should be placed parenthetically somewhere in or at the end of sentences (see page 132 in Chapter 7). Authors should be the subjects of sentences when there is a clear need to delineate between the separate contributions or competing theories of different researchers or to vary your writing style. You could write:

> Sternberg and Grajek (1984) examined three models designed to reveal the structural nature of love.

Just make certain that relatively few sentences focus on researchers.

Students learning to use APA style often organize a literature review chronologically (Thaiss & Sanford, 2000). The earliest study is cited and discussed first, then the next earliest, and so on up to the most recent, relevant publication. A better solution is to review prior research thematically, by topic (e.g., Thaiss & Sanford, 2000). If several studies relied on the same methodology, review them together. Conceptually grouping prior research that shares common themes highlights those themes and makes their link to your study easier to understand.

Inevitably, you will need to comment on the shortcomings of earlier studies. Shortcomings that seem obvious now were probably not so obvious when past research was conducted. And in any case, criticism cannot be speculative; you must prove your concerns empirically. Thus, do not be too harsh in your criticism of earlier work ("It is not at all clear why previous researchers completely neglected to examine the role of friendship in romantic attraction"). Instead, raise questions about previous research by examining problems in methodology, reinterpret past results using recent findings, or highlight inconsistencies present among different studies. Criticism must be professional and constructive, never personal. It is entirely possible to acknowledge the contributions of others while indicating shortcomings. The key is to do so by exploring empirical challenges to what is known, not by offering unsubstantiated (and unkind) opinions (see also Sternberg, 2002).

The last paragraph or two of the introduction should clearly state the study's hypothesis and anticipated results, and include a brief preview of the methodology used to test it. Instead of the tried and true (but tired), "This study's hypothesis was that private forms of emotional disclosure should accelerate romance between dating partners . . .," try stating it simply: "Private forms of emotional disclosure are anticipated to accelerate romantic ties between dating partners." Besides stating the hypothesis, be sure to mention the anticipated results: "Dating partners who listen to an emotional rather than a neutral disclosure should report higher levels of romantic attraction for their partners." Methodology is described in the Method section, so the preview here should be short but descriptive: "To determine the role of emotion disclosure in romantic attraction, some dating partners were asked to describe a past emotional turning point to one another. Other dating couples were told to share the reason they chose their current major rather than another major."

Finally, students who are new to APA style often believe that they should not reveal the study's methodology in the introduction, that each section must stand apart from the others. In order for any section of the paper to truly stand alone, however, it necessarily needs to share some common information with the others. A study's hypothesis, for example, will make little sense unless it is linked to the research methodology being used to examine it.

QUICK SUMMARY FOR WRITING AN INTRODUCTION

- The introduction is not labeled by name.
- According to the *Publication Manual* (APA, 2001), the paper's title is double-spaced and centered at the top of page 3, the page where the introduction begins.
- An introduction is usually written in the past tense because it reports on published research and your own research, which has (presumably) already been conducted.
- The introduction contains three main elements: An overview of the topic, a literature review, and the hypothesis (with brief mention of anticipated results and the methodology employed).

- An introduction is shown in the sample research paper (see pages 107 to 108).
- For more information on writing an introduction, see section 1.08 of the *Publication Manual* (APA, 2001).

Method

Any Method section is a blueprint for readers who want to evaluate what was done in a study or to replicate it from start to finish. A thorough Method section allows readers to mentally walk through a study, to imagine the experience of research participants who took part in it. Readers can also assess the reliability and validity of an empirical investigation by carefully reading its Method section (APA, 2001).

A Method section is like a script for a play: lines are recited by some actors (i.e., experimenters) and listened to by other actors (i.e., participants), and all action is coordinated by stage directions. These directions include identifying which variables are measured or manipulated; what the experimenters and participants do; what stimuli, personality inventories, surveys, or questionnaires are employed; and when the participants' debriefing occurs.

WRITING A METHOD SECTION

A Method section should be appropriately descriptive but not so exhaustive that it results in an overly detailed paragraph that could have been better said in a crisp sentence. Method sections can contain the following subsections, labeled by subheading, and usually in this order:

- **Participants** or **Subjects.** Describes human participants (whether men and/or women, children, toddlers or infants, how many, their average age and age range, how and where they were recruited, and other pertinent information) or animal subjects (sex, weight, genus, species, strain number or the animal supplier and stock name, how many, and any other relevant details, especially their physical condition and the treatment they experienced).

Here is a brief participants section from Gasper and Clore (2002, p. 35):

Participants
Fifty-six men, 51 women, and 1 respondent who did not indicate his or her sex participated in the experiment for credit toward a course requirement.

- **Apparatus** or **Materials.** Apparatus refers to any special laboratory equipment, computer software, or other equipment that readers should know about. Manufacturer names and models should be provided. A specially created apparatus (e.g., a unique animal maze) should be illustrated in a drawing or photograph or described in an appendix. Materials often refer to surveys, questionnaires, or other stimuli that are shown to participants. Previously published instruments (i.e., personality or other standardized tests) also fall under materials and should be included in the References section. Novel measures should be described in an appropriate level of detail allowing for replication (a facsimile can be placed in an appendix).

This sample apparatus section includes information about the stimuli used in the research (from Bergeson & Trehub, 2002, p. 72):

Stimuli and Apparatus
Digital audio recordings were made in a large IAC sound-attenuating booth by means of a SHURE 5155D microphone in the booth, which was linked to a Denon PMA-680R stereo amplifier and Radius 81/110 computer with SoundScope software (GW Instruments, Inc., Somerville, MA). Test sessions were videotaped to ensure that infants' mood was comparable across sessions (to preclude maternal vocal changes arising from infants' mood change).

- **Procedure.** The procedure provides a chronology of what took place in a study. A thorough procedure should include a general description of the experimental design and task(s) used; how participants were assigned to particular conditions (if any); the most essential details of instructions given to participants; a description of all independent and dependent variables, as well as any additional variables that were controlled in the experiment; and mention of the study's debriefing and that ethical guidelines required by the APA were observed (see Table 5.2).

This procedure section is combined with information about the apparatus used in the study (from Kimchi & Hadad, 2002, p. 42):

Table 5.2. Following Procedure: Writing About Research Design Issues

Reis (2000) summarizes some basic questions about design issues that should be addressed in the Procedure subsection of any Method section appearing in a research paper. Use these questions to shape the beginning of your procedure section, the place where design issues are usually explained.

1. **What sort of research design was it?** Was the research conducted using a correlational, a quasi-experimental, or an experimental design? How many independent variables with how many levels were there? Were the independent variables presented between-participants or within-participants, or was a mixed-participants approach taken? When an unfamiliar research design is used, provide a general reference for it.

2. **How were the participants assigned?** How were the participants or animal subjects placed within the conditions in the study?

3. **What was the independent variable(s)?** What independent variable(s) was used in the study? Which conditions in the experiment, for example, represented the independent variable(s)? What aspects of the research setting (i.e., laboratory or field) were controlled or assessed?

4. **What was the dependent variable(s)?** What variable(s) was used to assess the influence of the independent variable(s)?

Source: Kendall, Silk, and Chu, Guide to Publishing in Psychology Journals, ed. R.J. Sternberg, p. 87. Copyright © 2000. Reprinted with permission of Cambridge University Press.

Procedure and Apparatus

Each trial consisted of the following sequence of events. First, a central fixation dot appeared for 250 ms. After a 250-ms interval, a priming stimulus (an upright or inverted letter, or an array of random dots) appeared for a variable duration, followed immediately by the test display, which stayed on until the participant responded.

As quickly and as accurately as possible, the participant made a same/different judgment about the two test figures by pressing one of two keys. Response times (RTs) were recorded by the computer. Feedback about an incorrect response was provided by an auditory tone presented as soon as the participant responded. Trials on which the response was incorrect were repeated at the end of the block. The screen was viewed through a circular aperture (14 cm in diameter) in a matte black cardboard sheet.

Note that it is not necessary to have all these sections in every APA-style Method section. Basic papers have a participants or a subjects section, as well as a procedure section. Apparatus and materials are optional, depending on the nature of the project. Flexibility is important, and many papers include unique subheadings that make understanding the reported research easier to follow (see the respective examples for apparatus and procedure shown above).

Brevity can be introduced into writing a Method section if the study relied on materials (e.g., instructions, procedure, measures) that were published previously:

> We relied on the identical materials and procedure used by Sternberg and Grajek (1984).

Include a brief synopsis of your methodology and then refer readers to the Method section of the previous publication for more specific details:

> Participants completed a demographic and family history questionnaire, as well as several standardized instruments and measures of liking and loving (see Sternberg & Grajek, 1984).

If you are using a previously published paradigm for a student paper, check with your instructor to make certain that referring readers to a previous publication is acceptable. Your instructor may still want you to write a detailed Method section to gain experience.

QUICK SUMMARY FOR WRITING A METHOD SECTION

- The Method section immediately follows the introduction.
- As a section heading, "Method" is centered.
- The Method section contains subsections, which are labeled with left-justified subheadings, including *Participants* (for humans) or *Subjects* (for animals), *Apparatus* or *Materials*, and *Procedure*; where necessary, novel section subheadings can be created. The research design (see Table 5.2) is usually explained early in the Procedure subsection.
- A Method section is shown in the sample research paper (see pages 109 to 110).
- For more detail on crafting a Method section, review journal articles cited in the introduction of your paper or consult section 1.09 of the *Publication Manual* (APA, 2001).

WRITER'S GUIDEPOST   5.2
A Little Is Enough When Writing a Method Section

Students sometimes include too much detail in their Method sections. It is no exaggeration to say that some come close to documenting every eye blink or breath taken. That much detail is too, too much. Assume your readers are knowledgeable. Here are a few suggestions to help you do so.

1. **Don't belabor the ordinary.** Some things do not need to be mentioned because they are implied by the demands of the situation. If participants are completing a survey, there is no need to indicate whether they used pens or pencils (number 2 at that!) or where the writing instruments came from.

2. **There is no need to explain standard experimental design, terms, or methodology.** Assume that your readers are familiar with psychological research. Do not explain random assignment or the counterbalancing of stimulus materials in any detail. Instead, just state that participants were randomly assigned to condition and that stimulus materials were counterbalanced to rule out any order effects.

3. **In general, describe the procedure from the participants' point of view.** Although you might be the experimenter, the research is about the participants' experiences. Your role, including what you did and said, is important, but the bulk of the description should highlight research procedures as the participants saw them.

4. **When something is used more than once, do not describe it again.** When anything is mentioned more than once in a Method section, such as rating scales, instructions, surveys, or instruments, refer back to the original description. If an experimenter repeats the same instructions several times, provide the verbatim instruction once, referring back to it as needed.

5. **Look for economies in words and phrases.** Whenever possible, leave out unnecessary details. If participants were told to read a passage as fast as possible without making any mistakes, simply indicate in the Method that the instructions stressed speed and accuracy (Szuchman, 2002).

Results

The Results section presents research findings based upon statistical analyses of the study's data. This section tells readers "what happened" in terms of the hypothesis being investigated. Did the obtained results confirm or defy expectations? Chapter 6 in this book presents detailed guidelines for selecting appropriate statistical tests and writing a Results section, so the presentation here is relatively brief.

WRITING A RESULTS SECTION

A good Results section proceeds in a straightforward manner. Readers are first reminded about the study's hypothesis, the analysis used to statistically test the hypothesis is noted, and then the actual results are presented. When presenting results, it is essential to describe them verbally (what happened is explained in words), statistically (what happened is explained using statistical symbols and numerical values of test statistics), and numerically (what happened is shown using numbers, as when averages are compared). Results sections often contain tables and figures, illustrating data relationships using numbers or graphs, respectively (see Chapter 8).

A Results section should be a factual account of what was found, not why. The writing should be clear and declarative, focusing on what did or did not happen behaviorally. Interpretation, speculation, or commentary regarding any findings is saved for the discussion section. Whether a hypothesis was confirmed is mentioned, for example, but not explored further until the Discussion section.

Only the results of data analyses are reported in the Results section, not the actual data. Statistical analyses summarize what was found, so raw data have no place there or anywhere in an APA-style paper. Do hold onto your data, however. Some instructors like to see raw data included in an appendix, whereas others just want to know that it is accessible (indeed, APA encourages researchers to hold onto their raw data for at least 5 years following publication; APA, 2001, p. 137).

QUICK SUMMARY FOR WRITING A RESULTS SECTION

- As a section heading, "Results" is centered.
- The Results section should open by restating the main hypothesis for readers. If there is more than one hypothesis, each is reviewed in turn (see Table 6.3 on page 126).

- Any statistical information must also be explained in clear, descriptive terms highlighting behavior (i.e., how research participants behaved in concrete terms).
- Whenever feasible, descriptive statistics (i.e., means, standard deviations, ranges) should be used to support inferential statistics (i.e., whether an observation is characteristic of one population or another).
- Any tables or figures appearing in the Results section must be referred to—and their contents explained—in the text.
- Detailed advice about choosing appropriate test statistics, organizing findings, and organizing a Results section can be found in chapter 6.
- A Results section is shown in the sample research paper (see pages 110 to 111).
- For more detail on writing a Results section, consult section 1.10 of the *Publication Manual* (APA, 2001).

Discussion

> Discussion sections of published articles exhibit science at work.
> —Norman H. Anderson (2001, p. 7)

> What can you say after you've said everything that you've already said?
> —Robert Calfee (2000, p. 133)

The Discussion section comes at the end of the APA-style paper, yet it is something of a beginning: What *does* it all mean, anyway? Discussion sections serve the important purpose of reflecting on an entire study, from reviewing the hypothesis and results to thinking about the "big picture," the implications of the findings for existing and future scholarship. Traditionally, little advice is offered about how to write a thorough Discussion section (Calfee, 2000); even the *Publication Manual* does not provide much guidance.

WRITING A DISCUSSION SECTION

There are four things you must do when writing a Discussion section:

- **Restate the hypothesis and results.** What did you expect to find? Did you find it? Why or why not? When describing a hypothesis that matches up with the (anticipated) results, call on prior research and theory for explanatory support. This part is easy; supporting evidence lies in the introduction and the Results sections. When predictions go awry, however, you must search for reasons to explain the null findings. The research methodology is usually the best place to begin, but it is also a good idea to consider the possibility that the logic you used to develop the hypothesis could be wrong. You cannot be certain unless you conduct a separate experiment to test this possibility, but you can certainly speculate a bit about it in writing.

- **Consider the wider implications of the study's findings.** Now that you know something about behavior, what does it mean? What else does it tell us about behavior? This second feature of the Discussion section is much more creative than the first (Szuchman, 2002), hence it is sometimes more difficult to write. When results support a hypothesis, a creative researcher thinks long and hard about what they mean and whether they are related to other behaviors. In other words, do the results have implications for more or less complex levels of analysis regarding behavior (APA, 2001)? Unsupported hypotheses: Does a problem exist in the theory, or in how it was tested, or do the negative results suggest other possibilities? Although null results do not point to clear explanations of why a hypothesis failed, significant results pointing to an interpretation *opposite* a hypothesis invite a researcher to think through other explanations, even other parts of the literature. Should you reconsider and revise a hypothesis or even revisit the larger theory from which it was drawn? If your results failed to replicate prior research, could there be something about your participants that affected the outcome?

- **Acknowledge what did not work or whether any problems exist.** No study is the last word on a topic; no research, no matter how well done or how good the results, is perfect. Good researchers are upfront and honest about a study's shortcomings. There is virtually always some limitation associated with the methodology, its execution, or possibly the pattern of the findings. Avoid mentioning trivial problems, however. Many studies can be criticized for relying on relatively nondiverse, homogeneous populations (i.e., the proverbial white, middle-class college sophomore; see Dawes, 1991; Sears, 1986). On the other hand, a restricted sample size can be worth mentioning when it probably had an effect on the statistical power in a study (see Dunn, 2001;

Rosenthal & Rosnow, 1991). Separate typical problems from those that pose a real threat to a study's validity.

- **Look ahead—what's next?** Far too many Discussion sections end with a vague call for "more research" on a topic. Such a conclusion adds little, as few topics in psychology do not require additional research. Be specific and provide a short but sensible direction for future research, particularly when your study's results imply what comes next. A thoughtful researcher who knows the research literature can point to related questions awaiting investigation.

Once you cover these four points, focus on making your discussion distinctive. After all, the Discussion section is the most personal part of an APA-style paper. Make an effort to write about what you believe is important and true about your work. Why do your findings matter? Why should readers care about them?

Woodzicka and LaFrance (2001, p. 28) wrote a distinctive concluding paragraph in a study examining real versus imagined sexual harassment. As you will see, these researchers identify problems and recommend solutions by highlighting why the research is important:

> Although experimental analogues and retrospective surveys provide important information about how women think they should respond and how they remember responding, they may overestimate rates of confronting compared with actual experience. Reliance on these methods may also miss complex emotional reactions that are directly linked to short-term and long-term responses. We advocate the use of multiple modes of investigating feelings and responses to sexual harassment. Realistic experimental harassment paradigms, diary studies, and structured interviews of harassment victims coupled with retrospective survey data would paint a more accurate picture of women's reactions to sexual harassment. Continued understanding of women's emotional reactions to harassment and public acknowledgment of how most women actually respond to harassment would help alleviate some of the stigma associated with being a target of harassment.

QUICK SUMMARY FOR WRITING A DISCUSSION SECTION

- As a section heading, "Discussion" is centered.
- Start any Discussion section by reviewing the main hypothesis and whether the results support it (additional hypotheses and findings should also be considered).

- Discuss the larger implications of the findings, if any, and acknowledge problems associated with the study (avoid trivial ones).
- Identify a future, specific direction for research (don't bother if you can only be general).
- A Discussion section is shown in the sample research paper (pages 111 to 112).
- For more detail on writing a Results section, consult section 1.11 of the *Publication Manual* (APA, 2001) or Calfee (2000).

References

Scientific references bolster a writer's arguments and are thus an essential part of the APA-style paper. Careful use of references establishes your credibility and familiarity with the psychological literature. Their presence in APA-style papers also serves an educational function: Readers can go to primary sources to retrace your steps. The philosophy of citing prior research and accurately reporting references in the required format is presented in detail in Chapter 7.

QUICK SUMMARY FOR ORGANIZING REFERENCES
- As a section heading, "References" is centered.
- Cite only publications that are directly relevant to your study and that you have actually read.
- The information contained in any citation must be accurate and conform precisely to APA-style guidelines for References (see chapter 7).
- Detailed guidelines for a variety of citations are provided in chapter 7 (see also the References section in the sample research paper, page 113).
- Exhaustive guidelines for citing previous research, including rare or obscure citations, can be found in sections 4.01–4.16 of the *Publication Manual* (APA, 2001).

Tables and Figures

Tables and figures are used to convey information about data (or relationships therein) simply, clearly, and sparingly. Tables contain statistics, not raw data, while figures graphically illustrate relationships using scatterplots, line graphs, patterns, and the like derived from the data. Thus, tables must convey precise numerical information whereas figures provide quick, visual summaries that are not meant to be as exact as those found in tables (APA, 2001). Chapter 8 provides guidance for constructing accurate tables and figures in accordance with APA style.

QUICK SUMMARY FOR TABLES AND FIGURES

- Tables contain numbers, which are usually presented as descriptive statistics (e.g., means, standard deviations) or inferential statistics (e.g., the results of some t-tests).
- Figures are quick, visual representations of results that do not necessarily contain numbers. When numbers are present, they are often less precise than those found in tables.
- Detailed guidelines for preparing tables or figures are provided in chapter 8.
- Further information about tables and figures can be found in sections 3.62–3.86 in the *Publication Manual* (APA, 2001).

Appendix

In APA style, an Appendix contains information that might otherwise draw readers' attention away from the main text, taking up too much space or not being appropriate for it. Appendixes are rare in student papers.

QUICK SUMMARY FOR PREPARING AN APPENDIX

- As a section heading, "Appendix" is centered.
- An appendix contains specialized materials that are not appropriate for the main body of APA-style papers (for further detail, see section 1.14 of the *Publication Manual*; APA, 2001).

Author Note

The Author Note should be short, sweet, and straightforward: author departmental affiliation, source of funding for research, acknowledgments, and whom to contact for further information about the work. Most student papers will probably not require one, but some may, especially when projects are collaborative. Here is a basic Author Note appropriate for a student's APA-style paper:

Author Note

Steven J. Student, Department of Psychology.

I am grateful to our chapter of Psi Chi for providing funds to make copies of the questionnaire used in this study. Professor Jones and the students in Research Methods 202 provided helpful comments on earlier versions of this paper.

Correspondence concerning this research should be sent to Steven J. Student, Box 222, Bigtime University, Anytown, USA, 11111; e-mail: sjs@bigtime.edu.

QUICK SUMMARY FOR WRITING AN AUTHOR NOTE

- As a section heading, "Author Note" is centered.
- Indicate the departmental affiliation of the author or authors.
- Identify financial support used in the research (i.e., grants, scholarships). Undergraduate papers rarely have such support, but some graduate student papers do.
- Acknowledge collegial help. It is a professional courtesy to thank individuals who provided constructive comments on your paper or assisted with the research.
- Provide a contact for further information about the research. Share your mailing address and e-mail address so that anyone interested in your work can contact you (this is especially helpful for conference presentations or journal submissions; see chapter 10).
- An Author Note is shown in the sample research paper (see page 114). For further guidelines, see sections 1.15, 3.89, and 5.20 in the *Publication Manual* (APA, 2001).

A SAMPLE RESEARCH PAPER

The sample paper that follows represents a student's first attempt at writing in APA style. The marginal comments describe style rules and the accompanying arrows highlight examples in the paper.

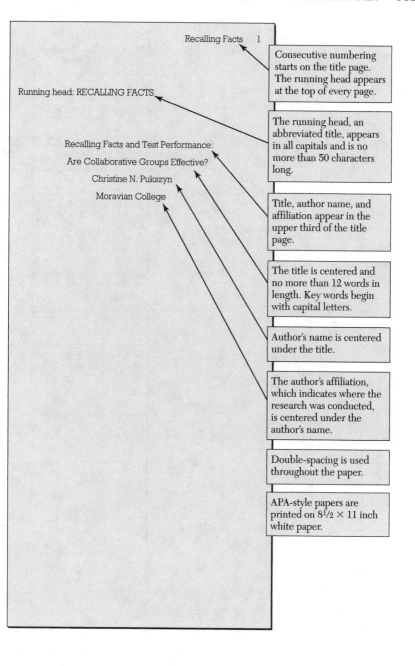

Recalling Facts   1

Running head: RECALLING FACTS

Recalling Facts and Test Performance:

Are Collaborative Groups Effective?

Christine N. Pukszyn

Moravian College

Consecutive numbering starts on the title page. The running head appears at the top of every page.

The running head, an abbreviated title, appears in all capitals and is no more than 50 characters long.

Title, author name, and affiliation appear in the upper third of the title page.

The title is centered and no more than 12 words in length. Key words begin with capital letters.

Author's name is centered under the title.

The author's affiliation, which indicates where the research was conducted, is centered under the author's name.

Double-spacing is used throughout the paper.

APA-style papers are printed on $8^1/_2 \times 11$ inch white paper.

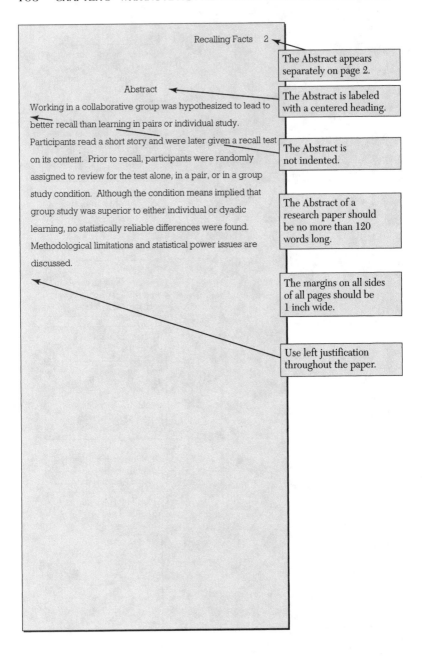

Recalling Facts   2

The Abstract appears separately on page 2.

Abstract

Working in a collaborative group was hypothesized to lead to better recall than learning in pairs or individual study. Participants read a short story and were later given a recall test on its content. Prior to recall, participants were randomly assigned to review for the test alone, in a pair, or in a group study condition. Although the condition means implied that group study was superior to either individual or dyadic learning, no statistically reliable differences were found. Methodological limitations and statistical power issues are discussed.

The Abstract is labeled with a centered heading.

The Abstract is not indented.

The Abstract of a research paper should be no more than 120 words long.

The margins on all sides of all pages should be 1 inch wide.

Use left justification throughout the paper.

Recalling Facts   3

Recalling Facts and Test Performance:

Are Collaborative Groups Effective?

Educational standards in America's classrooms currently focus on assessing and demonstrating learning through testing. As academic standards increase, students are encouraged to learn and retain larger amounts of information. Teachers are motivated to identify efficient strategies promoting the recall of the information that students learn. A familiar classroom strategy involves emphasizing group interaction over solitary study. Whether group dynamics, notably collaborative learning, actually enhance student recall and subsequent test performance remains an open question.

Groups do provide some educational benefits, notably those resulting from mutual cooperation. When working in groups, students often share their thoughts and ideas, increase their motivation, and better pursue goals than individuals working alone (Anderson & Thomas, 1996; Brodbeck & Greitemeyer, 2000). Group cooperation, " ... might lead to better performance, including sharing of ideas about approaches to solving the problem identification of different categories of information, and increased monitoring of the solution process" (Barron, 2000, p. 392). If students working in groups are actively engaged, they should work together cooperatively, identifying errors while searching for correct solutions. Groups are also capable of considering more ideas than an individual working alone. And as students collaborate to solve problems, such teamwork increases the group's sense of unity.

The size of a group influences the nature of the collaboration, if any, occurring within it. A collaborative group consists of at least two people. When a group has two members, a problem's solution must be determined in the absence of a majority vote, an

---

The introduction begins on page 3.

The paper's title is repeated and centered above the opening sentence of the introduction. Note that the title's main words are capitalized.

Citations appearing within parentheses are listed alphabetically and separated by a semicolon.

Parenthetical citations use an ampersand (&) in place of "and" but citations outside parentheses use "and."

An example of how to cite a quotation of fewer than 40 words. Longer quotations appear in an indented block without quotation marks.

Recalling Facts   4

often-necessary component of groups comprised of three or more people (Clark, Hori, Putnam, & Martin, 2000). Presumably, a group of two people must discuss a decision more thoroughly than a larger group, where dissent can be overlooked in favor of majority choice. Yet larger groups can be expected to yield a greater diversity of opinions, which can influence the nature of their collaborative interactions.

> Cite all authors up to six the first time their work is used.

Collaboration, then, involves cooperating as a group, but does cooperation enhance information recall? Some research finds an unexpected difference in the free recall of information following group collaboration (Clark et al., 2000). Ironically, some collaborative groups show lower levels of recall than noncollaborative groups. Perhaps high levels of cohesiveness lead to the sharing of trivial rather than consequential information during group interaction. Other research demonstrates, however, that the amount of correctly recalled information in any collaborative group should still exceed that of an average individual (e.g., Basden, Basden, Bryner, & Thomas, 1997). As long as a collaborative group remains focused on a topic, relevant knowledge shared by some of its members can be considered by the other members.

> With three or more authors, use "et al." following the first citation.

> e.g. ("exempli gratia") means "for example."

Based on previous research examining cooperative learning and recall, I hypothesized that three or more individuals studying together in a collaborative group would perform better on a recall test than those working in pairs or alone. Participants read a short story and then later prepared for a multiple-choice recall test in one of three randomly assigned study conditions: in a group, paired with a partner, or alone. Average recall scores were predicted to be highest for the group study condition, followed by those working in pairs. Recall scores were anticipated to be lowest in the individual study condition.

> Writing in the first person is acceptable in APA style.

> The hypothesis is clearly stated prior to the Method section.

Method

Participants

Participants were 20 (10 men, 10 women) student volunteers who received extra course credit. All participants were enrolled as part or full-time students at a small liberal arts college. Participants were White and ranged in age from 18 to 28 years ($M = 19.2$, $SD = 2.35$).

Materials

The materials used in this experiment included a 20-item multiple-choice recall test based on the short story, "Shiloh" (Mason, 1997). The questions dealt with characters and the story's plot; some were relatively easy (e.g., "What was Leroy's wife doing when the story begins?"), others were more challenging (e.g., "What was Norma Jean's mother's name?"). After reading the story but before taking a recall test, all participants received a list of seven short answer review questions to prepare for the recall test (e.g., "Think about the characters in the story: What were their names? How were they related to one another?"). Following the recall test, participants completed a 10-item manipulation check assessing their feelings about working alone or in groups, whether they perceived the study time as helpful, and their general reaction to taking tests. Responses to the manipulation check were based on a five-point rating scale, anchored from (1) strongly disagree to (5) strongly agree. Participants completed a standard informed consent form and received an extra-credit form at the study's conclusion.

The Method section is written in the past tense.

First-level headings are centered but not italicized.

Second-level headings appear at the left margin and are italicized.

Participant information includes number, gender, race, age, selection procedure, and any reason for participation.

Statistical symbols are italicized.

Arabic numerals are used for numbers of 10 or more.

The materials section describes the nature and function of the materials used in an experiment.

Procedure

Participants were greeted by two experimenters and then handed the informed consent and extra credit forms. After choosing their own seats, the participants were informed they would read a short story and then answer questions about it. Participants were then given the story and 25 min to read it.

When participants finished reading, they were randomly assigned to one of three study groups and given a copy of the review questions. Participants assigned to prepare for the recall test alone constituted a control group. A second group consisted of participants who studied for the test by working in pairs. The third group was comprised of three or four participants who prepared collaboratively. Following the study time for review, participants were given the recall test and the manipulation check. All participants were then debriefed according to the guidelines for the ethical treatment of research participants endorsed by the American Psychological Association.

Results

Preliminary analyses revealed that there were no effects due to the sex of the participants. Consequently, this variable will not be discussed further.

Preparing for the recall test in a collaborative group was predicted to lead to better recall than studying in a pair or individually. In general, participants scored quite well on the recall test; the lowest recall score was a 16 and four participants achieved perfect scores of 20. Although participants who studied in groups had slightly higher scores on the recall test ($M = 19.20$) than those working in pairs ($M = 18.00$) or individually ($M = 19.00$) a one-way analysis of variance (ANOVA) found no significant differences among the three conditions, $F(2, 17) = 1.01, p > .05$.

Given the basic research design and straightforward results, no table or figure were needed.

Standard units of measurement are abbreviated.

Sections of the APA-style paper appear with no page breaks.

The Results section is written in the past tense.

Note that a verbal description of the findings accompanies the means and the statistical results.

An abbreviation is identified the first time it appears.

Participants' responses to items on the manipulation check indicated that they took the review session seriously. Ninety-five percent of the participants disagreed with the statement that the review "confused me more than helped me" prior to the recall test. Most respondents (90%) agreed that the study session provided "clarity and insight" into the short story. Finally, all participants either agreed or strongly agreed with a statement indicating that they felt "comfortable" taking multiple-choice tests.

Discussion

The results of this study did not confirm prior research indicating that collaborative group work leads to better recall of learned information. Although increased motivation and idea sharing were expected to lead to heightened test performance in the group study condition (e.g., Brodbeck & Greitmeyer, 2000; Willoughby, Wood, McDermott, & McLaren, 2000), no supporting results were obtained. Participants who studied in a group did not have a significantly higher mean recall score than those who prepared in pairs or individually. Despite the absence of significant differences among the three groups in this study, the observed results were suggestive: Students preparing in pairs or individually had slightly lower (though not reliably so) average recall scores than those who collaborated in a group.

Lack of support for the hypothesis can be explained in several ways. First, when studying together in groups, students are forced to adopt the style of most group members. Perhaps the participants' recall suffered because their innate learning styles differed from the condition to which they were assigned (Basden et al., 1997). A second possibility is that no pretesting of the short story's multiple choice test was conducted. It is possible that the test was

> The Discussion is written in the present tense.

> The Discussion indicates what the findings did and did not reveal.

Recalling Facts   8

too easy, as indicated by the relatively similar—and quite high—recall scores found in each of the three conditions. Indeed, the three condition means were very close to the test's possible high score of 20. A ceiling effect might have masked any real differences attributable to the effects of how students prepared for the recall test. In retrospect, too, exposure to the study questions could have inflated recall scores. Having more difficult questions on the test might have highlighted recall differences among individual, pair, or group study methods. Finally, too few participants took part in this study; statistical power was too low to reliably detect any between group differences. Addressing these shortcomings in a replication could lead to results aligned with both the favored hypothesis and the existing literature.

A replication of this experiment might also examine what participants are actually doing during the study period prior to the recall test. Any study period is supposed to enhance performance on a test, but only if the available time is used appropriately. The present study did not specifically observe or track participant activities during their time in group, pair, or individual preparation. Tighter control should be exercised so that a more fine-grained analysis of activities occurring during the study time can be subsequently and constructively linked to student performance at recall.

> A study's limitations should be noted in the Discussion.

> Directions for future research are offered in the Discussion.

References

Anderson, N., & Thomas, H. D. C. (1996). Work group socialization. In M. A. West (Ed.), *Handbook of work group psychology* (pp. 423-449). Chichester, UK: Wiley.

Barron, B. (2000). Problem solving in video-based microworlds: Collaborative and individual outcomes of high-achieving sixth-grade students. *Journal of Educational Psychology, 92,* 391-398.

Basden, B. H., Basden, D. R., Bryner, S., & Thomas, R. L., III. (1997). A comparision of group and individual remembering: Does collaboration disrupt retrieval strategies? *Journal of Experimental Psychology: Learning, Memory, & Cognition, 23,* 1176-1191.

Brodbeck, F. C., & Greitemeyer, T. (2000). Effects of individual versus mixed individual and group experience in rule induction on group member learning and group performance. *Journal of Experimental Social Psychology, 36,* 621-648.

Clark, S. E., Hori, A., Putnam, A., & Martin, T. P. (2000). Group collaboration in recognition memory. *Journal of Experimental Psychology: Learning, Memory, & Cognition, 26,* 1578-1588.

Mason, B. A., (1997). Shiloh. In D. Hunt (Ed.), *The Riverside anthology of literature* (pp. 460-471). Boston: Houghton Mifflin.

Willoughby, T., Wood, E., McDermott, C., & McLaren, J. (2000). Enhancing learning through strategy instruction and group interaction: Is active generation of elaborations critical? *Applied Cognitive Psychology, 14,* 19-30.

The References section begins on a new page.

APA-style References appear in alphabetical order.

APA-style References are double-spaced and should have a hanging-indent.

Only the first word in titles or subtitles, as well as any proper nouns, are capitalized.

Italicize journal names, book titles, and volume numbers.

A multiple author reference uses an ampersand (&) in place of "and."

Recalling Facts   10

Author Note

Christine N. Pukszyn, Department of Psychology.

I am grateful to class peers and to Professor Robert T. Brill for reading and commenting on an earlier draft of this paper. Copies of the short story test, manipulation check questionnaire, study review sheet, and informed consent form are available from the author.

Correspondence concerning this research should be sent to Christine N. Pukszyn, c/o the Department of Psychology, Moravian College, 1200 Main Street, Bethlehem, PA 18018-6650, or by electronic mail to cpk@mc.edu.

> The Author Note appears on a separate page following the References section.

> The first paragraph identifies author and departmental affiliation.

> The second paragraph contains any acknowledgments and offers to share materials with readers.

> The third paragraph provides contact information regarding the author.

WRITING AN ARTICLE CRITIQUE

An **article critique** is a short, focused paper (usually 4 to 6 double-spaced pages) that analytically evaluates a published journal article. Writing an article critique allows you to become familiar with the strengths and weaknesses of a single project. By identifying problem issues in published writings, you can learn style points and techniques to improve your own writing. Article critiques are relatively informal, though most contain the following sections that address specific questions:

- **Thesis or hypothesis.** What is the central question explored in this article? What is the study's main hypothesis?
- **Method.** What are the most important procedures the researcher(s) used to test the hypothesis? Were these methods suited to the task? Were the methods used appropriately? Were there enough participants? Were they drawn from an appropriate population? Were there any other problems? Be specific.
- **Evidence offered in support of the thesis or hypothesis.** How would you concisely summarize the main results of the research? Do the findings support the hypothesis? What are the strengths and weaknesses of the results? Were appropriate statistical tests used? How well do the results support the author's thesis?
- **Contribution to the psychological literature.** What are the major conclusions the researcher(s) draws from this study? How does this research affect the existing literature? Does it promote future research in a new or merely consistent direction? Are there any limitations to this work?
- **Assessment and recommendations.** Are the author's conclusions legitimate and scientifically valid? What audience will benefit from reading this article? What are the specific benefits? Can the findings be generalized to other times, places, and populations?

Your article critique can be organized around these sections. Ask your instructor for additional formatting instructions.

WRITING A RESEARCH PROPOSAL

In preparation for conducting an APA-style research project, some instructors require their students to write a research proposal (sometimes known as a "prospectus"). Some instructors assign proposals to give

Table 5.3. Parts of an APA-Style Research Proposal

Title page—page 1

Abstract page—page 2

Introduction (with centered title at the top of the page)—begins on page 3

- Identification of research problem or thesis
- Review of the literature
- Hypothesis, short description of methodology, and anticipated findings

Method (immediately following the introduction)

Anticipated Results (optional)

References

Note: Research proposals are abbreviated versions of standard APA-style manuscripts (cf. Table 4.2).

students a chance to design an experiment; others do so as a first step toward conducting one. A research proposal is a plan, an outline of what you intend to do and why. In practical terms, an APA-style research proposal is a research paper that lacks Results and Discussion sections. The Method section is usually the last main section of the paper, though some students add a section labeled "Anticipated Results" in which they outline what they expect to find once data are collected and analyzed.

When writing such a proposal, the recommended steps for drafting (see Table 4.6 on page 68) can be modified. Because the study is still on the drawing board, you may find it easier to draft the introduction first (i.e., begin at step 3 in Table 4.6) and then the Method (back to step 1), followed by the Anticipated Results (if included) and References (see Table 5.3).

A decided benefit of writing a proposal is that you get to really think things through before the actual research takes place. The parts of the proposal shown in Table 5.3 probably receive a little more scrutiny and revision than they do in those research papers written once data collection is underway. When (or if) the research project is actually conducted, you can focus most of your energy on writing the Results and Discussion sections.

WRITING A LITERATURE REVIEW PAPER

A literature review, the traditional "term paper," examines published research pertaining to a focused topic. Imagine, for example, that you were interested in the effects of parental divorce on the academic performance of adolescents. You would search the psychological literature for all studies examining the relationship between scholastic performance of teenagers and divorce. In doing so, you would state your hypothesis, and all the studies included in your paper would somehow refer back to it.

The *Publication Manual* (APA, 2001, pp. 7–8) indicates the requirements of any review article:

- Describe and refine a research issue.
- Review prior studies covering the research issue (i.e., what is known about it).
- Designate relationships among relevant variables, highlight contradictory findings, point out issues requiring investigation, and highlight any inconsistencies in the available studies.
- Provide a concrete suggestion about how research should proceed to address the issue.

According to Thaiss and Sanford[1] a good student-written review paper has three basic parts:

1. **Topic overview:** Statement of theme and purpose of review.
2. **Bulk of paper:** Review of specific topics drawn from critical reading of existing studies.
3. **Closing section:** Critical assessment of conclusions drawn from review and recommendations for future research.

Each section of the review would liberally use headings and subheadings (drawn from a detailed outline) to organize the literature for readers. As noted earlier, research studies should be reviewed by topic and not chronologically. Good sources of sample literature reviews are found in *Psychological Bulletin, Annual Review of Psychology*, and *Personality and Social Psychology Review*, among other sources. Take a look at a

---

[1]From C. Thaiss and J. F. Stanford, *Writing for Psychology,* p. 88. Published by Allyn and Bacon, Boston, MA. Copyright © 2000 by Pearson Education. Adapted by permission of the publisher.

sample of articles from these sources, and do not be put off by their length, depth, or scholarly detail. You are learning to write a literature review paper. No one, including your instructor, expects a flawless work the first time around. For further advice on writing a literature review, see Eisenberg (1997, 2000; see also Bem, 1995).

The main question students ask regarding literature reviews is, "How long does the paper have to be?" The answer, of course, is up to your instructor, but it is not unusual to be assigned a 10- to 20-page term paper. Writing a literature review paper is not terribly different than doing an empirical study, except that it usually requires more library work. You will save some time, however; no experiment needs to be designed and run, no data collected or analyzed. The processes for identifying a topic, outlining, drafting, writing, revising, and editing empirical papers shift only slightly to accommodate doing review papers.

Writing a Theory Paper

A variation of the literature review paper is the theory paper—a paper that focuses on explaining the results attributed to some phenomenon by advancing a new theory for it. Whereas a literature review organizes existing research in terms of a binding theme, a theory paper tries to explain often-disparate findings by reexamining them from a new perspective. Theory papers are difficult to write, but the challenge can be both educational and rewarding. They are generally structured this way:

1. Presentation of detailed theory and predictions.
2. Review of existing research in light of the new theory.
3. Recommendations outlining future studies to test the theory.

Sample theoretical papers can be found in *Psychological Review*, the APA journal devoted to theoretically innovative ideas. Go to the library and examine recent issues of this journal for high-quality theoretical papers. Do not be intimidated by the length and depth of the contributions in this journal. Your goal is to mimic the style of *Psychological Review* articles on a smaller scale, one appropriate to your situation as a student learning the ropes of the discipline. As always, practice and experience are the best teachers.

EXERCISES

1. Go to the periodicals section of the library. Look through some psychology journals until you find an article that you believe is an exemplary example of APA style and one that is less so.
2. Read a research article. Using your own words and ideas, write a new opening paragraph for the article's introduction and a new concluding paragraph for its Discussion.
3. Select a Method section from a published research article. In your research notebook, try to rewrite the Method, condensing it without losing any important details.
4. Locate the Results section from a journal article. Create an outline of the Results section that you believe might present the findings more clearly for readers.
5. Write a critique of an article.
6. Draft an outline for a paper that reviews the literature concerning some psychological issue or question.

6

WRITING UP RESULTS

Written interpretation of statistical results is the focus of this chapter. I cannot teach you to perform statistical analyses, but I can provide guidance about reporting numerical results in words. I will assume that you have already taken an introductory statistics course or that your instructor will provide necessary help with data analyses. When you complete this chapter, you will be well prepared to write a clear APA-style Results section (additional suggestions are presented in Chapter 5).

CONVEYING STATISTICAL RESULTS IN WORDS

When you cannot quickly and concisely explain the result of some statistical test, then you do not really understand that test. If you do not understand the test, then you cannot accurately interpret a result derived from it. If you cannot interpret the result, then what should you do?

First, never, never panic. Second, take your time to carefully read and think things through. Third, consult someone who understands statistical results better than you do, such as your instructor, a trusted peer, or someone who routinely does data analyses. Fourth, keep things in perspective by remembering that statistics are tools, guides to inference and scientific judgment that help us to develop written conclusions about behavior. The psychological interpretation we make in our writing is inherently more important than the statistical analyses leading up to it.

Starting with a Hypothetical Research Result

Let's review a hypothetical research result, focusing on interpreting and writing it up. Perhaps a student researcher decides to replicate existing research on the informal but personal space people like to maintain around themselves. Hall (1966; see also Hall, 1963) argued that in Western cultures, individuals only let their closest friends and intimates into the small "bubble" of space that surrounds them. It follows that if a stranger or mere acquaintance enters this zone of intimacy, the entry should create discomfort, leading the affected person to move away from the invader. If someone you do not know well has ever gotten too close to you and like most people you felt minor distress and tried to back away, then Hall's claim seems valid.

A simple study is conducted where friends or strangers are induced to get close to each other. An experimenter surreptitiously observes the proceedings, counting the number of floor tiles separating one person from another. According to Hall's (1966) theory, the observed distance should be smaller between friends than between strangers. In practical terms, the average number of floor tiles should be smaller between people who know each other well than between those who do not. Imagine that these observational data were collected in a public setting, say, a lounge in a student union.

Once the data were analyzed, you would write down concrete, behavior-focused sentences indicating what the result means. Table 6.1 will help you do so. The first step in Table 6.1 directs you to identify the test used in the data analysis, prompting you to remember the test's function and its statistical symbol (see step 1). The present study involves two independent participant groups: friends standing near friends and strangers standing near strangers. The appropriate statistical test for analyzing the average distance between the participant pairs is the independent groups t test. The data are the number of counted floor tiles lying between each pair of participants. Following the space-invasion hypothesis, the t test is used to determine whether the average number of tiles falling between friends is significantly less than the average observed between strangers.

Perhaps the descriptive statistics imply that Hall (1966) was correct. The average distance between friends was smaller (3.2 tiles) than that observed between strangers (4.5 tiles). Will this relationship be statistically significant? Back to the analysis: The second step in Table 6.1 involves pulling together statistical information. Besides jotting down the symbol associated with your test statistic (i.e., the independent groups t-test, identified back in step 1), you would need to do the following:

- Record the test's degrees of freedom and critical value (both are necessary parts of any hand t-test calculation or can be found on a computer printout of an analysis).
- Indicate the value of the test statistic (based on your calculation or computer printout).
- Accept or reject the null hypothesis.
- Make note of the observed significance level.

Table 6.1. Putting Results onto Paper: Turning Statistics into Words

Step 1—Identify your statistical test (check one below):

Test	What the Test Does	Statistical Symbol
_____ Chi-square	Tests for categorical differences	χ^2
_____ Factorial ANOVA	Tests for mean difference(s)	F
_____ Independent groups t-test	Tests for mean difference	t
_____ Dependent groups t-test	Tests for mean difference	t
_____ Repeated measures ANOVA	Tests for mean difference(s)	F
_____ One-way ANOVA	Tests for mean difference(s)	F
_____ Pearson correlation coefficient	Assesses association between variables	r

Step 2—Organizing statistical notation information (fill in each blank below):

a. Test symbol (from step 1)   _____

b. Degrees of freedom (df)   _____

c. Critical value (from statistical table or computer printout)   _____

d. Calculated value of test statistic (from calculation or computer printout)   _____

e. Status of null hypothesis (circle one)   Accept or Reject

f. Obtained significance level (e.g., $p < .05$)   _____

Step 3—Describe the result in words, incorporating any statistical information (including means as well as statistical notation from step 2) as appropriate.

Source: Adapted from Dana S. Dunn, The Practical Researcher: A Student Guide to Conducting Psychological Research, *Table 8.5, p. 280, McGraw-Hill, 1999. Copyright © 1999 by Dana Dunn. Reprinted with permission of The McGraw-Hill Companies, Inc.*

All the information outlined in step 2 of Table 6.1 is a standard part of any statistical analysis, whether it is done by hand or by computer. Let's assume that we are drawing the information from a computer printout, filling in the blanks in step 2 accordingly. If the degrees of freedom were 20, then the critical value for a two-tailed test would be 2.086 (parts b and c in step 2). In order to reach statistical significance at the .05 level, the calculated t-test statistic would need to equal or exceed this critical value. Imagine that the obtained test statistic is equal to 2.35, which does indeed exceed the 2.086 critical value—we can reject the null hypothesis at the .05 level of significance (see parts d, e, and f of step 2).

Step 3 in Table 6.1 involves writing a summary sentence describing what happened behaviorally, making certain to include the statistical information from steps 1 and 2. Following APA style, of course, the results should make explicit reference to the hypothesis being tested. The descriptive summary of a result should have two qualities:

- **Brevity**—Use as few words as possible to explain what happened.
- **Simplicity**—Readers who know nothing about statistics should have a clear sense of what happened; those with statistical training should concur with the data analyses.

Here is one way to write up our hypothetical result, making clear mention of the original hypothesis, the behavior and how it was measured, and the statistical results:

> We tested Hall's (1966) claim that only close friends and family members are welcome in the so-called "zone of intimacy," the small bubble extending a few feet around each person. Replicating Hall's observations, friends allowed other friends to be physically closer than did relative strangers. In a staged, casual encounter, friends permitted a significantly smaller number of floor tiles between one another ($M = 3.2$) than did strangers ($M = 4.5$), $t (20) = 2.35$, $p < .05$.

As shown here, a result is easier to understand when it is summarized in words prior to citing the test statistic's calculated value, degrees of freedom, and significance level. Indeed, the statistical information found in any Results section is there only to support the prose—meaning matters more than numbers. For a straightforward analysis like the t-test, it is often easier to cite the group means in the descriptive sentence accounting for the result. In this example, the reader quickly appreciates that fewer tiles lie between friends than between strangers. Reporting the actual averages allows readers to visualize this scene of closer proximity. For more complex statistical relationships, presenting data in a table is often easier for readers to follow (see Chapter 8). Other examples illustrating written summaries of statistical results can be found in psychology journals (see the appendix) and the *Publication Manual* (APA, 2001).

One oddity about APA style must be mentioned here: When reporting basic sample statistics (e.g., a mean and its standard deviation, a measure of spread or dispersion of observations) within written text rather than tables, statistical symbols like $\bar{x}$ (the statistical symbol for a mean) and s (the statistical symbol for the standard deviation of a sample) are not used. Instead, the mean is symbolized by capital M, and SD is used to denote a standard deviation (see the *Publication Manual* for related examples). Other helpful rules for writing about results using APA style are shown in Table 6.2.

Organizing the Results Section

Salovey (2000) reminds us that a well-written Results section tells a good story, and such stories always have an organization making them compelling and clear. Salovey recommends that writers follow these steps when organizing a Results section:

- Always begin with what is most important, the study's main finding.
- Present findings in the same order they are considered in other sections of the paper.
- Give readers "top-down" structure at the beginning of the Results: Remind them what was done, why, and what will follow.
- Let the meaning of the findings organize the Results section, not the nature of the statistical analyses; again, meaning matters more than any numbers.
- Justify the choice of any statistical analysis.

All these valuable suggestions point to a larger principle: Tell readers what you did and why you did it. The art involved in doing so is in being logical and hitting the right level of detail. Other good suggestions can be found in Salovey (2000).

What if you have several findings to summarize and share? Larger studies will have more detailed Results sections than smaller studies. The basic guidelines for putting together a Results section are presented in Chapter 5. We can supplement them, however, by recommending a hierarchical outline for more detailed research efforts. Table 6.3 illustrates such an outline, one that can be adapted or expanded as needed. As you

Table 6.2. Additional Helpful Rules for Writing About Results in APA Style

- Just as *datum* is singular while *data* is plural, the word *analysis* is singular ("I performed one statistical analysis"); the plural form of this word is *analyses* ("I performed several statistical analyses on my data").

- The word *between* refers to a relationship existing between only two things (e.g., "There was a positive correlation between variables X and Y"). Use the word *among* for relationships involving three or more things (e.g., "Correlations were computed among the three variables").

- Statistical or mathematical symbols cannot be used as substitutes for words in sentences. Never write: The n of participants in the experimental condition $= 20$.

- A zero (0) always appears before a decimal point when the value of the number is less than 1.0 except in cases where it could never exceed 1 (as is true for p values, correlation coefficients, and so on).

- When referring to numbers in written text, use words for the numbers nine and below; use the arabic numbers for 10 and higher (i.e., nine participants, 20 stimuli).

- Never begin sentences with arabic numerals—use a word if you must (e.g., "Eleven participants . . .") or alter the sentence (e.g., "There were 11 participants . . .").

- Always italicize statistical symbols (e.g., χ^2, N, p, x as on p.122 in Table 6.1 under "Statistical Symbol").

- When referring to descriptive statistics in parenthetical comments or in a table, use the APA-style abbreviations (e.g., M, SD); in written text, however, use words to denote these statistics (e.g., mean, standard deviation).

---

can see, Salovey's (2000) recommendations are reflected in Table 6.3. At the top of the hierarchy, an opening paragraph reminds readers about the study's purpose (remember, each section of the APA-style paper must stand alone), thereby preparing readers for the detailed review of results that follows (see Table 6.3). Following presentation of a main result and its supporting information, for example, secondary and tertiary results are reviewed. Based on the hourglass model, of course, the Results section broadens toward the necessary transition to the Discussions section.

A glance at the articles in almost any psychology journal will reveal that there is a pronounced trend to "package" studies, so that many articles contain not one but two, three, or even more studies. Few student papers are

Table 6.3. Outlining a Hierarchical APA-Style Results Section

Opening Paragraph Review of Results—Overview

Brief review of overall hypothesis and research method

Explanation of what aspect of behavior (human or animal) is being investigated

Specific mention of independent variable(s) and dependent variable(s)

Concrete description of the nature of the data

Main Result

Specific statistical test used and brief rationale for it

Concrete description of behavioral finding and link back to hypothesis

Statistical notation (symbol, degrees of freedom, obtained value, significance level) supporting the result

Table(s) and/or figure(s) supporting the statistical result(s)

Secondary and Tertiary Results (if any)

Specific statistical test(s) used and brief rationale(s)

Concrete description of behavioral finding(s) and link back to hypothesis(es)

Statistical notation (symbol, degrees of freedom, obtained value, significance level) supporting each result

Table(s) and/or figure(s) supporting the statistical result(s)

Transition to Discussion Section

Source: Adapted from Dana S. Dunn, Statistics and Data Analysis for the Behavioral Sciences, *Table C.1, p. C-9, McGraw-Hill, 2001. Copyright © 2001 by The McGraw-Hill Companies, Inc. Reprinted with permission of The McGraw-Hill Companies, Inc.*

apt to contain multiple experiments. Should you ever need to do so, though, be aware that APA style is appropriately flexible (see Section 1.12 in the *Publication Manual*). Each study has a separate introduction (usually quite brief, as a standard one still opens the paper), Method, Results, and Discussion section. When a study is very short and to the point, the Results and Discussion sections can be combined into one section. A centered heading labels each study (e.g., Experiment 1, Study 2). Articles containing more than one study conclude with a General Discussion, an attempt to highlight the most important issues collectively raised by the research.

REFLECTING FURTHER ON YOUR RESULTS

Once the draft of a Results section is finished, you should address the finer points that require a bit of reflection on your part. Remember, your goal is not just to report results but also to think about larger issues relating to them. I have two sources for doing so: new APA guidelines on statistical methods and five criteria for presenting results.

New APA Guidelines on Statistical Methods

Not too long ago, the APA brought together a group of experts to discuss how psychologists use (and occasionally abuse) statistical procedures (Azar, 1999; Wilkinson & the Task Force on Statistical Inference, 1999). Their reflections were crafted with an eye to improving scientific communication in journals, which means there were also a few implications for writing in APA style. As you think about writing up your research results, a few observations made by the Task Force can help you to do so more clearly (other, more technical issues can be found in Wilkinson et al., 1999):

- **Be careful about drawing any causal conclusions.** When writing about results, individuals have a tendency to simplify findings, to make them seem more definitive than they really are. Statistical results identify what is likely to be true, not what is true. In the same way, your writing can identify possible causal links between variables, but it should not imply that they are clear and absolute. There is always a possible, rival hypothesis waiting in the wings to account for some set of findings.
- **Identify problems in your research procedure before discussing results.** As noted in Chapter 5, no set of research results is ever perfect. There is bound to be some minor problem in the execution of the research procedure, research participants' behavior, and so on. Mention such issues prior to discussing any results. Such disclosure is honest, preparing readers to think about how or whether any problem poses threats to the interpretation or acceptance of your results.
- **Define all variables and explain their relevance to the research.** All independent and dependent variables present in any research must be clearly defined, their relevance documented. To do this, you must present them in the right context, one in which identifying and discussing them improves a reader's comprehension

of your arguments. No variable should be mentioned casually or introduced in an off-hand manner; their presence and relevance to the research must be justified completely and concretely.

• **Think about the generalizability and the utility of the results.** What do the results tell you about behavior? How do they extend, change, or otherwise inform what is already known about behavior? Can they be applied to broaden our understanding of psychology?

Meaning Before Numbers: The MAGIC Criteria

When writing up results, a good writer-researcher gives serious thought to their interpretation and meaning. How did the research participants behave? What, if anything, changed their behavior? What does their behavior mean for understanding some aspect of human or animal psychology? Again, besides focusing on what happened behaviorally, a writer must think about the wider implications that findings may have.

To establish the "meaningfulness" of research results for readers, the late Robert Abelson (1995) offered the MAGIC criteria. Representing five useful traits to consider when deciding how well some results support a hypothesis, the acronym MAGIC stands for **magnitude**, **articulation**, **generality**, **interestingness**, and **credibility**. Table 6.4,

---

Table 6.4. Abelson's MAGIC Criteria for Writing About Results

Magnitude—How strong are the results? How well do the results support the hypothesis?

Articulation—What is the simplest, most direct way to summarize a finding in words? As long as important information is not lost or misconstrued, briefer explanations are preferable to detailed ones.

Generality—Can the findings tell us anything about behavior in other places and at other times? How generalizable are the results? Are they broad or narrow in scope?

Interestingness—Who will care about, want to learn about, the findings? Will psychologists, educators, your instructor, and peers? Why? Be specific. To Abelson truly interesting results change the way people think about a research issue.

Credibility—Can the findings be supported and believed? Are the logic and method used to determine the results reasonable? How will critics interpret the results?

Source: Adapted from Abelson (1995). Adapted with permission.

which describes each of the five criteria, should be a helpful resource when reviewing the results you wrote using words.

EXERCISES

1. Write a paragraph in your research notebook explaining why a particular statistical test is the appropriate choice for analyzing some data.
2. Draft a Results section using Salovey's (2000) organizational recommendations.
3. Evaluate a Results section from a published journal article. Do conclusive phrases occur more often than hedged phrases? Revise any hedged phrases, writing conclusive versions in your research notebook.
4. Change any hedged phrases in your Results section into conclusive ones.
5. Use the MAGIC criteria to evaluate a Results section from a published journal article. How well do the Results meet the criteria? Identify passages in which the criteria could improve the text.
6. Revise a Results section you have written using the MAGIC criteria.

7

CITING REFERENCES
IN APA STYLE

The goal of writing in APA style is the clear communication of scientific information. This goal is aptly represented in the References section of any publication written according to APA style. References sections distill the citations that authors deem to be essential to *supporting* scientific arguments made in the body of their work. Naturally, authors must also fairly and impartially include those works whose scope or findings *contrast* with their own scientific positions. Ethically speaking, all sides of a scientific argument are entertained before one is chosen over another.

CITATIONS AND REFERENCES

Relevant citations referred to in the body of any APA-style paper must appear in a specified format in the work's accompanying References list. In turn, all references listed at the end of a work must be cited in the body of that work. In short, citations and references in APA-style papers must necessarily match each other (Smith, 2000).

Psychologists use particular references for specific purposes. As a result, no APA-style References list cites any and all possible works on a given topic. Instead, References sections include only the most appropriate works that pertain to the scientific question being investigated, reviewed, or discussed.

When writing, rely also on current references (Smith, 2000). Given the amount of available literature pertaining to most psychological topics, not to mention the relative ease with which you can search the literature housed in databases, online library catalogs, or the Internet (see Chapter 2), there is no excuse not to have up-to-date references. I am not suggesting that citing older or even "classic" references should be avoided, but rather that you should not have a great deal of difficulty locating recently published material pertaining to most topics.

Beyond the necessity of their presence and currency lies one other requirement: accuracy. References and citations must adhere to prescribed styles of presentation, and their content must be error-free. Any reader must be able to track down one of your cited works, which means that the References section must be flawless.

Learning the Psychological Literature by Reading References Sections

As you research a topic by reading selections from the available literature, its pays to skim References sections. As you do so, you will soon recognize the important or sometimes "classic" citations dealing with your topic due to the frequency with which authors rely on them. You may also discover a few gems, references that will help your work even though they are cited infrequently.

What makes a citation "classic" or influential? Surveys of academic psychologists reveal they believe that high impact articles are well written and theoretically significant, possess practical relevance, are attention-grabbing and methodologically interesting, and have value for generating future research (Sternberg & Gordeeva, 1996). Many articles are never cited, which does not mean that they are not read or that their ideas are unimportant. Most pieces of research are cited only a few times. The Social Science Citation Index (SSCI) and the Science Citation Index (SCI) actually track the frequency with which authors and their works are cited. There are even a few published lists of the most widely cited references in the field of psychology (see Kintsch & Cacioppo, 1994; Sternberg, 1992; see also Shadish, 1989).

Scientific references can be powerful and influential when properly used in your writing. As a result, of course, you are duty bound to provide readers with correct citations. Why? First, because it is your minimum responsibility to demonstrate publicly that you are familiar with the literature on some topic and that you know how to use it. Second, you want to share what you know with others, perhaps motivating them to read some of the relevant articles you used. To learn from these same references, readers must be able to locate them, tracking them down with little or no fuss. If you provide them with incorrect or limited bibliographic information, they will be unable to find what they need. It is in your interest as a student of psychology, then, to learn the ins and outs of citing references using APA style.

BASIC CITATION MECHANICS

Like the rest of APA style, the approach to citing references is meant to be easy on both writers and readers. In practice, it is a bit easier on readers than on writers. Writers must not only keep accurate track of all the references (see Chapter 2), they must know how citing journal articles differs from referencing books, Web sites, or even letters to the editor. Initially, learning the citation style can seem a bit intimidating—so many details, such precise and ordered structure. With a little experience, however, you will improve quickly and learn to reference effortlessly. You can rely on this chapter of the book for 12 categories of the most commonly used reference styles. For more exotic types of references, consult a copy of the *Publication Manual* (APA, 2001).

Citing References Within Text

When do writers need to reference a source in something they are writing? Like most researchers, psychologists are a conservative bunch. Most are concerned about giving scientific credit where credit is due. When they read research relating to questions they are investigating, psychologists cite those references that inform their work. As a writer and reader delving into this published literature, you must be certain to cite any research that helped you or guided your thinking about your chosen topic. Table 7.1 lists questions to help you decide whether to cite a reference in your writing.

There are two basic ways to cite a reference within some text. One approach relies on parenthetical citation:

> The positive psychology movement was created to address an imbalance in psychology, to examine beneficial processes over the more traditional focus on negative aspects of human behavior (Seligman, 2000).

Here, the relevant reference is parenthetically cited at the end of a declarative statement, letting the reader know where to look for support for the claim being made.

Naturally, more than one reference can be cited parenthetically. Multiple parenthetical references must be listed alphabetically, however:

> People generally present their public selves to others in much the same way they perceive themselves to be in their private thoughts (e.g., Buss & Briggs, 1984; Schlenker, 1986; Tesser & Moore, 1986).

Table 7.1. Citing Citations: When and Why?

To determine whether to include a citation in a piece of writing, ask yourself the following questions. Anytime you answer *yes*, including the citation is a good idea.

1. After reading a reference, did you use any hypothesis, research finding, or definition from it in your work?

2. After reading a reference, did it shape your thinking about the theory guiding your work?

3. After reading a reference, did you replicate or adapt any research methods presented therein for your work?

4. After reading a reference, did you borrow any statistical, analytical, or stylistic techniques from it for your work?

Source: Adapted from Dana S. Dunn, The Practical Researcher: A Student Guide to Conducting Psychological Research, *McGraw-Hill, 1999, p. 89. Copyright © 1999 by Dana Dunn. Reprinted with permission of The McGraw-Hill Companies, Inc.*

In this instance, "e.g." (*exempli gratia,* Latin for "for example") is included parenthetically to indicate that the cited references are examples that support the claim being made. Please take note of the fact that an ampersand (&) appears in any multiple author citation appearing within parentheses, as well as the fact that a semicolon (;) separates each reference from the others.

When two or more authors' names appear directly in text, the names are separated by "and" rather than an ampersand:

Robins and John (1997) found that most students predict their course grades will be higher than they actually turn out to be.

More than one parenthetical reference can also appear earlier in a sentence:

Research on self-knowledge (e.g., Baumeister, 1986), self-esteem (e.g., Rosenberg, 1965), and self-monitoring (e.g., Snyder, 1974) continues to be used in comprehensive reviews of self processes (Brown, 1998).

The alternative approach to basic citation involves making a reference a key part of the text, often the subject of a sentence:

> Following Chwalisz and Vaux (2000), rehabilitation researchers and practitioners are advised to consider how social support can enhance physical as well as psychological well-being.

Naturally, if a reference has more than one author (but fewer than six), each one should be cited the first time a reference is used:

> Ericsson, Chase, and Faloon (1980) described the unique memory skills of a research participant who chunked digits into meaningful running times.

Citations with one or two authors always provide the author names. When a citation has three, four, or five authors, however, subsequent citations need only cite the first author's last name and the Latin abbreviation "et al.," which means "and others." Thus, a second citation would look like this (and be sure to add a period after "al"):

> The participant in the Ericsson et al. (1980) study memorized collections of random digits over a period of several months.

When the same citation is cited more than once within a paragraph, the publication date is added only to the reference's first appearance in that paragraph:

> The participant in the Ericsson et al. (1980) study memorized collections of random digits over a period of several months. A detailed description of the training method can be found in Ericsson et al.

For more on how to cite a work written by multiple authors, see Writer's Guidepost 7.1.

Quoting and Paraphrasing

A quotation involves citing a collection of words and ideas drawn directly from some published or unpublished work. Shorter quotations—those fewer than 40 words—are placed directly within the text of a paper and enclosed in double quotation marks (APA, 2001, p. 117):

> In a particularly dark passage within *Civilization and Its Discontents*, Sigmund Freud (1930/1961, p. 23) claimed that, "Life, as we find it, is too hard for us . . . "

The date of publication and the page number from which the quote is drawn are provided. Why? Some readers will be interested in locating and reading the phrase in the original text. In this instance, two publication dates are noted—the date of the original German language edition

WRITER'S GUIDEPOST   7.1
Citing Multiple Works by the Same Author and Citing Multiple Authors

MULTIPLE WORKS

Single author publications by the same person are ordered in an APA-style Reference list by year of publication (earliest to latest):

Tufte, E. R. (1983).

Tufte, E. R. (1990).

- Single author entries come before multiple-author citations that start with the same last name:

Johnson, D. W. (1991).

Johnson, D. W., & Johnson, F. P. (1987).

- Citations with the same first author but different second or third authors appear in alphabetical order by the last name of the second author or, if the second author is identical, by the third author's last name, and so on:

Lincoln, Y. S., & Denzin, N. K. (1994).

Lincoln, Y. S., & Guba, E. G. (1985).

Tourangeau, R., & Rasinski, K. A. (1988).

Tourangeau, R., Rasinski, K. A., Bradburn, N., & D'Andrade, R. (1989).

Tourangeau, R., Rasinski, K. A., & D'Andrade, R. (1991).

MULTIPLE AUTHORS

Scientific investigations often involve a large number of researchers. As a result, it is not at all unusual to encounter empirical work that has several co-authors. As described here and elsewhere in the text of this chapter, the rules for citing a single work by two to five authors are not complicated—but what happens when a reference has six or more authors?

- When citing a reference with six or more authors within written text, you cite only the first author's last name—followed by

(continued)

(continued)

"et al."—and the year of publication for the *first* and all later citations.

Six-author reference: Sandberg et al. (2001).

Seven-author reference: Tucker et al. (2001).

Eight-author reference: Ahn et al. (2001).

- In the APA-style Reference list, however, provide the initials and surnames for the first six authors, shortening any other additional authors to "et al."

Six-author reference:

Sandberg, D. E., Meyer-Bahlburg, H. F. L., Hensle, T. W., Levitt, S. B., Kogan, S. J., & Reda, E. F. (2001). Psychosocial adaptation of middle childhood boys with hypospadias after genital surgery. *Journal of Pediatric Psychology, 26,* 465–475.

Seven-author reference (first six names listed, one name indicated by "et al."):

Tucker, C. M., Petersen, S., Herman, K. C., Fennell, R. S., Bowling, B., Pedersen, T., et al. (2001). Self-regulation predictor of medication adherence among ethnically different pediatric patients with renal transplants. *Journal of Pediatric Psychology, 26,* 455–464.

Eight-author reference (first six names listed, two names indicated by "et al."):

Ahn, W-K., Kalish, C., Gelman, S. A., Medin, D. L., Luhman, C., Atran, S., et al. (2001). Why essences are essential in the psychology of concepts. *Cognition, 82,* 56–69.

(i.e., 1930), followed by a slash (/) and the date of the English translation used here (i.e., 1961).

Note that I used three ellipsis points (. . .) at the end of Freud's (1930/1961, p. 23) quote to let you know that I quoted only part of his original sentence. If I had quoted the entire sentence, then I would not use any ellipsis points and the sentence would end with a period or other standard punctuation mark (APA, 2001, p. 119).

Quotations that have 40 or more words must appear in an indented block of double-spaced, typewritten lines—no quotation marks are necessary. The quote block should be indented about 1/2 inch (or 5 spaces) from the left margin. Here is a longer block quote from *Civilization and Its Discontents* (Freud, 1930/1961, p. 23–24), including the previously cited line:

> In a famously bleak passage, Freud (1930/1961, pp. 23–24) wrote that:
>
>> Life, as we find it, is too hard for us; it brings us too many pains, disappointments and impossible tasks. In order to bear it we cannot dispense with palliative measures. . . . There are perhaps three such measures: powerful deflections, which cause us to make light of our misery; substitutive satisfactions, which diminish it; and intoxicating substances, which make us insensitive to it.

Notice that I used four ellipsis points (. . . .) this time, thereby indicating that I intentionally left out more than just a sentence fragment. Four ellipsis points indicates that some material—at least one whole sentence, possibly more—was dropped *between* sentences present in the quotation. The first ellipsis point represents the actual period ending a sentence from the quoted source, whereas the subsequent three points indicate that material falling between *two* sentences was left out (APA, 2001).

Again, always be sure to carefully document where a quotation is found. In the case of both short and long quotations, the author's name, publication date, and the page number (or range of pages) from which the quote is drawn must always be provided for readers. This information is usually provided parenthetically, as is the case in both the line and block quotes we just reviewed.

When quoting a source, a writer usually wants to precisely convey the point an author was trying to make (e.g., everyday life can be psychologically difficult) or to draw attention to some aspect of an author's argument or line of thought (e.g., perhaps Freud was *too* pessimistic in his assessment of daily human experience). Citing a quote allows a writer to agree, take issue with, or somehow examine the ideas of another for a specific purpose.

In general, quotations should be relatively brief and used only when necessary. The reason is simple: Too many quotes in a paper are distracting to readers. When I encounter a piece of writing with too many quotations, I always wonder why the author didn't save time by simply telling me to read the cited works before reading his or her comments on them. This complaint might sound cranky to you, but my concern is a legitimate one where developing writers are concerned. Lengthy quotations take up precious pages, reducing the available space for you to write and share your thoughts about a topic with readers. This concern is especially important when one reader, your instructor, is going to grade your work.

Writing teachers call the practice of tying bunches of quotations together **patchwriting**, meaning that such papers are basically collections of other writers' ideas surrounded by a little "filler" supplied by student authors (R. M. Howard, personal communication, September 5, 2001; see also, Howard, 1999). Such jumbled or quilted writing is usually boring to read and often difficult to understand.

If you do want to quote some source in a paper, just be sure that the quotation is both meaningful and useful. A good quote is one that supports your perspective in some way or, conversely, allows you to challenge the scientific views of another author or source. Unless absolutely necessary, do not use more than one quotation in a paper—and make sure it is a compelling one. For a more detailed discussion of the use of quotations within APA style, please see Sections 3.34 through 3.41 in the *Publication Manual* (APA, 2001).

A viable and often preferable alternative to directly quoting a source is **paraphrasing**—restating the meaning of some passage using different words and phrases than those found in the original. In other words, you put the words of another *into your own words*.

To present someone else's point of view in your own words requires a close and thoughtful reading of the original work. Bad paraphrases are easy to write and recognize—perhaps because they often verge on plagiarism—whereas good paraphrases take some worthwhile effort. In fact, the explicit goal of paraphrasing is to avoid plagiarizing the work of others (see pages 46–52 in Chapter 3), but such intentional summaries are also used to present technical material more clearly than was true in original texts. Similarly, dry writing can be made more interesting through careful paraphrasing; important points that might otherwise be missed can be "unpacked" or highlighted for readers.

Writing an APA-style paper involves quite a bit of paraphrasing because you, the writer, must discuss relevant research in terms of what has been done, why, what results were found, and what questions remain to be answered. A writer alerts readers to paraphrases in two ways: by using either a signal phrase or a parenthetical reference to identify a summary of another author's ideas (e.g., Hacker, 1991). Here is an example of a signal phrase:

> Cohen (2001) claimed that diverse environmental and ecological "niches," or life spaces, are largely responsible for cultural variation.

The signal phrase *Cohen (2001) claimed that* and the absence of quotation marks lets readers know that the author is paraphrasing. Use of a parenthetical reference, of course, achieves the same end:

> Distinct and different environmental and ecological niches are thought to introduce cultural variation (Cohen, 2001).

No signal phrase was needed here because the parenthetical presence of an author's surname and publication date points to paraphrasing.

Learning to properly paraphrase is not difficult but it does take practice, as well as adherence to helpful recommendations. A key recommendation is this one: Paraphrase from memory, *not* while reading the text (Hacker, 1991). If you read original text while writing, you increase the chances of borrowing too many words or phrases from it, thereby committing plagiarism (see Chapter 3). Instead, read the text you intend to paraphrase, close the book or put away the article, and only then begin to write about it. Once you have a rough draft of your paraphrase, you can turn back to the original text to be sure that you accurately represented an author's point of view while not copying it word-for-word.

Beyond the global warning to paraphrase from memory, Hult (1996, p. 43) offered five guidelines for appropriately paraphrasing the work of others:

1. Use synonyms of the words appearing in an original source.
2. Avoid overly technical terms (e.g., cathected) or jargon-laden phrases (e.g., "personological foundation of selfhood").
3. Change the structure of the sentences you are restating.
4. Reorder the information you are drawing from a source.
5. Reduce complex ideas into smaller thoughts that can be summarized in simpler sentences.

Adding an obvious but important sixth point is worthwhile:

6. Always include the citation you are paraphrasing.

Let's consider a paraphrased passage. Using Hult's (1996) advice, I rewrote but did not change the fundamental meaning of the "life is too hard for us" message presented earlier in the block quote from *Civilization and Its Discontents* (Freud, 1930/1961, pp. 23–24):

> Freud's (1930/1961) point is a good one: There is no denying that the demands of everyday life can be difficult for many of us. Practically everyone has a number of responsibilities to juggle or challenges to overcome, not to mention dealing with typical setbacks associated with modern life. How can we cope with it all? Regrettably, perhaps, many of us deny that any problems exist, or we seek creative ways to distract ourselves from reality. Some of us even blunt pain and anxiety by relying on drugs and alcohol.

The spirit of Freud's original message is retained, but his actual words are not repeated or, more importantly, copied. For more advice on paraphrasing, see Hacker (1991) or Hult (1996).

Citing Secondary Sources

In general, you should work with primary sources. If you plan to cite a particular article or book, for example, then you should read and understand the work before doing any writing about it. It is unwise to cite a work unless you are familiar with it. Citing something you have not read but that another person used is careless, even dangerous. Your second-hand discussion might be flawed or even completely in error.

I am not suggesting that secondary sources (see Writer's Guidepost 2.1 on page 21) are always a bad idea, just that you should make an effort to locate a primary source before falling back on using a secondary source to cite it. On occasion, you may be truly unable to obtain a given reference but you still want to use and, in fact, need it. Alternatively, you might also want to draw attention to and comment on another writer's point-of-view regarding the source. In either case, a sentence like the following would be appropriate:

> Smith (as cited in Jones, 1995) examined the relative frequency of certain surnames in the general population.

Although Smith's article or book was not available, findings from it are discussed in Jones's text. Only the citation for Jones, however, appears in the APA-style References section (APA, 2001).

FORMATS FOR APA-STYLE REFERENCES

The References section of an APA-style paper begins on a new page at the end of the paper, following the Discussion section and any Author Notes but before any tables, figures, or appendixes (see page 102 in Chapter 5). References must be set up as follows:

- Double-spaced and alphabetized by an author's last name (i.e., A to Z) and then arranged by date of publication (i.e., for multiple citations by the same author[s], earlier publications come before more recent ones).
- Formatted with a "hanging indent," which means that a citation's first line is against the left margin and any subsequent lines are indented (see Section 5.18 in the APA Manual).

The References section of most APA-style papers written by students contains four basic formats: journal articles, books, chapters within edited books, and online periodicals and documents. Please note that certain parts of a reference must be italicized. (I have set these in italics in the examples below.) If you do not have an *italicized font* at your disposal, use <u>underlining</u> instead.

Here is the citation format for a journal article:

> Author(s) last name, first and middle initials. (Year of publication). Title of the article. *Name of Journal,* *Volume number,* range of pages.

Books are cited in much the same way, though the publisher and the publisher's city are also included:

> Author(s) last name, first and middle initials. (Year of publication). *Title of the book* (with volume number or edition number when anything but the first). Publisher's city (with state abbreviation when the city is not a major one): Name of publisher.

Book chapters are a hybrid of these two formats:

> Author last name, first and middle initials. (Year of publication). Title of chapter. First and middle initials, followed by last name, of editor [(Ed.)] or editors

>[(Eds.)], *Title of edited book* (volume number and/or range of page numbers for chapter). Publisher's city (with state abbreviation when the city is not a major one): Name of publisher.

Online references are drawn from online journals, Web sites and Web pages, databases, Web-based discussion groups, electronic newsletters, and so on. Online references come in two basic types, one for periodicals and the other for documents. The basic format for an online periodical resembles that for a print journal:

>Author last name, first and middle initials. (Year of publication). Title of online article. *Title of Online Periodical, Volume number*, range of pages. Retrieved month day, year from source.

The only real addition here is information regarding when and where the citation was retrieved. This additional information is also present in the basic format for online documents:

>Author last name, first and middle initials. (Year of publication). *Title of document*. Retrieved month day, year, from source.

I will present specific examples of each of the basic citations, as well as the formats for other citations often found in the References sections of student papers. Please consult Section 4.16 in the *Publication Manual* (APA, 2001) for less common citation formats.

Journal Articles

One author:

>Kimmel, A. J. (1991). Predictable biases in the ethical decision making of American psychologists. *American Psychologist, 46*, 786–788.

Two authors:

>Anderson, J. R., & Matessa, M. (1997). A production system theory of serial memory. *Psychological Review, 104*, 728–748.

More than two authors:

> Tourangeau, R., Rasinski, K. A., Bradburn, N., & D'Andrade, R. (1989). Carryover effects in attitude surveys. *Public Opinion Quarterly, 53*, 495–524.

Books

For books written by one or two authors:

> Campbell, D. T., & Stanley, J. C. (1963). *Experimental and quasiexperimental designs for research.* Chicago: Rand McNally.
> Putnam, R. D. (2000). *Bowling alone: The collapse and revival of American community.* New York: Simon & Schuster.

For subsequent editions of the same book:

> Harris, R. J. (2001). *A primer of multivariate statistics* (3rd ed.). Mahwah, NJ: Erlbaum.

For an English translation of a book:

> Freud, S. (1961). *Civilization and its discontents* (J. Strachey, Trans.). New York: Norton. (Original work published 1930.)

As shown earlier in this chapter, when citing a translated work like this one in text, use the author's name, the year of original publication, and the year the translation appeared in print: Freud (1930/1961) or (Freud, 1930/1961).

Books without individuals as authors:

> American Psychological Association. (2001). *Publication manual of the American Psychological Association* (5th ed.). Washington, DC: Author.
> *The Merriam-Webster dictionary.* (1997). Springfield, MA: Merriam-Webster, Inc.

Edited Books

Books with one editor:

> Snyder, C. R. (Ed.). (1999). *Coping: The psychology of what works*. New York: Oxford University Press.

Books with more than one editor:

> Wegner, D. M., & Pennebaker, J. W. (Eds.). (1993). *Handbook of mental control*. Englewood Cliffs, NJ: Prentice Hall.

Chapters in Edited Books

Chapters appearing in an edited book:

> Nowlis, V. (1965). Research with the Mood Adjective Checklist. In S. S. Tompkins & C. E. Izard (Eds.), *Affect, cognition, and personality* (pp. 352–389). New York: Springer.

Chapters appearing in a volume of an ongoing series:

> McAdams, D. P. (1985). The "imago": A key narrative component of identity. In P. Shaver (Ed.), *Review of personality and social psychology* (Vol. 6, pp. 115–141). Beverly Hills, CA: Sage.

Magazine or Newspaper Articles

Magazine article by an author:

> Chatterjee, C. (2001, September/October). Overcoming sex: Can men and women be friends? *Psychology Today, 54*, 60–67.

Newspaper article by an author:

> Blakeslee, S. (2001, July 31). Car calls may leave brain short-handed. *The New York Times*, pp. D1, D7.

Magazine or newspaper articles with no author:

> Insurers pushed to cover eating disorders. (2001, July 31). *The New York Times*, p. D8.

Presentations at Professional Meetings or Conferences

For paper presentations:

> Beins, B. C. (1998, August). *Activities to introduce students to psychology faculty and psychological paradigms.* Paper presented at the annual meeting of the American Psychological Association, San Francisco, CA.

For unpublished works presented at a symposium:

> Faust, D. (2001, June). When science corrects common belief and hence is rejected: The sometimes sad case of the expert witness in psychology and psychiatry. In R. M. Dawes (Chair), *Unpopular results: Providing incremental validity at the price of being rejected.* Symposium conducted at the annual meeting of the American Psychological Society, Toronto, Canada.

For poster sessions:

> Meier, B., & Graf, P. (2001, June). *Transfer appropriate processing affects prospective memory performance.* Poster session presented at the annual meeting of the American Psychological Society, Toronto, Canada.

Electronic (Online) Sources

If you read and use an electronic version of an article that originally appeared in print, indicate this fact by adding "[Electronic version]" immediately following the title, as in:

> Dunn, D. S., & Dougherty, S. B. (2005). Prospects for a positive psychology of rehabilitation [Electronic version]. *Rehabilitation Psychology. 50*, 305–311.

For a periodical article retrieved online:

> Carpenter, S. (2001). A new reason for keeping a diary: Research offers intriguing evidence on why expressive writing boosts health. *Monitor on Psychology, 32*, 68–70. Retrieved September 11, 2001 from http://www.apa.org/monitor/sep01/keepdiary.html

Retrieval information about online sources typically ends with a period *except* when (as above) an Internet address is provided.

For an electronic version of an article from a daily newspaper:

> Franklin, D. (2006, August 15). Patient power: Making
> sure your doctor really hears you. *New York Times.*
> Retrieved August 25, 2006, from
> http://www.nytimes.com

For a document retrieved online:

> Committee on Disability Issues in Psychology (1992).
> *Guidelines for non-handicapping language in APA*
> *journals.* Retrieved September 11, 2001, from
> http://www.apastyle.org/disabilities.html

For an e-book published on the Internet and downloaded:

> Halonen, J. S., & Davis, S. F. (Eds.). *The many faces of*
> *psychological research in the 21st century.* Retrieved
> August 22, 2006, from the Society for the Teaching of
> Psychology at: http://teachpsych.lemoyne.edu/
> teachpsych/faces/script/index.html

For an e-book chapter published on the Internet and downloaded:

> Branscombe, N. R., & Spears, R. (2001). Social psychology:
> Past, present, and some predictions for the future.
> In J. S. Halonen & S. F. Davis (Eds.). *The many faces*
> *of psychological research in the 21st century.* (chap. 7).
> Retrieved August 22, 2006, from http://teachpsych.
> lemoyne.edu/teachpsych/faces/script/Ch07.htm

For articles appearing in journals published exclusively on the Internet:

> Haidt, J. (2000, March 7). The positive emotion of elevation.
> *Prevention & Treatment, 3,* Article 0003c. Retrieved
> October 31, 2005, from http://journals.apa.org/
> prevention/volume3/pre0030003c.html

Other citation formats for electronic sources can be found in section 4.16 of in Chapter 4 of the *Publication Manual* (APA, 2001).

Reviews

For book reviews:

> Jarvin, L. (2001). Statistics: *S* is for simplified [Review of the book *Visual statistics: A conceptual primer*]. *Contemporary Psychology: APA Review of Books, 46,* 207–208.

For motion picture reviews:

> Kael, P. (1991, February 11). The doctor and the director [Review of the motion picture *Awakenings*]. *The New Yorker, 66*(52), pp. 70–73.

Personal Communications

Personal communications are usually private sources of information, including phone calls, letters, e-mail messages, or conversations. Although it is important to document personal communications, such communications are irretrievable. As a result, personal communications are noted in text only, not in the References section. Identifying a source and date is all the detail needed for a personal communication. Here are two examples, one as the subject of a sentence and the other in the form of a parenthetical citation:

> J. S. Halonen (personal communication, July 10, 1999) suggested that . . .

> (D. M. Raves, personal communication, December 27, 2006)

Letters to the Editor

For letters to the editor:

> Wilson, V. (2001, September). On rediscovering lost data [Letter to the editor]. *Monitor on Psychology, 32,* pp. 8–9.

Dissertations and Master's Theses

For a dissertation that appears in the Dissertation Abstracts International (DAI) database:

> Tolson, T. F. J. (1993). Sequential analysis of mealtime conversation patterns in two- and three-generational African-American families. *Dissertation Abstracts International, 54* (5-B), 2788.

For an unpublished doctoral dissertation:

> Brill, R. T. (1992). *The effect of job knowledge and task complexity on information processing and rating ability.* Unpublished doctoral dissertation, Virginia Polytechnic Institute and State University.

For an unpublished master's thesis:

> DiLalla, D. L. (1986). *Naturalistic home behavior of abused, neglected, and adequately reared children.* Unpublished master's thesis, University of Virginia.

Unpublished Manuscripts or Data

For a manuscript that has not been submitted for review and publication:

> Zaremba, S. B., & Dunn, D. S. (2000). *Self-evaluation and class participation.* Unpublished manuscript, Moravian College.

For a manuscript that has been submitted for review and publication:

> Schmidt, M. E., DeMulder, E. K., & Denham, S. D. (2001). *Kindergarten social–emotional competence: Developmental predictors and psychosocial implications.* Manuscript submitted for publication.

For unpublished raw data for a study that is untitled:

> Wilson, T. D., & Kraft, D. (1988). [The effects of analyzing reasons on affectively- versus cognitively-based attitudes]. Unpublished raw data.

Table 7.2 is a quick checklist that will help you to verify that citations are properly constructed and appropriately referenced in the text and in the References section of APA-style papers.

Table 7.2. Checklist for Working with APA-Style References

In an APA-style paper:

_____ Does the citation information in the written text match that found in the References section?

_____ Are the cited names spelled the same as those found in the References section? Are the dates the same?

_____ Are the titles of all journals spelled out fully in the References section?

_____ Are all multiple references appearing in parenthetical citations in the text and in the References section ordered alphabetically by authors' last names?

_____ Do older references by the same author appear first in parenthetical citations and in the References section?

_____ Are page numbers provided for any articles and book chapters appearing in the References section?

WRITER'S GUIDEPOST   7.2
Keeping Up with Changes in APA Style

APA style continues to change, grow, and develop as a means for ideas in psychology and other disciplines to be shared with the scientific community. Many recent changes were documented in the fifth edition of the *Publication Manual* (APA, 2001). Innovation did not end when that book went to press, however. In order to help students, teachers, and researchers keep abreast of new information regarding APA style, the American Psychological Association created a Web site dedicated to documenting all changes between new editions of the *Publication Manual*. Here is the Web site's address:

http://www.apastyle.org

This site offers a variety of other helpful services pertaining to writing papers using APA style. There is now an "Ask the Expert" area, which allows anyone to submit style questions to and receive answers from APA's resident experts. Be sure to check out this Web site when writing your next APA-style paper.

Some last thoughts on citing references: At first, learning to use APA style correctly can be daunting. With experience, trepidation often turns into tedium. Stick with it. Eventually, citing references correctly will become second nature to you. Your effort ensures that others will learn from your work in psychology.

EXERCISES

1. In your research notebook, write a sentence that contains a parenthetical citation. Rewrite the sentence but make the citation the subject this time.
2. Using a Reference list, copy two citations by the same author in your research notebook. Locate two other citations with the same first author but that have two or more co-authors.
3. Write the proper citations for a book, a magazine article, a newspaper article, and a document from an online source into your research notebook.
4. Peruse the Reference section of a journal article or psychology book. How many errors in APA-style can you spot in the citations? Are the errors "logical" mistakes linked to APA style (i.e., using the wrong format for a given type of citation) or simply typographical errors?

8

DISPLAYING DATA IN TABLES AND FIGURES

Less is more.

—Robert Browning, *Andrea del Sarto*

The tables and figures found in psychology papers serve one purpose: to present data succinctly. On rare occasions, photographs or line drawings are also represented in these data displays. All displays should be carefully planned, used sparingly, and designed to enhance rather than disrupt a paper's narrative. Readers welcome data tables or figures within a paper, regarding them as additional detail clarifying an author's arguments.

Data displays should be a seamless part of any scientific paper, adding to the whole while concisely conveying important information in summary form. Let me dissuade you from creating any table or figure with too many "bells and whistles"—busy or fussy graphics forcing readers to linger too long while trying to interpret your intentions. When reading an empirical article, I never like getting the impression that a writer spent more time with a graphics program than refining his or her prose. Pretty pictures cannot save unclear writing. Ideal data displays can be understood with a glance and are supported by a clear narrative in the body of the paper.

TABLES

Tables contain numbers. In APA style, precise quantitative information is summarized in tables, which contain organized and labeled rows and columns (APA, 2001). A table serves the important purpose of removing essential numbers from written text while maintaining their availability for readers. Readers retain more information about a piece of research when there are fewer numbers to pore over. On the other hand, statistics are a big part of any research project in psychology, and readers need to be reassured that all data analyses were conducted properly. Tables constitute a happy compromise: Valuable space is saved but no technical information is sacrificed. As an added advantage, readers flipping through APA-style articles can get a quick sense of results by examining tables.

Following Nicol and Pexman (1999), a table serves two main purposes:

- To isolate data for further critical examination, even additional analysis, by readers.
- To remove specific results from the main text, encouraging readers to adopt a broader perspective on findings and their implications.

Without reading the supporting text in a Results or Discussion section, then, readers should be able to get a quick understanding of a table's contents. Any APA-style table should be able to stand on its own. Any acronyms, abbreviations, or other special qualities must be spelled out in the table itself or in notes appearing below the bottom of the table.

Constructing a Table

The most common table that student writers construct is one displaying means. A mean is a mathematical average of a group of observations, used to illustrate the "typical" or usual behavior found in some circumstance. Psychologists display tables of means so that readers can compare behavior in one experimental condition with that found in a study's other conditions. What did the average person in one group do behaviorally? How did typical responses in another group compare? A table of means generally needs to highlight both independent (i.e., manipulated) and dependent (i.e., measured) variables. Finally, tables of means often appear within a text prior to any statistical analysis comparing their relative magnitudes (see Chapter 6).

Table 8.1 is a sample table illustrating hypothetical data—means, standard deviations, and sample sizes (i.e., number of people in each experimental condition)—from an experiment on how stress leads to antisocial behavior. A researcher induced stress in groups of participants by exposing them to an aversive, loud noise. In the high-stress group, noise occurred randomly, whereas those in the low-stress group heard noise at predictable intervals (e.g., Glass, Singer, & Friedman, 1969). Take a look at Table 8.1: Can you size up the results with a glance? Participants in the study's high-stress condition, for example, expressed a higher average number of aggressive words during an experimental task than those present in a low-stress condition. Note that the data were further broken

Table 8.1. A Sample APA-Style Table Displaying Means

Table 1
Mean Aggressive Words Uttered as a Function of Sex and
High versus Low Stress

Sex	Mean		Standard deviation		Sample size	
	High	Low	High	Low	High	Low
Men	25.40	8.54	6.55	2.76	20	19[a]
Women	23.00	9.24	5.21	3.11	20	20

[a]One participant who failed to follow instructions was dropped from the analysis.

down by the gender of the participants in each condition, though this variable does not appear to have interacted with stress.

When using a table such as the one shown here, you would call readers' attention to it while briefly explaining its contents:

> The mean number of aggressive utterances made by men and women in the high- and low-stress conditions are shown in Table 1. On average, a greater number of aggressive words were spoken by participants in the high- rather than the low-stress condition. Contrary to expectation, however, men do not appear to have used aggressive language more frequently than women (see Table 1).

What about the formatting in our sample table? Note that all categories are carefully labeled (i.e., sex, stress level), as are the numerical entries (i.e., mean, standard deviation, and sample size), and everything is lined up in a block format. All the numbers, for example, are aligned along the placement of the decimal point. The table's title, too, is concrete. With a glance, a reader knows that, on average, both men and women uttered more aggressive words under conditions of high rather than low stress. Someone who examined this table but did not read the paper from which it was drawn would reach the same conclusion. Other formats for creating and presenting tables of means (or displaying results from particular statistical analyses) can be found in Nicol and Pexman (1999) or the *Publication Manual* (APA, 2001).

APA style no longer requires authors to indicate the relative placement of tables (or figures) within text. This responsibility is now left to typesetters (see Section 3.63 in the *Publication Manual*; APA, 2001). If desired, however, you can indicate where a table or figure belongs in your paper. The traditional way to do so looks like this:

- - - - - - - - - - - - - - - - - - -

Insert Table 1 About Here

- - - - - - - - - - - - - - - - - - -

Ask about your instructor's preference, if any, regarding table or figure "callouts" in your paper.

Here are some final thoughts about using tables:

- Include the minimum amount of detail that readers need in order to understand a table's content and its relationship to the whole study. To be useful, a table should be informative but not exhaustive or cluttered.
- Make sure that any table is clearly linked back to a text's narrative. A reader should be able to examine a table and then find some text discussion explaining it (and vice versa). Avoid redundancy, however; never repeat the information from a table in the text.
- Aim for including four or more descriptive statistics (e.g., means) or other summary statistics in a table. Fewer than four means are best reported in the text. The *Publication Manual* (APA, 2001) suggests that tables with two or fewer columns and rows should be avoided.
- Try to determine how many tables are too many. A 15- to 20-page student paper probably needs no more than a table or two. Exceptions to this rule exist, of course, but it must be obvious why additional tables are necessary.
- Place statistical calculations or raw data in an appendix rather than a table.
- Ideally, try to fit a table on one page of a manuscript. Though not an APA-style requirement, it does seem reasonable for student papers.
- Remember that tables appear at the end of the APA-style manuscript, following the Author Notes page of the paper. If

Table 8.2. A Checklist for Creating Tables

_____ Is a table really needed?

_____ Is each table referred to and discussed in the text?

_____ Have tables been used sparingly in the paper?

_____ Is each table numbered (use arabic numerals [1, 2, 3, . . .]) based on the order in which each table is mentioned in the paper?

_____ Is double-spacing used throughout every table?

_____ When displaying means in a table, are their standard deviations and sample sizes provided?

_____ Is a table's title brief but understandable?

_____ Are any abbreviations or symbols appearing within a table explained by a note underneath it?

_____ Is it clear that a table's contents are not redundant with those of another table or figure?

_____ Has every numerical entry within a table been double-checked for accuracy?

_____ Do any tables appear after the References section and any appendix, at the end of the APA-style manuscript (see Table 4.2)?

there is no such page, then place all tables after the References section.

Table 8.2 is a checklist for preparing tables in APA-style manuscripts. A quick summary regarding creating tables and figures appears in Chapter 5 on page 103. Additional guidelines for choosing and using tables are provided in Nicol and Pexman (1999) and in Sections 3.62 to 3.74 of the *Publication Manual* (APA, 2001).

FIGURES

Figures convey meaning using few words or numbers, graphically illustrating trends in behavior as well as statistical interactions between two or more variables. In APA style, the term *figure* refers to data displays that are not technically tables, including graphs, histograms, line graphs, bar graphs, frequency polygons, photographs, diagrams, pie charts, scatterplots, and line drawings. With the possible exception of the histogram (a bar graph where bars do not touch one another) or line graph, figures

WRITER'S GUIDEPOST   8.1
A Last Word on Tables

We are accustomed to thinking of tables as exclusively numerical in nature. Most are, but APA style does permit writers to use word tables. Instead of numbers, word tables contain qualitative or explanatory information (Nicol & Pexman, 1999). When a study contains a large number of variables or when a new personality measure is introduced, for example, psychologists need a convenient method to organize, present, and define important terms. Research papers that describe previously published studies, too, can rely on word tables.

Word tables are used only when discussing their contents within a paper's text would take up too much space or be otherwise unwieldy. These tables have no standard format, so they are readily adaptable to a writer's needs. Consider using one when you need to compartmentalize verbal materials. Here is a simple example:

Table 1: Factors and Sample Items from the Socioemotional Personality Scale

Factor	Sample Item (keyed in a positive direction)
Self-esteem	I feel that I am a good person.
Social Support	I have friends who help me with problems.
Emotional Intelligence	I recognize the effects my moods have on other people.
Social Intelligence	I always observe how others receive my comments.

Note: The factors and items in this scale are entirely hypothetical.

are probably less common in student papers than are tables. Whether you decide to use a figure or a table, never use both to illustrate the same finding in the same paper.

Constructing a Figure

Any good figure should possess three characteristics: accuracy, brevity, and clarity (Tufte, 1983). Figures should be lean on details so that readers can obtain a quick, pictorial sense of a finding. To achieve informational simplicity, use a graphics program instead of trying your hand at freeform drawing. Graphics programs are easy to use. Once you enter the data and make some choices, a program will do the work for you. If you own a computer, it probably has a graphics program. Alternatively, your campus network will have a graphing program or two (ask your instructor for recommendations).

To become familiar with figures that do a good job of illustrating clear summaries of or relationship present in data, take a trip to the periodicals section in your institution's library. Once there, look at current psychology journals (see the list in the appendix) to locate some examples you can emulate in your paper.

Once there, look at current psychology journals (see the list in the appendix) to locate examples you can emulate in your paper.

Here are some guidelines for constructing figures in a manuscript:

- In lieu of a title, a figure must have a brief but explanatory caption. The caption appears on an accompanying caption page rather than on the figure itself.
- Figures are always in black and white, never color, though different gray shades or stripes are permissible when necessary.
- Figures should be plain, even austere, with no distracting details or "chartjunk" (Tufte, 1983).
- Information appearing in a figure must be clearly labeled.
- Whatever unit of measurement is shown, it must be consistent throughout the figure.
- Any data appearing in a figure must be plotted accurately (using software is a good idea).
- Independent variables are always plotted on the horizontal or x-axis of a graph.
- Dependent variables are always plotted on the vertical or y-axis of a graph.

- When plotting data representing a dependent variable, the values should increase from lesser to greater, from the bottom to the top of the y-axis.
- Within a graph, the vertical (y-axis) should be approximately two-thirds the length of the horizontal (x-axis).
- When labeling the two axes in a graph, the labels should be brief (one or two words) and arranged like this:[1]

- A legend, the part of a figure explaining symbols that appear within it, must be integrated into the figure.

- The word *top* should be written at the top of the back page of a figure to indicate which way is up. The word *figure* and its specific number should be handwritten in light pencil on the figure.

Additional details about creating and displaying figures can be found in Sections 3.75 to 3.86 of the *Publication Manual* (APA, 2001) and in Nicol and Pexman (2003). Table 8.3 is a checklist of *Publication Manual* (APA, 2001) requirements worth reviewing when finalizing any figure.

EXERCISES

1. Locate examples of well-constructed and poorly constructed tables in the psychological literature. What makes the good examples so interpretable? What improvements would you make to the bad examples?
2. Locate examples of simple and cluttered figures in the psychological literature. Why are the simple examples so clear? How would you go about fixing the clarity of the cluttered figures?
3. Select a table or figure from the published literature. Write a paragraph in your research notebook that describes its contents.

---

[1]The "optimal" example graph is from page 196 of the *Publication Manual of the American Psychological Association* (2001). Reprinted with permission.

4. Construct a table or figure based on data that are available to you. Copy the table or figure into your research notebook and write a descriptive paragraph beneath it.
5. Locate an example of a word table in the published literature or create one of your own.

Table 8.3. A Checklist for Creating Figures

_____ Is a figure really needed?

_____ Is each figure referred to and discussed in the text?

_____ Is the figure clutter-free?

_____ Are the data plotted correctly?

_____ Does each figure have a brief but understandable caption?

_____ Are any abbreviations, symbols, or acronyms defined in a caption or legend accompanying the figure and on a separate page appearing prior to it?

_____ Is each figure numbered (use arabic numerals [1, 2, 3, . . .]) based on the order in which each table is mentioned in the paper?

_____ Are all lines and bars appearing in a figure clearly labeled?

_____ Do any figures appear after the References section, any appendix, any tables, and figure captions, at the end of the APA-style manuscript (see Table 4.2)?

9

FORMATTING AND PROOFREADING YOUR PAPER

Good writing is a matter of content and presentation. This chapter deals with formatting and proofreading the final version of a paper. Proofreading—marking the last corrections in a paper—is the "spit and polish" that separates high-quality work from average contributions. No writer wants readers to mentally correct spelling or punctuation, or to get lost in a thicket of questionable grammar.

Besides doing a final check of your writing, remember that the physical appearance of your paper also matters. As the saying goes, "neatness counts." We begin inside, focusing on grammar, punctuation, spelling, and related issues, working our way out to consider a paper's physical appearance.

GRAMMAR GUIDELINES

I still have trouble identifying grammatical structures by name, though I know them as matters of usage.

Robertson Davies (1913–1995)

Most of us are a lot like the late playwright and novelist Robertson Davies. We innately know grammar, even if we cannot rattle off the parts of speech or diagram a sentence. We sense what is grammatically right or wrong, even if we cannot explain why.

I won't try to teach you all the rules of grammar at this point in your education. There are countless books devoted to grammar issues, many of which you studied throughout your primary and secondary education (but see two wonderful, recent books: O'Conner, 1996, 1999). What I can do is review major grammatical guidelines and the errors students regularly encounter or, more precisely, commit. Before reviewing these guidelines,

I encourage you to go to your institution's student writing center for help if you struggle with grammar.

Table 9.1 defines some common grammar terms. Look them over before proceeding to the list of grammar guidelines below.

- **Subject-verb agreement.** When the subject of a sentence is plural, the verb must also be plural. Similarly, singular subjects require singular verbs.

  Incorrect: The *members* of the group *is* going to attend the meeting.

  Correct: The *members* of the group *are* going to attend the meeting.

  Incorrect: Based on departmental rules, the *involvement* of students in research *are* welcome.

  Correct: Based on departmental rules, the *involvement* of students in research *is* welcome.

- **Sentence fragment.** A sentence fragment is an incomplete sentence, one that does not express a complete thought. A demonstrative pronoun (i.e., *which, that, who*) can be a subject only when a sentence is phrased as a question.

  Incorrect: The psychologist studied cognition, development, and neuroscience. Which were the three strong areas at her university.

  Correct: The psychologist studied cognition, development, and neuroscience, the three strong areas at her university.

- **Run-on sentences.** Run-on sentences (sometimes called *fused sentences*; see Hacker, 1991) occur when a writer fails to separate independent clauses by using punctuation marks. As a result, a run-on sentence appears to just "keep on going."

  Incorrect: I wanted to let you know why there were several reasons that the meeting dragged on including the time it was held the attendees participating and the topic itself.

  Correct: There were several reasons that the meeting dragged on, including the time it was held, the attendees participating, and the topic itself.

- **Unclear references involving pronouns.** Readers struggle to understand a sentence when a pronoun stands in for a group of nouns

---

Table 9.1. Some Common Grammar Terms Defined

Subject—The person, idea, or thing that is the focus of a complete sentence (e.g., *Neuroscience* is the newest area of psychology).

Verb—A word denoting action or some state or way of being (e.g., *is, was, did, love, cried, sang*; Psychology *is* a popular college major).

Predicate—The portion of a clause or a sentence expressing what is said regarding a subject (e.g., Traditional psychotherapy *can go on for several years*).

Sentence—A coherent, grammatical assertion, question, wish, command, or exclamation (e.g., Psychology is both a social and a natural science).

Clause—A grouping of words containing a subject and predicate that is part of a larger sentence (e.g., *Psychologists work in a variety of settings / some teach / while others work in clinics or private practice*; there are three clauses in this sentence).

Noun—A person (e.g., Leon Festinger), place (e.g., Vienna), or thing (e.g., stopwatch).

Pronoun—A word that stands in for a noun (e.g., *he, she, it, we, you, they, his, her, him, them*).

Adjective—A word that modifies or describes a noun (e.g., *hot* water, *small* house, *old* tire, *wet* blanket).

Adverb—A word that acts as a modifier of a verb, an adjective, or another adverb (e.g., ran *quickly*, spoke *fast*).

Article—A word used with a noun to limit or provide distinctiveness to it (e.g., *a, an, the*).

Preposition—A word that relates a noun or pronoun to another word in a sentence (e.g., *into, on, through*).

Conjunction—A word that connects words, phrases, or clauses together (e.g., *and, but, or, nor*).

---

appearing in a sequence. The difficulty is that the reader is not sure which noun (or nouns) the pronoun is supposed to represent.

> ***Incorrect:*** The experimenters passed out surveys to the participants, and *they* were quickly collected.

Does *they* refer back to the surveys or to the participants?

> ***Correct:*** The experimenters passed out surveys to the participants; the surveys were then quickly collected.

- **Lack of agreement between pronouns and antecedents.** An antecedent is a noun that is replaced by a pronoun in a sentence. When an antecedent is singular, the pronoun must also be singular. Plural pronouns must in turn accompany plural antecedents.

WRITER'S GUIDEPOST   9.1
Creating Connections—with Fewer Words

First and last words in sentences and paragraphs matter a great deal, so sentences should not begin or end with superfluous words (Barrass, 1978). Extra words act as a helpful crutch, allowing us to connect thoughts together in early drafts. Later, however, they become distracting, excess baggage that should be edited out of subsequent drafts.

Below are common introductory and connecting phrases that can generally be removed without any loss of meaning (note that many are written in the passive voice; adapted from Barrass, Table 7, p. 39). As you tighten up the grammar in your paper, lighten your load by deleting superfluous phrases. Space is provided below for you to jot down any verbal crutches you repeatedly use. Record them here and look out for them in future writing.

In conclusion . . .	In the final analysis . . .
It was found that . . .	It can be seen that . . .
It may be noted that . . .	It is apparent that . . .
From this point of view . . .	Research shows that . . .
From these results we can now see that . . .	When we consider . . .
	Next we need to consider . . .
For your information . . .	To summarize . . .
In summary . . .	
The results in this study provide evidence that . . .	

Your frequent connecting phrases:

_____   _____

_____   _____

Incorrect: The researcher must submit the grant on time and then wait six months to receive their feedback.

The subject of the sentence (*researcher*) is singular, but the pronoun (*they*) is plural.

Correct: The researcher must submit the grant on time and then wait six months to receive his or her feedback.

Unless the gender of the researcher is known, citing both possibilities is preferable to citing one. APA-style advocates gender neutrality by using plural pronouns (see below) except in cases where focus on one gender is warranted (APA, 2001).

Better yet: Researchers must submit grants on time and then wait six months to receive their feedback.

- **Misplaced modifiers.** Modifiers are either adjectives or adverbs (see Table 9.1). To be grammatically correct and informative, a modifier must identify the word it is describing without ambiguity.

Incorrect: The participant responded to the experimenter using the questionnaire.

Who used the questionnaire here—the participant or the experimenter? The issue is clarified for the reader in this sentence:

Correct: Using the questionnaire, the participant responded to the experimenter.

PUNCTUATION BASICS

Punctuation marks clarify meaning and separate ideas from one another in written text. They are the traffic signals in sentences and paragraphs, alerting readers about when to stop, pause, end, be excited, and so on. Without punctuation, our writing would be like our thought—a forever-flowing stream of consciousness. Punctuation imposes organization on our written thoughts.

Just as grammar is not arbitrary, neither is punctuation. Table 9.2 identifies the most common punctuation marks and describes how to use them. Please familiarize yourself with this table before continuing to read.

After teaching writing in psychology, I am aware of the simple punctuation mistakes made by student writers. Chief among these is confusing the colon with the semicolon (see Table 9.2 for usage guidelines). Other common problem areas in punctuation are listed below.

Table 9.2. Standard Punctuation Marks Defined

Apostrophe (')—Used to denote possession of singular (e.g., Tom's car) and plural nouns (the dogs' bones). When a noun ends in <u>s</u>, the general rule is to add an apostrophe after it (e.g., The Jones's boat). Exception: An apostrophe is *not* used with <u>its</u> to show possession (i.e., The dog got *its* bone) because *it's* is a contraction meaning "it is" (i.e., "*It's* hot today" is the same as saying, "It is hot today").

Colon (:)—Introduces a list, a statement, or a long quotation (e.g., When shopping, I bought several items: bread, milk, cheese, fruit, and salad).

Comma (,)—A comma separates words or phrases in some series (e.g., I ran into Ted, Jim, George, and Susan).

Exclamation point (!)—An exclamation point is used for emphasis, to draw attention to some word, phrase, or sentence (e.g.,Yipes! Avoid using exclamation points in psychology papers! They rarely belong!).

Parentheses ( )—Parentheses are used to isolate information that can remain independent from the rest of a sentence (like this parenthetical comment). In APA style, parentheses often enclose author names and/or publication dates, as well as page numbers (see Chapter 7).

Period (.)—A period marks the end of a complete sentence.

Semicolon (;)—A semicolon separates two independent clauses that are not joined by a conjunction (e.g., William James' monumental *Principles of Psychology* was often referred to as "James"; the abridged version was jokingly called "Jimmy.").

- **The comma.** The comma, too, is often misapplied. Some writers use far too many, others rarely bother to use any at all. Any commas must be judiciously placed to split up the words or phrases located in a series (see below and Table 9.2). One thing that commas do is encourage readers to take a breather in a sentence.

    Incorrect: I ate some lunch, and then went to the store.

  The comma looks all right here but it is incorrect; it separates the subject from its predicate.

Correct: I ate some lunch and then went to the store.

Commas are appropriately used in this extended version of the sentence:

Correct: I ate some lunch, made a few phone calls, and then I went to the store.

- **The exclamation point.** Another shared error involves the use of exclamation points, which should be used only occasionally, when the content of some writing must shout.

   Incorrect: Help me, I'm hurt.

   Correct: Help me! I'm hurt!

   Unless they are present in some emotional quote, however, exclamation points are seldom needed in an APA-style paper. If you decide to use one, make certain that it is truly needed.
- **Comma splices.** A comma splice occurs when this punctuation mark is inappropriately used to connect two complete sentences.

   Incorrect: Social cognition is a hybrid of social and cognitive psychology, it examines topics including stereotyping, prejudice, and judgment and decision making.

   Correct: Social cognition is a hybrid of social and cognitive psychology. It examines topics including stereotyping, prejudice, and judgment and decision making.

   Here is another correct alternative:

   Correct: Social cognition, a hybrid of social and cognitive psychology, examines topics including stereotyping, prejudice, and judgment and decision making.
- **Missing commas in nonrestrictive phrases or clauses.** When a comma appears at the beginning of a noun phrase or a clause, another comma is used to close the phrase or clause.

   Incorrect: Cognitive dissonance, the theory that conflicting thoughts lead to psychological tension and subsequent rationalization has been researched for over 40 years.

   Correct: Cognitive dissonance, the theory that conflicting thoughts lead to psychological tension and subsequent rationalization, has been researched for over 40 years.

SOME COMMON USAGE ERRORS IN STUDENT WRITING

Every writing teacher can identify frequent errors found in student writing. I am no different. Four of my pet peeves are confusing *affect* and *effect*; *that* with *which*; *while* with *although*, *but*, and *whereas*; and *since* with *because*. A fifth involves knowing the correct meaning and use of the much-abused word *data*.

- **Affect** and **effect.** *Affect* and *effect* sound alike but have different meanings and uses in writing. In general, *affect* is a verb that means "exerting some influence":

  As anticipated by the hypothesis, the control group was not *affected* by the weak stimulus.

  Within academic psychology, however, *affect* can be a noun, a synonym referring to "mood states" or "emotion," as in this sentence:

  The longitudinal study examined links between *affect* and heart rate.

  In contrast, the word *effect* is a verb meaning "to cause to happen or occur":

  The engineer effected repairs on the damaged motor.

  When used as a noun, *effect* refers to "meaning or intention." In psychology, *effect* is often used as a synonym for statistical "results" or "findings," as in:

  A significant main *effect* for gender was found in Study 3, revealing that men asked fewer questions than women.

  Psychology students often find themselves using *effect* when they mean *affect*, and vice versa. Always check to see that *affect* or *effect* fits the interpretive need of the sentence. Making the right choice takes practice.

- **That** versus **which.** Knowing when to use *that* or *which* is an even stickier problem than the distinction between *affect* and *effect*. The word *that* is used within restrictive clauses where it provides vital meaning to sentences. Here is an example:

  The software *that* organized the data was quite expensive.

  The word *which* is used with unrestrictive clauses because it adds *additional*, not essential, meaning to a sentence. Commas are used to offset unrestrictive clauses:

The new software, *which* was quite expensive, kept the project on schedule.

The clause "which was quite expensive" is not essential to the rest of the sentence.

- **While, although, but, and whereas.** The word *while* is often used in place of the words *although, but,* and *whereas.* It shouldn't be. *While* is temporal—that is, time related—and it means "at the same moment as":

    While I cooked dinner I talked on the phone.

    The other words are not temporal: *although* means "in spite of," *but* can mean "however" or "on the other hand," and *whereas* is a substitute for phrases like "in contrast to" or "it is true that." When proofreading a paper, be sure that *while* is used only to convey time-bound information.

- ***Since* versus *because.*** *Since* and *because* are often used interchangeably in student writing, despite the fact that they mean different things. The word *since* is temporal, meaning "after that period in time," as in:

    Since the semester started, my office phone rings all the time.

    There is no temporal quality to the word *because,* which means "for the reason that":

    Because I missed the appointment, I could not schedule another one for two months.

    When proofreading, be sure that *since* refers to a period in the past and is not a rationale for some event.

- **The data on the word *data.*** The word *data* is a synonym for information, particularly facts, figures, and statistics. Scientists have always cozied up to this word, and many psychologists routinely use it when discussing their research. Investigators, teachers, businesspeople, journalists, students, and many writers routinely misuse the word, treating it as singular when it is in fact plural.

    Incorrect: Where *is* the data?

    Correct: Where *are* the data?

    The singular form of *data* is *datum.* A *datum* is a single piece of information, whereas the word *data* involves a collection of facts. Thus, it would be appropriate to write:

    Correct: Where is the *datum*?

> *Correct:* The age of one participant is a *datum*, while the ages of all the participants are *data*.

Data and *datum* are perfectly fine words, but they should be used sparingly—their overuse can make a paper sound pretentious.

CHECKING YOUR SPELLING

Most word-processing software includes some sort of spell-checker, a tool that searches through text, highlighting misspelled or unknown words along the way. Spell-checkers are a blessing and a curse. On the one hand, they can proofread your writing in a few seconds and catch many typos and errors quickly. Yet spell-checkers routinely miss things.

A big-ticket item among the missing turns out to be homophones, as in this clever bit of doggerel (S. Daubs, personal communication, February 13, 2002):

> Eye halve a spelling chequer
> It came with my pea sea
> It plainly marques four my revue
> Miss steaks eye kin knot sea.

A **homophone** is a word that sounds the same as (but is spelled differently than) some other word. Naturally, the meanings of two homophonic words are usually unrelated, as in the following examples (for a comprehensive list, see Hacker, 1991):

affect – effect	by – bye	doe – dough
here – hear	its – it's	to – too – two
there – their – they're	cite – sight – site	brake – break

Never trust your spell-checker to make the correct selection for you. If a homophone is spelled correctly, it will usually be ignored.

Besides pure homophones, spell-checkers routinely fail to notice other types of near-miss spellings. A word may be spelled correctly but be contextually inappropriate. When writing quickly, I often type *you* in place of *your*, for example. Unless I do a careful proofread of the paper, neither the spell-checker nor I catch the dropped *r*. Words with *oo* in the middle are also likely candidates to be missed, as in:

chose – choose	lose – loose	nose – noose

After all, one cannot be hung from a nose until dead. I just wrote that sentence and immediately turned on my spell-checker, which has a much-touted grammar-checking function. Was the error caught? Not by a nose. To my spell-checker, the word *nose* is fine here, even if it is not a *noose*.

What is the best way to catch spelling errors without electronic intervention? Try this boring but very accurate method: Start on the last page in the last sentence of your paper and read backward (Hult, 1996; Thaiss & Sanford, 2000). Doing so is an odd experience, but it will ensure that you can concentrate on one word at a time instead of being distracted by familiar prose.

CHECKING YOUR WRITING VOICE: BE ACTIVE, NOT PASSIVE

Writers convey a presence in what they write. Grammatically, this presence is commonly called the **active voice** or the **passive voice**. Writers use the passive voice when they are not sure what happened or when they want to fade into the background of their writing. The passive voice often leaves the impression that things "just happened" by themselves:

> *Passive voice:* The participants were randomly assigned to one of three experimental groups.

In contrast, the active voice is lively, focused, and self-assured. Reader and writer alike know who did what so there is no confusion:

> *Active voice:* We randomly assigned participants to one of three experimental groups.

Sentences using the passive voice tend to have more words than those written in the active voice:

> *Passive voice:* In the present study, the findings were found to confirm prior research.

> *Active voice:* The findings confirmed prior research.

Many student writers adopt the passive voice because they erroneously believe that it makes their writing sound "more scientific." It only does so if one associates dull writing with science (sadly, there is ample evidence in this direction). Other students rely on the passive voice because their psychology instructors discourage use of personal pronouns in APA-style writing, despite the fact no such prohibition exists. The following sentence, for example, might be off-putting to some instructors:

Active voice: I detected two unexpected but intriguing results.

There is a way around the personal pronoun in this sentence. To please an instructor, you could write a less personal but still active sentence like this one:

Active voice: This experimenter detected two unexpected but intriguing results.

One problem remains, of course. The first example sounds more authentic and natural than the second. Still, a little awkwardness is acceptable, but you would not want to fill your paper with too many of these impersonal, though still active, sentences.

USING INCLUSIVE LANGUAGE

When studying behavior, we must describe research participants, students, clients, cases, even whole cultures or ethnic groups. We must be mindful of how we refer to people, whether individually or as members of distinct groups. When writing about groups, students as well as researchers should

> . . . avoid perpetuating demeaning attitudes and biased assumptions about people in their writing. Constructions that might imply bias against persons on the basis of gender, sexual orientation, racial or ethnic group, disability or age should be avoided. Scientific writing should be free of implied or irrelevant evaluation of the group or groups being studied (APA, 2001, p. 61).

When you write, be vigilant and eliminate any possible bias in the way you refer to groups.

There are three keys for avoiding bias when writing about particular groups (APA, 2001):

- **Do not rely on labels.** People are people, not things; we refer to people who take part in research as *participants*, not *subjects* (only animals are subjects in psychological research; however, prior to 1994, this outdated term was used to describe humans). When referring to people or writing about them, you must always treat them respectfully, as unique individuals, not objects of study. What does the group you are studying prefer to be called? Individuals who have a physical (e.g., quadriplegia) or mental (e.g., schizophrenia) disability prefer to be described as *people with disabilities* or a *person with quadriplegia* or an *individual with* *schizophrenia*, and not as *quadriplegics* or *schizophrenics*. Never equate people with conditions that are only one part of their lives (Wright, 1991; see also, Dunn, 2000; Dunn & Elliott, 2005). Similarly, do not describe groups in monolithic ways. Instead of saying *the elderly*, try *elderly people* or be more specific still by writing *elderly women*. For the same reason, the term *gay males* is preferable to *gays*, *retired persons* is better than *retirees*, and so on.

- **Be precise, specific, and sensitive.** Try to individualize the group you are describing (e.g., Maggio, 1991). Characteristics including sexual orientation, marital status, age, education, racial and ethnic identity, and the like can be effectively used to individualize people and groups. Just be sure when you highlight one or more such characteristics in your writing and that you do so for a legitimate purpose. Never mention a person's or a group's characteristic in a wanton or flippant manner. If participants in your study were of Japanese ancestry, be clear as to whether they were Japanese (i.e., from the nation of Japan but currently in the United States) or Japanese Americans (i.e., people of Japanese ancestry who are Americans). Consider another example: In a generic sense, the term *gay* does encompass both men and women, but deeper clarity is warranted. Try using *gay men* and *lesbians*, accepted terms that denote sexual orientation and gender.

- **Recognize participation.** Taking part in any research study takes time, energy, and work on the part of any participant. As a writer-researcher, you owe it to participants to be grateful for their efforts on your behalf. Not only is it your responsibility to thank them in person for being a part of your research, you must also acknowledge their contributions in writing. Never refer to them impersonally as *subjects*; instead, choose a neutral or active descriptor, such as *participants*, *respondents*, *students*, *individuals*, and the like. Further, describe their contributions actively: they *did* things, things were not *done* to them (again, promote the active, not the passive, voice). Noting that the "parents *completed* the sibling personality survey" is superior to "parents *were given* the sibling personality survey." And in any case, never write, "subjects were run" when you can indicate that "the experimenters collected responses from the participants." Be factual, not judgmental, in your writing: Don't say, "two students failed to complete the dependent measure"; be concise and direct, noting that, "two students did not finish the dependent measure" (see also Knatterud, 1991).

Gender and Sex

Historically, academic psychology emphasized men over women in its use of written language. Terms like *man* and *mankind* were conventionally used to encompass all men and women. Although most people understood this attempt at a universal referent, a subtle masculine priority was established. We eschew such parochial terms today, relying on intentionally inclusive ones (e.g., humanity, human beings, humankind, human species) to collectively refer to all people.

Among students, there is often confusion about the correct way to refer to males and females within particular contexts. Specifically, when is the term **gender** a more appropriate choice than **sex**? Gender refers to how an individual thinks about him- or herself, whereas sex is a term referring to a person's biological identity based upon the presence of a male or female reproductive system. Unless you are specifically writing about reproductive or sexual orientation issues, terms denoting gender and sex will probably not cause you much trouble.

The American Psychological Association advocates a gender-neutral, nonsexist approach in writing, one wherein men and women are treated equally and without bias. You will have to contend with deciding when and where to specifically refer to men and women, which pronouns to use, and so on. The American Psychological Association offers simple advice: Avoid using gender-specific pronouns except in those situations where they are absolutely necessary. Instead, rely on gender-neutral, plural pronouns, such as *they* or *them*.

Consider the following example of a first-draft sentence:

When a person perceives stress, he is likely to respond by using both problem-focused and emotion-focused coping.

One way to redress the situation is to indicate that stressed people can be either male or female. Here is a second pass at the sentence:

When a person perceives stress, he or she is likely to respond by using both problem-focused and emotion-focused coping.

The inclusion of both a masculine and a feminine pronoun certainly supports equality, but it also breaks up the cadence of the sentence. Besides, the phrase *he or she* is awkward and should be used sparingly.

A better solution is to eliminate the two gender-specific pronouns in favor of a neutral, plural one. To do so, the sentence must be revised slightly:

People who perceive stress are likely to respond by using both problem-focused and emotion-focused coping.

In this case, everyone (people) can perceive stress and all of them (they) can respond by using both forms of coping. Unless there is a specific reason to focus on one gender or the other within some specific example, stick with plural pronouns.

Occasionally, describing the experience of an individual is necessary (e.g., case studies, narratives). Use of a singular masculine or feminine pronoun is called for, but with one additional caveat. Presumably, more than one example will be present in the writing, allowing you to use *he* or *him* in one instance and *she* or *her* in another. Such balance is welcome as

---

WRITER'S GUIDEPOST   9.2
Choosing Your Words Well—Seeking Simplicity

The goal of scientific writing in psychology is clarity. Whenever possible, choose simple, preferably short, words. Here is a rule to consider: *Prefer a short word to a long one unless the long word is truly a better choice* (Flesch, 1962, cited in Barrass, 1978). Below is a list of simple words and their more complex cousins. You need not revise every one found in your writing, but consider changing a few when proofreading.

Use this word	*in place of this word*
do	accomplish
extra	additional
expect	anticipate
help	assist
simple	simplistic
use	usage, utilize, application
about	concerning, regarding
build	construct
show	demonstrate, exhibit, reveal
suggest	hypothesize
change	modify
ease	facilitate

Source: Adapted from Barrass (1978, p. 56, Table 9). Adapted with permission.

long as you avoid a singsong quality when switching back and forth from *he* to *she*. In any case, do not use "creative" pronoun constructions like *he/she* or *(s)he* in your writing because they slow readers down and do not conform to APA style.

Of course, it almost goes without saying that terms like *boys* and *girls* are used exclusively to describe children, never adolescents or adults. When writing about humans, use of *men* and *women* is preferred over *males* and *females*. Terms like *ladies* and *gentlemen* are antiquated and should not be used in research writing.

Race and Ethnicity

The designations used to refer to various racial and ethnic groups are fluid; what was acceptable at one point in time is suddenly out of date. Groups change their collective minds about acceptable labels. A writer's job is to stay abreast of the changes. Americans of African ancestry prefer to be described as *Black* or *African American*; older terms like *Negro* and *Afro-American* are out of date and rarely used (APA, 2001). The best approach is to rely on the three aforementioned keys to avoiding bias (especially the call for being specific and sensitive), but there is one other working rule: Racial and ethnic groups are proper nouns, so they must be capitalized within written text. Thus, as racial designations, *Blacks*, *Whites*, and *Asians* (do not use *Orientals*) are all capitalized, as are ethnic groupings: *Portuguese*, *Koreans*, *Laplanders*, and *Afghans*. For more specific advice on this topic, consult Section 2.15 of the *Publication Manual* (APA, 2001).

GUIDELINES FOR FORMATTING IN APA STYLE

The order and outline for empirical papers written in APA style are presented in Chapter 4 (see Table 4.2 on page 60). Please refer to Table 4.2 when organizing a paper, verifying the ordering of sections, page location requirements, and so on. Here is a list of other basic requirements for formatting APA-style papers based on the *Publication Manual* (APA, 2001):

- Double-space throughout a paper—never single-space.
- Type or print your paper on 8 1/2-by-11-inch white paper of good quality.
- Use a 12-point font or typescript.
- Type or print on only one side of each sheet of paper.

- The left margin of the paper should be even (i.e., use a left-justified margin).
- The right margin of the paper should appear jagged or uneven (i.e., do not use a right-justified margin, which wastes space and makes any text look like it was printed in a block).
- Use 1-inch margins around the four sides of each page.
- All paragraphs (except for the Abstract) are indented 5 spaces (1/2 inch) from the left margin.

We now turn to more specific issues regarding the physical layout of APA-style papers.

Title Page

The title should be centered in the upper half of the title page. Brief titles appear on one line of text; longer titles (especially those containing a colon) require two lines of text. All the words in a title except articles are capitalized (an exception is an article appearing as the first word in the line of a title or subtitle). Double-spaced and centered beneath the title is your name and, two spaces below that, the full name of your institution (multiple authors hailing from the same or different institutions also appear on the title page; see Section 5.15 of the *Publication Manual* [APA, 2001] for formatting examples). The format of the center of a title page looks like this:

Reason and Cognition in Toddlers: Problem Solving at Two Years

Jane C. Smith

Montwell University

Another example can be found in the sample paper (see page 105).

A second element appearing on the title page is the page header. A **page header** consists of the first few words of a paper's title. These two or three words appear in the upper right-hand corner of each page, adjacent to the page number. Why bother with page headers? Sometimes the pages in a paper become separated and page headers ensure that none become lost. Here is an example of a page header—this one appears on the title page because it accompanies the page number, 1.

Reason and Cognition 1

Besides a title, author name(s), institutional affiliation, and page header, a title page must also have a **running head**, which is a shortened title appearing at the top of each page in a printed article. Running heads help readers locate or keep track of articles within journals. A running head is no more than 50 characters in length (all letters, spaces between words, and any punctuation marks figure in this count). The running head appears flush left with the top of the title page (but one double-space below the right-justified page header and number appearing on the first line). Here is an example of a running head, appropriately located below a page header. Note that the word *Running* is capitalized but *head* is not, and that the short title appears in all capital letters:

Reason and Cognition 1

Running head: REASON AND COGNITION IN TODDLERS

The sample title page illustrating all these features is found on page 105.

Page Numbering

Page numbering in APA style is straightforward: Pages are numbered consecutively, starting with the title page. Page numbers appear in the upper-right corner of each page, at least 1 inch from the right-hand edge of the paper and to the right of the page header (see above example). Page numbering using Arabic numerals (i.e., 1, 2, 3, 4, . . .) does not stop until the manuscript page for the first table or figure, if any, is reached or the paper ends.

Headings and Subheadings

All APA-style papers rely on headings and subheadings to internally organize a paper's text (recall the discussion of outlining in Chapter 4). By now you are well versed in the major sections found within APA-style papers, each of which—except for the introduction—is marked by a centered heading. **Centered headings** contain both capital and lowercase letters but are not underlined. Here are some examples:

Abstract

Method

Results

Discussion

References

Centered headings can also be found within any one section of the paper. Thus, an introduction might contain a heading like this one:

Cognition in Infancy

Major sections of a paper are further divided by using **subheadings**, which are placed flush with the left margin, include both upper- and lowercase letters, and are italicized. A second-level subheading appears at the beginning of a paragraph (i.e., indented from the margin), is italicized, begins with a capital letter, and is followed by a period (the text begins two spaces later). Here are the two levels of subheadings placed under a centered heading:

Cognition in Infancy

Reasoning in Early Infancy

   Defining cognition. Studying thinking in newborn infants is . . .

There are other heading levels that APA style sanctions (infants See student section 5.10 in the *Publication Manual* [APA, 2001]), but most student papers require only basic centered headings and subheadings. Further examples of both heading types can be found in the sample paper (see page 109).

Quickly Checking a Paper's Format

Table 9.3 is a checklist for formatting APA-style manuscript pages, a summary of the *Publication Manual* (APA, 2001) requirements just reviewed. Following this checklist during the final stages of preparing a manuscript will ensure that it is legible and consistent with APA-style requirements.

PROOFREADING THE PENULTIMATE DRAFT: ONCE MORE WITH FEELING

Proofreading the penultimate, or next to the last, draft is an important exercise, one last pass to verify that everything is in order. Doing a final proofread of your paper should occur only after you have completed all but the last two steps in Table 9.4. To begin the final edit, print out a clean copy of the paper, grab a pencil or pen, and retreat

Table 9.3. Checklist: Formatting Rules for APA-Style
Manuscript Pages

_____ Good-quality white paper is used.

_____ Pages are typed or printed on one side only and in a 12 point font
or typescript.

_____ All pages are double-spaced—no single-spacing is used.

_____ Paragraphs are indent 5 spaces.

_____ The paper's left margin is justified, whereas the right margin is uneven
(i.e., do not right- or full-justify the text).

_____ There are 1-inch margins around the four sides of each page.

_____ Page numbers appear in the upper-right corner of each page.
Beginning with the title page, Arabic numerals (i.e., 1, 2, 3, 4, . . .)
continue until the manuscript page for the first table or figure (if any)
is reached at the manuscript's end.

_____ The title page has a page heading and number (i.e., 1); a running
head; and a title, author name, and institutional affiliation.

_____ Each section immediately follows the previous one (i.e., Method after
introduction, Results after Method, Discussion after Results). Do not
skip to the top of a new page unless a section heading appears without
the first two lines of its text (see Table 4.2).

_____ Centered headings and subheadings are used, appearing in APA style.

to a quiet place. Once there, begin reading from the Title page forward, marking any final, necessary changes in the writing or the APA
style.

What sort of marks should you make on the penultimate draft? Try
your hand at learning to use the common proofreader's symbols shown in
Table 9.5. Editors and copy editors use these symbols to mark up manuscripts for revision prior to publication (see Chapter 7 of the *Publication
Manual*; APA, 2001).

Proofreader's marks are very helpful and, like many writers, you
will quickly find yourself using them when revising any draft. The top
of Figure 9.1 shows the first draft of a paragraph fragment, edited using proofreader's marks. The bottom of Figure 9.1 illustrates the corrected, final copy of the paragraph fragment. Editing and proofreading reduced the number of unnecessary words present in the earlier
version.

Table 9.4. Checklist: Steps to Follow When Preparing to Submit a Final Version of an APA-Style Paper

_____ Does the paper conform to the hourglass model (see Figure 5.1, page 83)?

_____ Is the paper's hypothesis clear (see pages 65–66)?

_____ Does each paragraph have a main point, linking it to previous and subsequent paragraphs (see pages 66–67)?

_____ Did you create, read, and revise several drafts of the paper (see Table 4.6, page 68)?

_____ Did you share a draft with an instructor, tutor, or peer? Were their comments incorporated into a subsequent draft (see pages 77–80)?

_____ Did you use fewer and simpler words whenever possible (see Writer's Guideposts 9.1 and 9.2)?

_____ Did you proofread the paper for errors in grammar (see pages 160–164)?

_____ Did you proofread the paper for errors in punctuation (see pages 164–166)?

_____ Did you proofread the paper for errors in spelling (see pages 169–170)?

_____ Did you use spelling- and/or grammar-correcting software to analyze the paper (see pages 169–170)?

_____ Did you rely on the active voice where possible and appropriate (see pages 170–171; see also the discussion of tone, page 70)?

_____ Did you use inclusive, nonsexist language throughout the paper (see pages 171–175)?

_____ Do all references and citations conform to APA style (see Chapter 7)?

_____ Did you read the paper aloud, slowly, from beginning to end, listening for cadence in the flow of the words and ideas (see page 72)?

_____ Did you make certain that the paper conformed to APA-style formatting requirements (see pages 175–178)?

_____ Did you make certain that any tables and figures conformed to APA style (see Chapter 8)?

_____ Did you do one final proofread of the paper from start to finish using proofreader's marks (see Table 9.5)?

_____ Did you make final changes and submit the final draft?

Table 9.5. Common Proofreader's Marks Used to Revise Manuscript Copy

1. Insert word that has been omitted	∧ caret	*the* Study describes ∧ effect
2. Insert letter that has been omitted	∧ caret	that b̥o̥k
3. Transpose letters	∿	fo͡rm the sea
4. Transpose words	∿	was only exposed
5. Capitalize letter	≡ (three short underlines)	these data
6. Change letter to lowercase	/ (slash)	These Ɖata
7. Change to italics	_____ (underline once)	Homo sapiens
8. Separate words that are run together	ǀ (draw vertical line in between)	edit|carefully
9. Delete word	_____ℊ (draw line through)	the ~~nice~~ data
10. Close up space	⌢ (sideways parentheses)	the e͜nd
11. Change wrong letter	/ (draw line through and add correct letter above)	ƒ̷emale
12. Change wrong word	_____ (draw line through and add correct word above)	*These* ~~This~~ data
13. Begin a new paragraph	¶ (paragraph symbol)	female. ¶ In contrast
14. Restore original	(STET)	(STET) the ~~energy~~ needs • • •

Source: Adapted from Pechenik (2001, pp. 128–129, chapter 5, Table 1). Reprinted with permission.

Sample paragraph fragment marked for corrections:
¶ This experiment was designed to determine whether Physically
attractive and extroverted applicants would influence an interviewers
perceptions and hiring decisions. Contrary to our preliminary
predictions, physical attractiveness and extroversion had no effect on
employment decision. Specifically, the results indicated that
applicants' extroversion did have a significant impact on the
participants' reactions and decision making to hire . . .

Corrected copy of sample paragraph fragment:
This experiment was designed to determine whether physically
attractive and extroverted applicants would influence an interviewer's
perceptions and hiring decisions. Contrary to our predictions,
physical attractiveness and extroversion had no effect on employment
decisions. Specifically, the results indicated that applicants' extroversion did not have a significant impact on the participants' reactions
and decision to hire . . .

Figure 9.1 Learning to Use Proofreader's Marks.

Source: Adapted from Dougherty (2001, p. 14). Used with permission.

EXERCISES

1. In your research notebook, write a few paragraphs about the grammar and punctuation errors you typically make. What can you do to
   avoid them?
2. Find some examples of the passive voice in published research or in
   your own writing. Rewrite these examples in the active voice in your
   research notebook.
3. Use the checklist in Table 9.3 to review the formatting of a paper.
4. Review a paper draft to remove any connecting phrases or complex
   words.
5. Edit a piece of your writing using the proofreader's marks shown in
   Table 9.5.

10

BEYOND WRITING: PRESENTING PSYCHOLOGICAL RESEARCH

Writing in psychology is not limited to creating papers—it is also an essential part of delivering a presentation—another form of communication, of sharing results. Psychological presentations are usually public events, such as lectures, discussions, poster sessions, and symposia. Psychologists speak in classes, at professional conferences, and in colloquia (invited research presentations given at colleges and universities).

Students, too, are called upon to present. Like writing a paper, giving a presentation is a learned skill based on guidelines and experience. This final chapter contains advice to help you give a professional, discipline-based presentation, whether in a psychology class or at a conference. I discuss how to give a "talk," the term psychologists use to refer to a research presentation, and how to participate in a student symposium or conference poster session. I also offer suggestions for submitting your research to a psychology journal.

THE CALL FOR PAPERS

A "Call for Papers" is an announcement of some meeting, usually a conference, that arrives in the form of a public invitation. Most Calls appear in poster form (check the bulletin boards in your institution's psychology department) or in the announcements section of psychology periodicals. With increasing frequency, conference invitations are appearing in e-mails or electronic newsletters.

There are many conferences designed for student presenters and aimed at student audiences. Check with the faculty in your psychology department to see if there are any local conferences where you can submit your work. Many professional conferences also reserve special sessions for student presentations. A list of both sorts of conferences is shown in Table 10.1.

Understanding Call Types and Requirements

A Call can be specific, inviting papers dealing with a specific research area (e.g., organizational psychology) or issue (e.g., teen depression), or it can be general, welcoming presentation on any area in the discipline. A Call will specify what sort of information authors must submit in order to have their work included. It will also indicate whether presentations are to be spoken (a talk), presented in the form of a poster (poster session), or presented by some other method (symposium, panel, workshop). Some conferences are competitive, meaning that only a portion of the total number of submissions is accepted for presentation. Other gatherings are open: As long as you supply the requisite materials on time, you are assured a place in the proceedings. Here is a list of the usual requirements found in a Call for Papers:

- **A short abstract.** A short summary of the research, usually in the range of 100 to 200 words. You can edit your paper's Abstract, adding or subtracting words as necessary. Never exceed the stated limits or you risk having your work rejected because you did not comply with guidelines.
- **A long abstract.** A long abstract is *not* your entire paper; rather it is a very short summary of the paper. Some Calls set limits according to number of words (e.g., 1,000 words), others according to number of pages (e.g., six double-spaced, typed pages, including references). Please note that you must condense your paper (yes, *all* those detailed pages) into a short, concise summary. Never exceed the stated limits.
- **Contact information.** The conference organizers will need your name, mailing address, e-mail address, and so on to let you know whether your work is accepted and to inform you when and where you will present it. For this reason, you may be asked to supply a self-addressed, stamped envelope or two.
- **Instructor or advisor support.** Student conferences often require that one of your instructors (preferably the individual who supervised your research) sign off on it, indicating that it was competently done. Larger regional and national conferences usually require that you be a member of their organization or that you secure a signature from a person who already belongs (again, a faculty advisor is the best bet). In both cases, the conference

THE CALL FOR PAPERS   185

Table 10.1. Some Psychology Conferences that Promote Student Involvement

STUDENT CONFERENCES IN PSYCHOLOGY:

Arkansas Symposium for Psychology Students
Carolinas Psychology Conference
Delaware Valley Undergraduate Research Conference
Great Plains Students' Psychology Convention
ILLOWA Undergraduate Psychology Conference
Kwantlen University College Undergraduate Psychology Research Conference
Lehigh Valley Undergraduate Psychology Research Conference
Michigan Undergraduate Psychology Paper Reading Conference
Mid-America Undergraduate Psychology Research Conference
Minnesota Undergraduate Psychology Conference
Southeastern Undergraduate Psychology Research Conference
University of Winnipeg Undergraduate Psychology Research Conference

NATIONAL STUDENT SCIENCE CONFERENCE WITH A PSYCHOLOGY COMPONENT:

National Council on Undergraduate Research (NCUR) Conference

NATIONAL AND REGIONAL PSYCHOLOGY CONFERENCES THAT WELCOME STUDENT PARTICIPATION:

American Psychological Association (APA) Annual Conference
Association for Psychological Science (APS) Annual Conference

Eastern Psychological Association
Midwestern Psychological Association
Rocky Mountain Psychological Association
Southeastern Psychological Association
Southwestern Psychological Association
Western Psychological Association

Note. Dates and contact information for many of these conferences are available in APA publications, including the APA Monitor on Psychology *and the journal* American Psychologist. *Details can also be found in the journal* Teaching of Psychology.

organizers are looking for some indication that the submitted work was carried out scientifically, ethically, and according to APA guidelines.

- **A submission deadline.** Putting together any professional gathering involves an incredible amount of work and countless details. As a result, submission deadlines are established so that the conference can occur on time. Be sure to submit all requested materials on time. If you are late, do not be surprised if your work is rejected.

Most conferences are interested in hearing finished research, not work in progress. If you are not certain that your research project will be finished before the presentation date, then you should probably not answer a Call for Papers. If your work is accepted, you are obligated to present it. To miss doing so because your research "isn't done yet" is not only unprofessional, it is unethical, especially because your acceptance might have prevented another submission from being accepted for presentation. If you cannot be there due to some truly unforeseen reason, a coauthor, possibly your faculty advisor, should go in your place.

Outside of giving a class presentation, answering a Call for Papers is the usual way to begin presenting your work. Wherever you have the chance to speak, though, you must take your listeners into account.

Knowing Your Audience

> The more you know your audience, and the more you can adjust your remarks to fit your audience, the better you are likely to be received.
>
> Robert J. Sternberg (1993, p. 204)

To whom are you speaking? Your instructor? A panel of judges? Classmates? Conference participants or faculty at your school? Knowing the members of your audience will determine the content, depth, and detail of your presentation. Speaking to a group of friends or family members is a very different experience than talking in front of a vast auditorium filled with attentive strangers. Your parents are apt to forgive nervous stumblings and numerous "ums" and "ers," but a group of professionals may be less charitable.

Consider these questions when planning a presentation:

- **Is your audience composed of professionals or peers?** Students will require more background explanation than will teachers or researchers. Professionals will expect you to demonstrate a higher degree of familiarity with the psychological literature.
- **What does your audience already know about psychology?** You can take some liberties if you know your audience is familiar

with the field. Otherwise, you will need to adjust the level of the presentation, making it more basic and introductory.

- **What does your audience know about your topic?** When presenting to class members, for example, you can focus almost exclusively on the research question and your project. If the audience is unknown to you, broaden your presentation by providing an appropriate level of background information to make your specific project understandable.

- **What do you want the audience to know?** In other words, what is your "take home" message? What should they leave knowing that they did not know before they heard your presentation? The amount of technical detail involved will determine how much you need to "set up" an audience before delivering the main message.

There is one other audience member you must satisfy, the person you are really writing and speaking for—yourself (Zinsser, 1990). Whatever you do when speaking to an audience, you must remain true to your instincts as a writer. Make sure that your talk is really the one you want to give.

Table 10.2 presents a checklist of questions to consider when answering a Call for Papers.

Table 10.2. A Checklist for Answering a Call for Papers

_____ 1. Review your paper: Will it make a good submission in answer to a Call for Papers?

_____ 2. What will you submit in answer to a Call? Can you choose from among papers (talks), poster sessions, and/or symposia?

_____ 3. Did you identify an audience (professional or peer) before writing a submission?

_____ 4. Are any short or long Abstracts you wrote within requested word limits?

_____ 5. Have you asked an academic advisor or a few peers to read and comment on your submission?

_____ 6. Did you prepare all supporting documents, such as contact information and self-addressed, stamped envelopes?

_____ 7. Did you carefully proofread all materials one last time before submission?

_____ 8. Did you note and follow all submission deadlines?

THE TALK

Every presentation should have an easy-to-understand, main message. The audience should leave your talk knowing one "big" thing, not a host of smaller, hard-to-remember details. Keep the main message simple—identify it at the beginning, somewhere in the middle, and again when wrapping up your presentation. Remember, too, that listening to a talk is not like reading a paper. A reader can read a confusing passage over and over until its meaning is clear, but a listener's only option is to look puzzled. Many people are hesitant to ask for clarification until the end of a presentation, when it is too late to correct a misunderstanding. The best line of defense is detailed preparation so that complex issues are made as concrete as possible and main ideas are repeated.

Table 10.3 identifies the basic steps necessary for putting together a research talk. Unless it has been awhile since you thought about your project or you are creating a talk from scratch, step 1 is probably already accomplished. If you are writing a talk from scratch, it is likely to be about a topic already covered in the literature rather than a novel empirical effort. If so, then library research and reading (see Chapters 2 and 3) will constitute step 1. The second step highlights the importance of knowing who will be listening to your talk. Having a firm grasp of a main message—step 3—is important because it represents the core of your presentation. Before proceeding on to step 4, the actual outlining and drafting of the talk, you must write down the main message.

Table 10.3. Six Steps for Preparing a Research Talk in Psychology

1. Read your APA-style paper (or, alternatively, select and refine a talk topic).

2. Identify and think about the audience.

3. Identify the talk's main message.

4. Outline and draft the talk.

5. Practice the talk; return to step 4 as needed.

6. Deliver the talk.

Source: From B. E. Gronbeck et al., Principles and Types of Speech Communication, *13/e. Published by Allyn and Bacon, Boston, MA. Copyright © 1997 by Pearson Education. Adapted by permission of the publisher.*

When you go to the fourth step, of course, some editing is also involved. Only a fraction of all the information present in an original paper will be retained for a talk. Once a working outline and draft of the talk is available, you should begin to practice delivering it (step 5 in Table 10.3). Such practice will help you decide what changes, if any, are necessary to improve the presentation. Finally, the actual presentation of the talk occurs as step 6.

Outlining a Talk

How do you outline a talk? Doesn't that mean reducing a detailed paper down into a concise version of its former self? Yes—and also no. Although many talks grow out of papers, no talk is supposed to completely reflect the content of a given paper. Once again, reading is not the same as listening, so you must take your audience into account when developing an outline.

The easiest way to begin an outline is with the hourglass model for APA-style manuscripts (see Figure 5.1 on page 83). Reread the introduction, Method, Results, and Discussion sections of your paper and identify the essential points within each one. You cannot describe every detail found in the Method, for example, but you can summarize the basic procedure, emphasizing any manipulated and measured variables. As you read through the paper, underline key points.

Write the presentation around the outline formed by the hourglass model and any key points, especially those found in the Results section. Results are really the heart of any good talk, and the bulk of your presentation should be focused on them. To be sure, material from the introduction and Method leads into the Results, and points raised in the Discussion provide context for the Results, but the actual findings are really the main message in any talk. When you discuss the Results, revisit the hypothesis, highlight the dependent measure (again), make note of the statistical analysis you used, and then describe what happened. By "what happened," I mean what did the participants in your research do *behaviorally*. When pointing to differences between means, for example, characterize the relationship behaviorally (e.g., how many times on average did the experimental group blink in response to a stimulus as compared to a control group).

Keep in mind that your goal is not to repeat or even paraphrase the information found in the original paper. The text is only a starting point for you to reorganize and rethink the work. Do not hesitate to drop old material in favor of new views. Similar to the outline you originally created for the paper (see outlining guidelines on pages 58–63), the one drafted for a presentation must also be refined and revised. Remember, you are not "married" to the paper you wrote earlier, so you need not recapitulate all of its points in a talk. Highlighting one or two main points rather than exhaustive details will ensure that the audience walks away knowing something about your topic.

Preparing Overheads, Slides, and Handouts

Too many tables and figures in a paper is cumbersome, and the same rule holds true for the overheads or slides speakers use when giving a talk. Keep them to a minimum, making sure that the ones you use can be understood with a glance or two. The last thing any good speaker wants is to have the audience puzzling over poorly presented numbers in a cluttered table shown on a screen or in a handout. You want people to listen to what you have to say with minimal distractions. By all means prepare good graphics (see Chapter 8), but do not become dependent on them. The purpose of a talk is to enable your audience learn from you, not from your props.

If you decide to prepare handouts, consider when to pass them out. Sharing handouts at the start of your talk invites the audience to page through the materials instead of listening to you. Do not wait until the bitter end of your presentation to pass them out, however. No one will have much to say if your data remain unavailable until the talk is over. Ideally, ask a peer to distribute handouts when you give some prearranged signal during your talk—a nod of the head or a simple request is sufficient. Enlisting the help of another ensures that the flow of your talk is not disrupted (asking someone to change slides or overheads for you is not a bad idea, either).

Computer-Aided Presentations

To some observers, the use of slides, overheads, and handouts is a dated exercise. Why struggle with upside-down overheads or jammed slide trays when a preprogrammed presentation can help almost anyone look like a polished speaker? Why not rely on new technologies and create a computer-aided presentation? I am of two minds on this issue. On the one hand, anything that helps a professional presentation come together sounds like a good idea. On the other, I wonder about overrelying on

Table 10.4. Guidelines for Effective Electronic Slide Presentations

1. **Avoid overloading slides**. Do not overload the slides with text. Summarize your research using keywords and brief definitions in an outline format.

2. **Do not read the slides**. Use slides to supplement, not replace, your role as speaker.

3. **Avoid flashy, distracting gimmicks**. Rely on simple backgrounds, simple fonts, and simple transitions between slides and sections of your talk.

4. **Use pictures and video clips sparingly, if at all**. Only use images that truly and effectively demonstrate the point you want to make. Limit yourself to one and no more than two images per talk.

5. **Do not distract your audience from the point of your talk**. Although technological "bells and whistles" are tempting, rely on your own wit and wisdom rather than a cartoon or odd noises.

6. **Do not forget about your delivery—rehearse your talk**. Remember, people came to see and hear you, not the slide show.

Source: Adapted from Daniel, D. B. (2005). How to ruin a perfectly good lecture. In B. Perlman, L. McCann, & W. Buskist (Eds.), Voices of NITOP: Favorite talks from the National Institute on the Teaching of Psychology *(pp. 119-130). Washington, DC: American Psychological Society.*

technology. Does a speaker end up worrying more about programming, pretty graphics, and dancing letters than giving an animated lecture? What happens if the laptop computer containing the presentation "crashes"? My notes, overheads, and slides have yet to fail me, and I prefer to rely on my brain as my processor.

Most, if not all, readers are probably quite familiar with PowerPoint presentations. Although space constraints preclude me from explaining how to set up presentations using this helpful software, I briefly offer suggestions in Table 10.4 on what *not* to do when using PowerPoint (drawn from Daniel, 2005; see also Ludwig, Daniel, Froman, & Mathie, 2005). Daniel (2005) vividly highlights the main perils of using any slide-dependent software, especially PowerPoint:

> In the hands of certain people . . . slideware can indeed be counterproductive. We have all sat through busy, text-laden presentations staring at someone's back while [he or she] read 3-foot tall paragraphs to us. The fault lies in the execution more than the software itself (p. 120).

If technology frees you to focus on the quality of a talk's content, then it may be a great thing. I recommend that you rely on whatever type of presentation aid makes you the most comfortable. If that happens to be a briefcase-sized computer, so be it. But do let me make one suggestion: Have a backup plan just in case technology fails you. Carry a packet of overheads based on the computerized presentation.

Practice, Practice, Practice

Practicing the talk is the fifth step in Table 10.3. By practicing your talk, I mean that you must say what you are planning to say *out loud*. To start, you can deliver your talk in front of a mirror. It usually takes a few minutes to get over the heightened self-awareness associated with watching your own reflection, which is helpful; you will feel a similar sense of self-consciousness when speaking in front of a live audience. After a few trials in front of the mirror, branch out and try to speak in front of a friendly group, say, a few friends or possibly your instructor or academic advisor. Ask one of them to time you so that you stay within the allotted time frame. Allowing 5 or so minutes for questions at the end, a 20-minute talk must be done in 15 minutes. Be sure to go over the outlines and notes for your talk several times so that you do not have to read them for the actual presentation. Before then, however, remember to practice, practice, practice. (If possible, rehearse in the room where you will give the talk; familiarity with this space will reduce your anxiety.)

Giving the Talk: Be a Pro, Avoid the Cons

Your talk outline is written, the visual aids are prepared, technology is (or is not) a part of the proceedings, and you have practiced what you intend to say many times. What's next? Giving the actual presentation, of course. Here are some qualities associated with being an effective speaker:

- **Begin on a strong, positive note.** Communication specialists claim that a strong, credible start will interest listeners (Lucas, 1995). Even if you rely on notes for the rest of a presentation, have the opening gambit memorized.
- **Know that anxiety is normal.** Even polished presenters routinely report having stage fright before they give talks (Goleman, 1984; Hahner, Sokoloff, & Salisch, 1993). Anxiety is understandable when all eyes are on you. Some speaking specialists actually

believe that a small case of the jitters before going on is a good thing, that it keeps a speaker focused, attentive, and alert (Lucas, 1995). Overconfident speakers can be dull speakers because they have done it all before, perhaps one too many times.

- **Never read a talk.** No one wants to watch you read your paper out loud. Giving a talk should have some spontaneity. Be conversational rather than formal.
- **Speak up.** Do not mumble or mutter, and never turn your back while talking to an audience. Speak in louder tones than normal, but do so more slowly than your accustomed speed.
- **Tell people what makes the topic so interesting.** If you do not make the case that your work, your topic, is interesting, no one will make it for you. Why do you care about this research? Why should others?
- **Be organized and efficient.** Know your outline. Your audience should always have a sense of where you are and where you are headed. Don't dither over details unless asked to explain some specific point.
- **Watch your time but avoid rushing.** Novice speakers routinely run out of time before they even get to the main results. Don't make this mistake. Practice your talk, fine-tuning it until you finish with 5 minutes left for questions. Ask a friend in the audience to let you know when you have 5 minutes left to speak (and don't infringe on the time reserved for questions and answers or the next presenter). If you find yourself rushing, then streamline the talk.
- **Move around.** Don't just stand there in front of a blackboard or behind a podium—do something to spark audience interest in what you have to say.
- **Make eye contact.** Focus on the faces of your audience, pick a few friendly ones, and speak directly to them. Making eye contact with the audience establishes a personal element in any presentation.
- **Use numerous examples.** The best way to maintain appropriate focus when speaking is to pepper the presentation with well-chosen examples. Illustrate concepts with good examples that will stay with listeners throughout the talk and beyond.
- **Summarize the main point throughout the presentation.** Tell the audience at the beginning what you intend to demonstrate, draw their attention to it again when you review the results,

WRITER'S GUIDEPOST   10.1
Becoming a Persuasive Speaker

Believe an expert.

Virgil, *The Aeneid* (19 B.C.E.)

Persuasion—how messages alter our attitudes, beliefs, or actions—is powerful. Ample social-psychological research on attitudes and behavior reveals that persuasive speakers possess particular characteristics that make them appealing to an audience. I am not suggesting that you adopt the mannerisms of a sideshow barker or an infomercial actor, but they can supplement the speaker guidelines we already reviewed. Where spoken presentations are concerned, persuasion often occurs when a speaker is an expert on some topic (for a review of persuasive communications, see Myers, 2002).

Here are some tips for becoming a persuasive speaker:

- Appear confident.
- Convey credibility and trustworthiness.
- Know your topics well.
- Strive for an attractive appearance (i.e., "dress for success" the day you speak).
- Look audience members right in the eye.
- Speak without hesitation—quickly but not in a rushed manner.
- Avoid long or awkward pauses.
- Appear spontaneous, not overly rehearsed.

Of course, persuasive speakers are often persuasive writers. Items from the above list can be adjusted for use in written communications as well.

and remind them of the main point as you conclude. Try to make the same point in a slightly different way each time.

- **Don't be defensive—welcome and use criticism.** Just as peer review improves writing, the questions and comments given by an audience can improve a presentation. Seasoned speakers know that even critical comments are offered in the spirit of intellectual exchange, of improving understanding. It is normal to be a little defensive when someone questions something you did or neglected to do in your research (remember, no study is perfect). Try to view such comments as helpful.

- **Never panic if you cannot answer a question.** No one expects you to know everything, nor can you anticipate every possible question. It is perfectly fine and entirely professional to admit when you don't know something. Be honest and admit that (until now) you never considered the question and need time to reflect on it. Tough questions are often the starting point for subsequent investigations.

- **End well.** Besides a good start, you need a good ending. The last thing you say is what people remember (Lucas, 1995), so let them know you are finishing up the presentation before you hit home the main point(s) one more time. Like a practiced opening, having the last few things you say committed to memory makes a favorable impression on listeners.

Table 10.5. A Checklist for Preparing and Giving a Talk

_____ 1. Does your talk fit the scope of a Call for Papers or other venue?

_____ 2. To what sort of audience (professional or peer) will you present?

_____ 3. Have you identified the main message of your research?

_____ 4. Have you followed the steps for preparing a presentation outlined in Table 10.3?

_____ 5. After some practice, does your presentation fit into the time allotted (e.g., 20 minutes, including the last 5 for questions)?

_____ 6. Are any handouts or supplementary aids (e.g., slides, overheads) prepared?

_____ 7. Have you reviewed the pros and cons for presenting outlined in this chapter?

Note: This checklist can also be used for preparing symposia.

Beyond practice and experience, the best teacher of public-speaking skills is observation. Watch those public speakers, teachers, invited lecturers, and even actors whose spoken delivery you admire. What do they do that gives them style while maintaining clarity and coherence in what they say? What can you borrow from their repertoire to improve your own speaking skills?

Table 10.5 presents a checklist of questions to consider when preparing and giving a talk.

SYMPOSIA: TALKS IN COMMON

An alternative to giving a talk is taking part in a **symposium**—an organized meeting where a group of talks related to a common theme is presented. Organizing themes for symposia can be broad (e.g., intelligence) or specific (e.g., declines in measured intelligence among women aged 80 and older). Symposia are frequently presented at psychological conferences, and they often highlight "cutting-edge" questions and empirical research. Attending a symposium allows a listener to learn multiple approaches to the study of a problem. Participating in a symposium affords speakers the opportunity to have a meaningful intellectual exchange with peers about a common question in psychology.

A symposium is usually comprised of three or more 20-minute talks. An organizer will usually start the session by introducing the general research area or question and then briefly introduce the speakers and their perspectives. Following these opening remarks, each speaker takes a turn presenting. Once all the speakers finish, a discussant usually reacts to the panelists' work, offering comments and criticisms, and giving a general summary of the symposium's scope. Symposium participants are not "attacking" one another's ideas or trying to "win" a speaking contest. Rather, they are sharing and occasionally challenging different ideas about a common topic. Table 10.5, the checklist for giving a talk, is useful for preparing to speak in a symposium as well.

Student Symposia

Student symposia at psychology conferences are much less common than individual talks. There is no reason, however, why you and a group of interested peers cannot organize a student symposium on your campus, in your home department, or in a single class. All you need is a question of common interest (which is often provided by the topic of a course or

Table 10.6. Considerations When Organizing a Symposium

1. **Assess interest in a symposium.** What is the theme? Who will present?

2. **Select an organizer and discussant.** Who will give an overview of the symposium topic and speakers? Who will serve as discussant?

3. **Pick a date, time, and place.** Will the symposium be held in or outside of a class? What location is best? When is a high level of attendance most likely to occur?

4. **Identify an audience.** Will classmates come? What about peers and instructors from other classes and departments?

5. **Organize and identify needed resources.** Must a room be reserved? Will slide and overhead projectors be available? Should refreshments be served (besides water for presenters)? Will presenters want to give handouts to the audience? How many copies are needed?

6. **Advertise.** Can posters be made? Can public invitations be sent over e-mail or in a campus newspaper?

Source. Adapted from Dana S. Dunn, The Practical Researcher: A Student Guide to Conducting Psychological Research, *McGraw-Hill, 1999, Table 9.2, p. 297. Copyright © 1999 by Dana Dunn. Reprinted with permission of The McGraw-Hill Companies, Inc.*

seminar), a group of speakers (three or four is ideal), perhaps a discussant (often an ideal role for a faculty advisor or invited scholar), and some venue for presentation (e.g., a classroom or lecture hall, or some lounge in the psychology department or campus student union). If the number of interested speakers is large, then you might want to stage several symposia. Avoid enlisting too many presenters for a single symposium or the audience (and even participants) will quickly lose interest.

One last piece of advice: Form a symposium committee. As shown by the questions and entries in Table 10.6, there are too many details for one person. Organize a committee and delegate responsibilities, using Table 10.6 as a starting point for planning the symposium. Be sure to invite interested peers and faculty from other social science departments or disciplines. You might just start a departmental tradition.

POSTER PRESENTATIONS

The final setting for presenting psychological research is the **poster session**—a collection of empirical studies conducted by different people and presented in a largely graphic format as posters. Poster sessions make research efforts more personal because the investigators are there to share their data with passersby. These sessions are increasingly common at psychology conferences, presumably because they provide an informal but highly informative setting for sharing research. When a researcher presents a poster, his or her research project is presented in an even shorter summary fashion than is the case for a talk. Indeed, the most essential information from the hourglass model is reduced to no more than a few paragraphs (usually three or fewer), and the introduction, Method, Results, and Discussion are presented in no more than one typed page each. Tables, figures, and occasionally photographs support this short text.

Knowing What to Expect

Most poster sessions take place in large convention halls or big rooms that allow interested people to mill around, moving from poster to poster. The space allotted for each poster is usually no more than 4 by 6 feet. Poster presenters stand by their work, prepared to answer any questions for an hour or so. What makes a poster distinct from a paper or talk is its inherently visual nature. Short research summaries and accompanying graphics are meant to entice viewer interest. Figure 10.1 illustrates one possible layout for a poster, which can be attached to a portable display board (most conferences use these) or a wall. The main message of a study can be gleaned quickly from a poster, allowing viewers to ask questions in an up-close and personal way.

Do viewers actually ask questions? Sometimes. Szuchman (2002) cleverly but truthfully notes that one of three things happens when a viewer gives your poster a quick look: The individual (1) walks away, (2) reads it, or (3) actually talks to you. In general, most people walk away, some read it, and a few engage you in conversation. You should not be offended or disappointed when people move on or only read the poster. Like you, people have different research interests and your topic might not attract their attention. Happily, some people will want to discuss your work. The funny thing is that some folks who ask about your work might not even take the trouble to read the poster. Instead, they want to hear about it directly from you (Szuchman, 2002). To prepare for this eventuality, you must have a quick, "canned" talk— no more than 2 or 3 minutes—that describes the work from conception to results and conclusions. Naturally, you can point to any data tables and figures in the poster as you go, just keep your comments short and

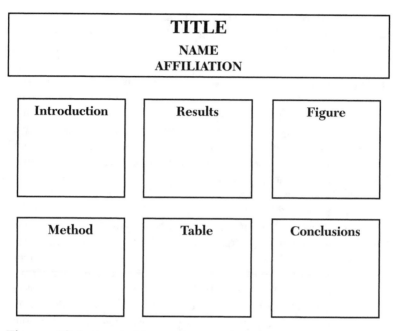

Figure 10.1 A typical layout for a psychology poster.

focused. Plan to repeat this mini-talk several times during the poster session.

To supplement the poster and your short speech, it is a good idea to have a handout to give away. This handout can be a short APA-style paper that is based on the poster content. There is no need to pass out copies of any original APA-style paper, but do put your contact information in the handout (i.e., e-mail and postal addresses) so that any interested party can ask for more details about your research.

Creating a Poster: Less Is More—and More Is a Bore

Technology, especially computer graphics and fonts, makes putting together a poster quite easy. Indeed, software exists that allows you to print out an entire poster display on a large sheet of paper. Many schools allow students to use special printers to create big, authoritative posters in several colors with graphs, photographs, text, and tables. There is nothing complicated, though, about using word-processing and graphics software to create separate sheets, tables, and figures. Remember, the goal is to provide a minimal amount of information, something that a viewer can assess quickly, understand, and "take home." Thus, your poster should be spare rather than cluttered and busy—less is more. Besides, you will be there to fill in the gaps, answer questions, and go beyond the level of detail available in the display.

Your poster must have a short, descriptive title, one that can easily be read from some distance, say, around 15 or 20 feet. Thus, the letters in the title will need to be between 1 and 2 inches tall (your name and institutional affiliation can appear in a slightly smaller font under the title). Remember, most psychology posters have an introduction, Method, and Results section (highlighting the main message), each of which is no more than a few short paragraphs. These sections can appear on individual sheets of paper and in a larger than usual font so that they can be read from a distance of about 3 feet. Some presenters prefer to have a "Conclusions" section in lieu of a Discussion (Szuchman, 2002), particularly since they are available to actually discuss their work. It's impossible to explain everything about your research on a poster, so it is quite acceptable to summarize main points in any section using bulleted or even numbered statements. Some authors use a bullet style in the earlier sections of their posters as well. Tables and figures (see Chapter 8) are apt to be linked with the Results section and should highlight clear relationships within the data. A table with numbers is fine, but a graphic figure is preferable if it conveys the main findings. Given the brevity of the poster, an Abstract is probably unnecessary (unless it is specifically requested by the conference organizers; cf. Szuchman, 2002), and any references cited in the poster's text could be provided in a handout (otherwise they can be distracting in the display).

Here are some ideas for presenting and organizing a poster's content:

- In the introduction, briefly describe the initial study concerning your topic as well as any relevant recent studies. Introduce your work as a replication or extension of this prior research, highlighting key differences or innovations. Make certain your hypothesis is clear to readers.
- In the Method section, include a short description of the participants (e.g., number of men and women, ages, and any other pertinent information). A description of the research design (e.g.,

experimental, correlational, observational), making note of manipulated and measured variables (behaviorally defined), is also needed. Be sure to mention whether a control group was used; if it was not, an explanation is probably warranted. An abbreviated procedure should lead readers through what happened to the participants. If any special materials were used (e.g., a survey, a personality inventory), having copies available is a good idea.

- In the Results section, briefly explain how the hypothesis was tested, making note of what statistical or other analyses were used. Significant, summary statistics should be included at the end of descriptive statements concerning what occurred behaviorally. These statements should in turn refer to the posted tables and figures illustrating the findings.

- In the Discussion or Conclusions, recapitulate what was found and speculate about what it means. Given space limitations, any speculation must be extremely brief, emphasizing observed ties between the hypothesis and obtained results. Save discussion of further implications and future directions for research for your prepared 2- to 3-minute speech.

All the individual components of the poster can be mounted on colored paper or poster board. A single color can unify a poster or, alternatively, a few different background colors can be used to highlight the different sections of the work (e.g., the Results, tables, and figures might be mounted on the same color). As to color choice, stick to the "less is more" dictum—colors that are garish or not found in nature are not only hard on one's eyes, they detract from the poster's findings. Remember, your goal is to arouse intellectual curiosity, not raise eyebrows.

When all the components are written and produced, play around with the layout a bit (see again Figure 10.1) until you achieve an easy-to-read display. You must decide whether viewers should read across the poster or up and down as they move from left to right. Selecting an appropriate format depends upon the amount of detail you have to share. Before you finalize it, ask a peer to read the layout to make sure it is easy to follow.

Here are a few final thoughts about putting together a poster presentation. Ideally, you should be able to put up and take down your poster in a few minutes. If you run out of handouts (a flattering circumstance), have a pad and pencil handy so that you can jot down names and addresses,

Table 10.7. A Checklist for Creating a Poster Presentation

_____ 1. Is the poster title short, descriptive, and legible from 15 to 20 feet away?

_____ 2. Do author (and any coauthor) name and institutional affiliation appear under the title?

_____ 3. Is the poster display attractive and organized (colorful but not garish or visually jarring)?

_____ 4. Is the written text in each section (introduction, Method, Results, Discussion or Conclusions) short, no more than three paragraphs in length?

_____ 5. Are all tables and figures simple and self-explanatory, as well as supported by the poster's text?

_____ 6. Is the main message or research finding clearly highlighted?

_____ 7. Are short, APA-style copies of the poster available as handouts (with your e-mail and mailing addresses included therein)?

_____ 8. Have the poster and handout been carefully and thoroughly checked for spelling and grammatical errors, as well as deviations from APA style?

_____ 9. Have you memorized a 2- to 3-minute summary of your work?

_____ 10. Do you have thumbtacks or tape for mounting the poster display?

then mail copies when you return home. Table 10.7 provides a checklist for creating a poster.

RETURN TO WRITING: SUBMITTING YOUR RESEARCH TO A JOURNAL

The ultimate form of public presentation is submitting your research to a psychology journal for review and possible publication. By doing so you are participating in the scientific enterprise and upholding a scholarly tradition. This road is not for the faint of heart or for individuals who demand instant gratification. As a form of public presentation, submitting to a journal takes time, energy, effort, stamina, and a willingness to wait. If you enjoy the process of writing and research, I hope that you will accept this last challenge and think about sharing your work in print.

Student Journals

There are two broad categories of journals in psychology: student journals and professional journals. Student journals are designed to publish the work of undergraduate students in psychology and, occasionally, graduate student efforts. Some student journals are published "in-house," that is, a faculty supervisor and a group of students (serving as reviewers and editors) create a departmental journal containing student papers. Such papers can be based on class projects and term papers, as well as on independent studies and honors projects. Other student journals are designed to have a wider audience than a single department or campus, soliciting student manuscripts from around the nation. Four of these national student journals and their addresses are listed in Table 10.8.

Professional Journals

Professional journals, of course, are the place where active researchers, scholars, and teachers publish their work (see the appendix; for a more extensive list, see APA, 1990). Besides their target audiences, a major difference between professional and student journals is the competition involved in getting papers accepted for publication. Professional journals

---

Table 10.8. Some National Undergraduate Student Journals

Journal of Undergraduate Studies	*Modern Psychological Studies: Journal of Undergraduate Research*
Department of Psychology	Department of Psychology
Pace University	University of Tennessee at Chattanooga
861 Bedford Road	Chattanooga, TN 37403-2598
Pleasantville, NY 10570	mpsedit@cecasun.utc.edu
The Journal of Psychology and the Behavioral Sciences	*The Psi Chi Journal of Undergraduate Research*
Department of Psychology	Psi Chi National Office
Fairleigh Dickinson University	407 East Fifth Street, Suite B
Madison, NJ 07904	Chattanooga, TN 37043-1823
http://view.fdu/default.aspx?id=784	http://www.psichi.org/pubs/journal

---

Note: These journals publish student writing and research in psychology. Information regarding manuscript preparation and submission deadlines can be obtained by contacting the journals directly.

often have extremely high rates of rejection so that only a relatively small number of submitted articles is accepted for eventual publication. Student journals are apt to be less competitive, though the submitted work must still be of high quality.

Can students publish their work in professional journals? Yes, indeed, they can. Faculty advisors frequently encourage their best students to write up and submit their work to mainstream journals. It is not unusual to see papers in print that involved some collaborative work between students and their teachers; the latter often appear as co-authors. Your instructor can probably give you some idea as to whether your work is an appropriate submission for a professional or a student journal.

Sternberg (1993; see also Sternberg, 2000a, 2000b) lists several matters to consider when a writer is deciding whether to submit a manuscript for publication:

- **Journal quality.** Not all journals are equal in quality or recognized prestige. It is difficult to get a paper accepted for publication by some journals; it is relatively easy to get one accepted by others. In general, difficulty is associated with quality, so an acceptance in a higher-quality journal means more to peers. As an author, you must determine your own publishing goals, including how you feel about coping with rejection and how much effort you are willing to put into revision and resubmission.

- **Journal content and scope.** All journals contain some statement of purpose or submission guidelines information for would-be authors about the sorts of papers that are desired for submission, review, and publication. Send your submission to the right kind of journal. A social psychology experiment is most appropriate for a social rather than a developmental journal, a data-less theory paper does not belong in an empirical journal, and so on. Read author instructions carefully and follow them to the letter.

- **Audience.** Who reads the journal? Does it have a wide readership or a relatively small circulation? Most authors want to be sure that their work is read and recognized by people who can both appreciate and use it. Take a look at the editorial board and the papers appearing in a recent issue—both will tell you something about the readership.

- **Paper length or word limits.** Some journals have no page limits for submissions, whereas others have strict requirements (e.g., no more than 6,000 words). Always make certain you are familiar with the required lengths. If no specific information is provided in a journal's submission guidelines, estimate the norm by looking at recently published articles or contact the journal's editor directly.

- **Time before publication.** It can take months for a submission to be reviewed and, once you receive feedback, time and care are usually necessary for a revision to be done. Resubmission usually means rereview, so it can take considerable time before a paper is accepted (if it is accepted—rejection is a more common experience). Imagine that your work is accepted: When will it appear in print? The sobering fact is that many quality journals have a publication time lag of between 12 and 18 months *after* acceptance. Academic publishing takes patience, and you must decide if you are willing to wait.

- **Submission and printing costs.** Well-established, high-quality journals cover postage and printing costs through subscriptions and advertising. Fledgling efforts or smaller journals must often charge both submission (review) costs and, once acceptance occurs, printing fees. Most psychologists adhere to the perception that fee-charging journals are of lower stature than no-cost journals. Choose wisely. Be sure you know whether any review or production costs exist before you submit your work to any journal.

- **Any author restrictions.** Some journals are by invitation only; others require an author to belong to an organization before a submission will be considered for review. Restrictions like these and others can usually be found in a journal's submission guidelines.

One more point merits mention: A manuscript can be submitted for review to only one journal at a time. It is both bad faith and bad form to submit the same paper for simultaneous review at different journals. Doing so is committing an ethical violation on a par with plagiarism.

Submission, Peer Review, and Editorial Decision: A Process Outline

Submitting a manuscript for review is not an arduous process, but it does require attention to detail. Much of your prior experience drafting and writing an APA-style paper is an important part of the process. You should reread or review any material from prior chapters that can help you prepare a final draft for submission.

Table 10.9. Process for Submitting a Manuscript for Editorial
Review and Publication Decision

  1. Identify an appropriate journal.
  2. Review journal's submission guidelines.
  3. Draft an APA-style manuscript in accordance with guidelines.
  4. Seek local peer feedback on manuscript.
  5. Revise manuscript into final draft based on peer feedback: Go back to step 4 as needed.
  6. Write cover letter to journal editor.
  7. Submit manuscript and cover letter to journal editor
  8. Receive journal decision (acceptance, request for revisions, or rejection) and peer reviewers' feedback: If manuscript is accepted, go to step 10.
  9. If manuscript revision is requested, go back to step 5; otherwise, go to step 1.
  10. Follow editorial directions, review copyedited manuscript or printed text, make necessary changes, and return to journal for publication: Article is then "in press."
  11. Wait for article to appear in print.

Table 10.9 outlines the usual steps involved in submitting and steering a manuscript through the review, editorial, and publication process. The steps shown here are somewhat truncated—there are many activities included within each one—but they represent a general account of the process. Step 1 involves a discussion with your instructor or academic advisor, and possibly a bit of library research, to select a journal that represents a "good fit" for your work (Warren, 2000). Submission to the wrong journal is a common reason that manuscripts are rejected. Choose well. The second step is just as important: Take the time to read the journal's "Instructions to Authors" or "Submission Guidelines" to learn what sort of work the journal accepts, any special conditions or requirements, and how to prepare the manuscript (see step 2). Steps 3 and 4 require that you draft a manuscript and seek peer feedback on it. Following review of the peer feedback, revising for the final manuscript occurs as step 5, though recursion back to step 4 for additional peer review is possible. Table 10.10 contains a checklist for preparing the final draft of a manuscript. The appearance of a manuscript does influence how it is received—and perceived—by editors and peer reviewers (APA, 2001; see also, Sternberg, 2000a).

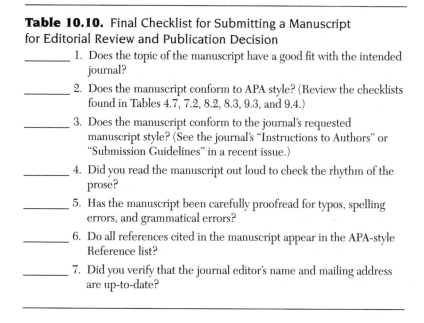

Table 10.10. Final Checklist for Submitting a Manuscript
for Editorial Review and Publication Decision

_____ 1. Does the topic of the manuscript have a good fit with the intended journal?

_____ 2. Does the manuscript conform to APA style? (Review the checklists found in Tables 4.7, 7.2, 8.2, 8.3, 9.3, and 9.4.)

_____ 3. Does the manuscript conform to the journal's requested manuscript style? (See the journal's "Instructions to Authors" or "Submission Guidelines" in a recent issue.)

_____ 4. Did you read the manuscript out loud to check the rhythm of the prose?

_____ 5. Has the manuscript been carefully proofread for typos, spelling errors, and grammatical errors?

_____ 6. Do all references cited in the manuscript appear in the APA-style Reference list?

_____ 7. Did you verify that the journal editor's name and mailing address are up-to-date?

Once the final manuscript is finished, a cover letter addressed to the journal's editor must be written (see step 6 in Table 10.9). Cover letters contain brief information for the editor, including the manuscript's title, length, number of tables and figures, whether the data have ever been presented at a conference, and contact information about you, the manuscript's author (e.g., postal and e-mail addresses and telephone number). (More-detailed information about cover letters can be found in Section 5.26 of the *Publication Manual*; APA, 2001.) Step 7 involves submitting the manuscript (and some specified number of photocopies) and the cover letter to the journal editor, who will initiate the review.

Patience, Patience, Patience

Following submission, authors need to do one thing: Be patient. The editorial review process can take several months. Generally, this waiting game reflects the amount of effort and detail that a journal's team puts into crafting fair and helpful reviews. Most editors will send a manuscript to three or more peer reviewers who will write detailed comments about the strengths and weaknesses of your work, highlighting its faults and ways it can be improved

(Calfee & Valencia, 1991). Three outcomes of an editorial review are possible (see step 8 in Table 10.9): **Acceptance** of your paper (there are always some minor revisions), a specific **request for revisions** based on the peer reviews (a good thing—you have a chance to revise and improve the manuscript and send it back for a second review), or **rejection** (never pleasant, but you can still use the reviews to revise the work for submission to some other journal). There are several common reasons for rejection or a request for revisions (e.g., Eichorn & VandenBos, 1985; Sternberg, 1993, 2000a):

- Limited literature review
- Research topic lacking empirical or theoretical depth
- Hard-to-understand research goal or hypothesis
- Incoherent writing
- Sloppy manuscript appearance
- Significant flaws in experimental procedures
- Inappropriate statistical analyses and interpretations
- Overly long or wordy manuscript
- Failure to follow APA style

Step 9, then, directs you to earlier parts of the submission process depending on whether a rejection or a request for revisions is the editorial decision. Steps 10 and 11 cover activities related to accepted manuscripts. By exerting effort and patience, there is always the happy chance that you will see your article appear in print. Contributing to the science of psychology through a fine piece of writing is a true achievement.

EXERCISES

1. Revise a research paper and turn it into a conference presentation. Write a short and a long Abstract based on the paper.
2. Outline a talk based on a paper. How does the talk differ from the written text?
3. Plan and then host a symposium with classmates.
4. Create a poster based on a paper.
5. Do some reflective writing in your research notebook: What have you learned about writing in psychology? How has your writing changed?

Appendix

SOME JOURNALS
IN PSYCHOLOGY

There are numerous journals that examine psychological topics. Below is a current list of some major psychology journals; your reading and library research will no doubt identify others.

GENERAL PSYCHOLOGY JOURNALS

American Psychologist
Contemporary Psychology: APA Review of Books
Current Directions in Psychological Science
Psychological Bulletin
Psychological Review
Psychological Science

CLINICAL PSYCHOLOGY

Cognitive Therapy and Research
Journal of Abnormal Psychology
Journal of Consulting and Clinical Psychology
Journal of Counseling Psychology
Prevention and Treatment
Professional Psychology: Research and Practice
Psychological Assessment

COGNITIVE PSYCHOLOGY

Cognitive Psychology
Journal of Memory and Language
Journal of Verbal Learning and Verbal Behavior
Perception and Psychophysics

DEVELOPMENTAL PSYCHOLOGY

Adolescence
Child Development
Cognitive Development
Developmental Psychology
Infant Behavior and Development
Journal of Experimental Child Psychology
Psychology and Aging

EXPERIMENTAL PSYCHOLOGY

Journal of Applied Behavior Analysis
Journal of Educational Psychology
Journal of Experimental Psychology: Animal Behavior Processes
Journal of Experimental Psychology: Applied
Journal of Experimental Psychology: General
Journal of Experimental Psychology: Human Perception and Performance
Journal of Experimental Psychology: Learning, Memory, and Cognition
Journal of the Experimental Analysis of Behavior

PSYCHOLOGY OF SEX AND GENDER

Psychology of Women Quarterly
Sex Roles

PSYCHOBIOLOGY AND NEUROSCIENCE

Animal Behavior
Animal Learning & Behavior
Behavioral Neuroscience
Biological Psychology
Brain and Cognition
Developmental Psychobiology
Experimental and Clinical Psychopharmacology
Neuropsychology
Psychobiology
Psychophysiology

SOCIAL AND PERSONALITY PSYCHOLOGY

Basic and Applied Social Psychology
Journal of Experimental Social Psychology

Journal of Personality and Social Psychology
Journal of Research in Personality
Journal of Social and Clinical Psychology
Personality and Social Psychology Bulletin
Social Cognition

OTHER MISCELLANEOUS JOURNALS

Emotion
Health Psychology
Journal of Applied Psychology
Journal of Comparative Psychology
Journal of Educational Psychology
Journal of Family Psychology
Journal of Social Issues
Personnel Psychology
Psychological Methods
Psychology, Public Policy, and Law
Rehabilitation Psychology
Teaching of Psychology

References

Abelson, R. P. (1995). *Statistics as principled argument*. Hillsdale, NJ: Erlbaum.

American Psychological Association. (1990). *Journals in psychology: A resource listing for authors* (3rd ed.). Washington, DC: Author.

American Psychological Association. (2001). *Publication manual of the American Psychological Association* (5th ed.). Washington, DC: Author.

Anderson, N. H. (2001). *Empirical direction in design and analysis.* Mahwah, NJ: Erlbaum.

Azar, B. (1999, May). APA statistics task force prepares to release recommendations for public comment. *APA Monitor,* 9.

Barker, J. (2001). *Finding information on the Internet: A tutorial: Metasearch engines.* Retrieved November 7, 2001, from University of California at Berkeley Library Web site: http://www.lib.berkeley.edu/TeachingLib/Guides/Internet/MetaSearch.html

Barrass, R. (1978). *Scientists must write: A guide to better writing for scientists, engineers and students.* London: Chapman and Hall.

Bem, D. J. (1987). Writing the empirical journal article. In M. P. Zanna & J. M. Darley (Eds.), *The compleat academic: A practical guide for the beginning social scientist* (pp. 171–201). New York: Random House.

Bem, D. J. (1995). Writing a review article for *Psychological Bulletin. Psychological Bulletin, 118,* 172–177.

Bem, D. J. (2000). Writing an empirical article. In R. J. Sternberg (Ed.), *Guide to publishing in psychology journals* (pp. 3–16). Cambridge: Cambridge University Press.

Benham, G., Woody, E. Z., Wilson, K. S., & Nash, M. R. (2006). Expect the unexpected: Ability, attitude, and responsiveness to hypnosis. *Journal of Personality and Social Psychology, 91*, 342–350.

Berger, K. S. (1988). *The developing person through the lifespan* (2nd ed.). New York: Worth.

Bergeson, T. R., & Trehub, S. E. (2002). Absolute pitch and tempo in mothers' songs to infants. *Psychological Science, 13*, 72–75.

Boice, R. (1990). Faculty resistance to writing-intensive courses. *Teaching of Psychology, 17*, 13–17.

Boice, R. (1994). *How writers journey to comfort and fluency: A psychological adventure.* Westport, CT: Praeger.

Booth, W. C., Colomb, G. G., & Williams, J. M. (1995). *The craft of research.* Chicago: University of Chicago Press.

Brooks, R., & Meltzoff, A. N. (2002). The importance of eyes: How infants interpret adult looking behavior. *Developmental Psychology, 38*, 958–966.

Calfee, R. (2000). What does it all mean: The Discussion. In R. J. Sternberg (Ed.), *Guide to publishing in psychology journals* (pp. 133–145). New York: Cambridge University Press.

Calfee, R. C., & Valencia, R. R. (1991). *APA guide to preparing manuscripts for journal publication.* Washington, DC: American Psychological Association.

Cameron, L., & Hart, J. (1992). Assessment of PsycLIT competence, attitudes, and instructional methods. *Teaching of Psychology, 19*, 239–242.

Cohen, J. (1990). Things I have learned (so far). *American Psychologist, 45*, 1304–1312.

Cross, K. P., & Angelo, T. A. (1988). *Classroom assessment techniques: A handbook for faculty.* Ann Arbor, MI: National Center for Research to Improve Postsecondary Teaching and Learning.

Cuseo, J. (2005). *The one-minute paper.* Retrieved September 9, 2005, from http://www.oncourseworkshop.com/Awareness012.htm

Daniel, D. B. (2005). How to ruin a perfectly good lecture. In B. Perlman, L. McCann, & W. Buskist (Eds.), *Voices of NITOP: Favorite talks from the National Institute on the Teaching of Psychology* (pp. 119–130). Washington, DC: American Psychological Society.

Dawes, R. M. (1991, June). *Discovering "human nature" versus discovering how people cope with the task of getting through college: An extension of Sears' argument.* Paper presented at the Third Annual Convention of the American Psychological Society, Washington, DC.

Diener, E., & Seligman, M. E. P. (2002). Very happy people. *Psychological Science, 13,* 81–84.

Dougherty, S. B. (2001). *Prejudice in hiring practices related to physical attractiveness and personality traits.* Unpublished student paper, Department of Psychology, Moravian College, Bethlehem, PA.

Dunn, D. S. (1994). Lessons learned from an interdisciplinary writing course: Implications for student writing in psychology. *Teaching of Psychology, 21,* 223–227.

Dunn, D. S. (1999). *The practical researcher: A student guide to conducting psychological research.* New York: McGraw-Hill.

Dunn, D. S. (2000). Social psychological issues in rehabilitation. In R. Frank & T. R. Elliott (Eds.), *Handbook of Rehabilitation Psychology* (pp. 565–584). Washington, DC: American Psychological Association.

Dunn, D. S. (2001). *Statistics and data analysis for the behavioral sciences.* New York: McGraw-Hill.

Dunn, D. S. (2001, February). *Writing in research methods, methods for research writing.* Invited presentation at the 13th Annual Southeastern Conference on the Teaching of Psychology, Atlanta, GA.

Dunn, D. S. (in preparation). *Research methods for social psychology.* London: Blackwell Publishing.

Dunn, D. S., & Elliott, T. R. (2005). Revisiting a constructive classic: Wright's *Physical disability: A psychosocial approach. Rehabilitation Psychology,* 50, 183–189.

Eichorn, D. H., & VandenBos, G. R. (1985). Dissemination of scientific and professional knowledge: Journal publication within APA. *American Psychologist, 40,* 1309–1316.

Eisenberg, N. (1997). Editorial. *Psychological Bulletin, 122,* 3–4.

Eisenberg, N. (2000). Writing a literature review. In R. J. Sternberg (Ed.), *Guide to publishing in psychology journals* (pp. 17–34). New York: Cambridge University Press.

Elbow, P., & Belanoff, P. (1995). *A community of writers: A workshop course in writing* (2nd ed.). New York: McGraw-Hill.

Fiske, S. T. (2002). What we know now about bias and intergroup conflict, the problem of the century. *Current Directions in Psychological Science, 11,* 123–128.

Flesch, R. F. (1962). *The art of plain talk.* London and New York: Collier-Macmillan.

Frank, E., & Brandstatter, V. (2002). Approach versus avoidance: Different types of commitment in intimate relationships. *Journal of Personality and Social Psychology, 82,* 208–221.

Gasper, K., & Clore, G. L. (2002). Attending to the big picture: Mood and global versus local processing of visual information. *Psychological Science, 13,* 34–40.

Gibaldi, J. (2003). *MLA handbook for writers of research papers* (6th ed.). New York: Modern Language Association of America.

Glass, D. C., Singer, J. E., & Friedman, L. N. (1969). Psychic cost of adaptation to an environmental stressor. *Journal of Personality and Social Psychology, 12,* 200–210.

Goleman, D. (1984, December 18). Social anxiety: New focus leads to insights and therapy. *The New York Times,* pp. C1, C14.

Gronbeck, B. E., McKerrow, R. E., Ehninger, D., & Monroe, A. H. (1997). *Principles and types of speech communication* (13th ed.). New York: Longman.

Hacker, D. (1991). *The Bedford handbook for writers* (3rd ed.). Boston: Bedford Books of St. Martin's Press.

Hahner, J. C., Sokoloff, M. A., & Salisch, S. L. (1993). *Speaking clearly: Improving voice and diction* (4th ed.). New York: McGraw-Hill.

Hall, E. T. (1963). A system for the notation of proxemic behavior. *American Anthropologist, 65,* 1003–1026.

Hall, E. T. (1966). *The hidden dimension.* Garden City, NY: Doubleday.

Hayes, J. R., & Flower, L. S. (1986). Writing research and the writer. *American Psychologist, 41,* 1106–1113.

Howard, R. M. (1999). *Standing in the shadows of giants: Plagiarists, authors, collaborators.* Stamford, CT: Ablex.

Howard, W. A., & Barton, J. H. (1986). *Thinking on paper.* New York: Morrow.

Hubbuch, S. M. (1985). *Writing research papers across the curriculum.* New York: Holt, Rinehart and Winston.

Hult, C. A. (1996). *Researching and writing in the social sciences.* Boston: Allyn and Bacon.

Jordan, C. H., & Zanna, M. P. (1999). Appendix: How to read a journal article in social psychology. In R. F. Baumeister (Ed.), *The self in social psychology* (pp. 461–470). Philadelphia: Taylor & Francis.

Joswick, K. E. (1994). Getting the most from PsycLIT: Recommendations for searching. *Teaching of Psychology, 21,* 49–53.

Kendall, P. C., Silk, J. S., & Chu, B. C. (2000). Introducing your research report: Writing the introduction. In R. J. Sternberg (Ed.), *Guide to publishing in psychology journals* (pp. 41–57). New York: Cambridge University Press.

Kimchi, R., & Hadad, B.-S. (2002). Influence of past experience on perceptual grouping. *Psychological Science, 13,* 41–47.

King, S. (2000). *On writing: A memoir of the craft.* New York: Pocket Books.

Kintsch, W., & Cacioppo, J. T. (1994). Introduction to the 100th anniversary issue of the *Psychological Review. Psychological Review, 101,* 195–199.

Kirby, M., & Miller, N. (1985). Medline searching on BRS Colleague: Search success of untrained end users in a medical school and hospital. In *National Online Meeting Proceedings (1985)* (pp. 255–263). Medford, NJ: Learned Information.

Knatterud, M. E. (1991, February). Writing with the patient in mind: Don't add insult to injury. *American Medical Writers Association Journal, 6,* 283–339.

Lepore, S. J., & Smyth, J. M. (Eds.). (2002). *The writing cure: How expressive writing promotes health and well-being.* Washington, DC: American Psychological Association.

Libby, L. K., & Eibach, R. P. (2002). Looking back in time: Self-concept change affects visual perspective in autobiographical memory. *Journal of Personality and Social Psychology, 82,* 167–179.

Library of Congress (2005). *Library of Congress Subject Headings* (28th ed.). Washington, DC: Author.

Lickel, B., Schmader, T., & Hamilton, D. L. (2003). A case of collective responsibility: Who else was to blame for the Columbine High School shootings? *Personality and Social Psychology Bulletin, 29,* 194–204.

Lucas, S. E. (1995). *The art of public speaking* (5th ed.). New York: McGraw-Hill.

Ludwig, T. E. Daniel, D. B., Froman, R., & Mathie, V. A. (2005). Using multimedia in classroom presentations: Best principles. Retrieved August 22, 2006, from http://www.teachpsych. lemoyne.edu/teachpsych/div/docs/classroommultimedia.rtf

Maggio, R. (1991). *The bias-free word finder: A dictionary of nondiscriminatory language.* Boston: Beacon Press.

Martin, D. W. (1996). *Doing psychology experiments* (4th ed.). Pacific Grove, CA: Brooks/Cole.

McCarthy, M., & Pusateri, T. P. (2006). Teaching students to use electronic databases. In W. Buskist & S. F. Davis (Eds.), *Handbook of the teaching of psychology* (pp. 107-111). Malden, MA: Blackwell.

Myers, D. G. (2002). *Social psychology* (7th ed.). New York: McGraw-Hill.

Nash, S., & Wilson, M. (1991). Value-added bibliographic instruction: Teaching students to find the right citations. *RSR: Reference Services Review, 19,* 87–92.

Nicol, A. A. M., & Pexman, P. M. (1999). *Presenting your findings: A practical guide for creating tables.* Washington, DC: American Psychological Association.

Nicol, A. A. M., & Pexman, P. M. (2003). *Displaying your findings: A practical guide for creating figures, posters, and presentations.* Washington, DC: American Psychological Association.

O'Conner, P. T. (1996). *Woe is I: The grammarphobe's guide to better English in plain English.* New York: Putnam.

O'Conner, P. T. (1999). *Words fail me: What everyone who writes should know about writing.* New York: Harcourt Brace.

Oskamp, S. (Ed.). (2000). *Reducing prejudice and discrimination.* Mahwah, NJ: Erlbaum.

Parrott, L., III. (1999). *How to write psychology papers* (2nd ed.). New York: Longman.

Pechenik, J. A. (2001). *A short guide to writing in biology* (4th ed.). New York: Addison Wesley Longman.

Pennebaker, J. W. (1997). *Opening up: The healing power of expressing emotions.* New York: Guilford.

Pennebaker, J. W., & Graybeal, A. (2001). Patterns of natural language use: Disclosure, personality, and social integration. *Current Directions in Psychological Science, 10,* 90–93.

Peterson, C. (1996). Writing rough drafts. In F. T. L. Leong & J. T. Austin (Eds.), *The psychology research handbook: A guide for graduate students and research assistants* (pp. 282–290). Thousand Oaks, CA: Sage.

Poincaré, H. (1913). *The foundation of science.* New York: Science Press.

Prohaska, V. (2001, October). *Exorcising plagiarism: Helping students avoid plagiarizing.* Paper presented at the Seventh Annual Northeast Conference for Teachers of Psychology, Danbury, CT.

Reich, J. (2001, October). *Teaching to learn and learning to teach.* Presentation at the Seventh Annual Northeast Conference for Teachers of Psychology, Danbury, CT.

Reis, H. T. (2000). Writing effectively about design. In R. J. Sternberg (Ed.), *Guide to publishing in psychology journals* (pp. 81–97). New York: Cambridge University Press.

Rosenthal, R., & Rosnow, R. L. (1991). *Essentials of behavioral research: Methods and data analysis* (2nd ed.). New York: McGraw-Hill.

Rosnow, R. L., & Rosenthal, R. (1996). *Beginning behavioral research* (2nd ed.). Upper Saddle River, NJ: Prentice Hall.

Salovey, P. (2000). Results that get results: Telling a good story. In R. J. Sternberg (Ed.), *Guide to publishing in psychology journals* (pp. 121–132). New York: Cambridge University Press.

Schultz, K., & Salomon, K. (1990, February 1). End users respond to CD-ROM. *Library Journal*, 56–57.

Scott, J. M., Koch, R. E., Scott, G. M., & Garrison, S. M. (1999). *The psychology student writer's manual.* Upper Saddle River, NJ: Prentice Hall.

Sears, D. O. (1986). College sophomores in the laboratory: Influences of a narrow data base on social psychology's view of human nature. *Journal of Personality and Social Psychology, 51,* 515–539.

Sewell, W., & Teitelbaum, S. (1986). Observations of end-user online searching behavior over eleven years. *Journal of the American Society for Information Science, 37,* 234–245.

Shadish, W. R., Jr. (1989). The perception and evaluation of quality in science. In B. Gholson, W. R. Shadish, Jr., R. A. Neimeyer, & A. C. Houts (Eds.), *Psychology of science: Contributions to metascience* (pp. 383–426). Cambridge: Cambridge University Press.

Shaughnessy, J. J., & Zechmeister, E. B. (1997). *Research methods in psychology* (4th ed.). New York: McGraw-Hill.

Silverman, J., Hughes, E., & Wienbroer, D. R. (2002). *Rules of thumb: A guide for writers* (5th ed.). New York: McGraw-Hill.

Skinner, B. F. (1981). How to discover what to say—a talk to students. *The Behavior Analyst, 4,* 1–7.

Slatcher, R. B., & Pennebaker, J. W. (2006). How do I love thee? Let me count the words: The social effects of expressive writing. *Psychological Science, 17,* 660–664.

Smith, R. A. (2000). Documenting your scholarship: Citations and references. In R. J. Sternberg (Ed.), *Guide to publishing in psychology journals* (pp. 146–157). New York: Cambridge University Press.

Sternberg, R. J. (1992). *Psychological Bulletin's* top 10 "Hit Parade." *Psychological Bulletin, 112,* 387–388.

Sternberg, R. (1993). *The psychologist's companion: A guide to scientific writing for students and researchers* (3rd ed.). New York: Cambridge University Press.

Sternberg, R. J. (2000a). Titles and Abstracts: They only sound unimportant. In R. J. Sternberg (Ed.), *Guide to publishing in psychology journals* (pp. 37–40). New York: Cambridge University Press.

Sternberg, R. J. (2000b). *Guide to publishing in psychology journals.* New York: Cambridge University Press.

Sternberg, R. J. (2000c). Article writing 101: A crib sheet of 50 tips for the final exam. In R. J. Sternberg (Ed.), *Guide to publishing in psychology journals* (pp. 199–206). New York: Cambridge University Press.

Sternberg, R. J. (2002, January). On civility in reviewing. *APS Observer, 15.*

Sternberg, R. J., & Gordeeva, T. (1996). The anatomy of impact: What makes an article influential? *Psychological Science, 7,* 69–75.

Sternberg, R. J., & Grajek, S. (1984). The nature of love. *Journal of Personality and Social Psychology, 47,* 312–329.

Strunk, W., Jr., & White, E. B. (1972). *The elements of style.* New York: Macmillan.

Szuchman, L. T. (2002). *Writing with style: APA style made easy.* (2nd ed.). Belmont, CA: Wadsworth/Thompson Learning.

Talarico J. M., & Rubin, D. G. (2003). Confidence, not consistency, characterizes flashbulb memories. *Psychological Science, 14,* 455–461.

Thaiss, C., & Sanford, J. F. (2000). *Writing for psychology.* Boston: Allyn and Bacon.

Tufte, E. R. (1983). *The visual display of quantitative information.* Cheshire, CT: Graphics Press.

University of Chicago Press. (2003). *The Chicago manual of style: The essential guide for writers, editors, and publishers* (15th ed.). Chicago: Author.

Walker, A., Jr. (Ed.). (1997). *Thesaurus of psychological index terms* (8th ed.). Washington, DC: American Psychological Association.

Wallas, G. (1926). *The art of thought.* New York: Harcourt, Brace.

Warren, M. G. (2000). Reading reviews, suffering rejection, and advocating for your paper. In R. J. Sternberg (Ed.), *Guide to publishing in psychology journals* (pp. 169–186). New York: Cambridge University Press.

Wegner, D. M. (1989). *White bears and other unwanted thoughts: Suppression, obsession, and the psychology of mental control.* New York: Guilford.

Wilkinson, L., & the Task Force on Statistical Inference. (1999). Statistical methods in psychology journals: Guidelines and explanations. *American Psychologist, 54,* 594–604.

Williamon, A., & Valentine, E. (2002). The role of retrieval structures in memorizing music. *Cognitive Psychology, 44,* 1–32.

Williams, B. T., & Brydon-Miller, M. (1997). *Concept to completion: Writing well in the social sciences.* Fort Worth, TX: Harcourt Brace.

Woodzicka, J. A., & LaFrance, M. (2001). Real versus imagined gender harassment. *Journal of Social Issues, 57,* 15–30.

Wright, B. A. (1991). Labeling: The need for greater person–environment individuation. In C. R. Snyder & D. R. Forsyth (Eds.), *Handbook of social and clinical psychology: The health perspective* (pp. 469–487). New York: Pergamon.

Zinsser, W. (1990). *On writing well: An information guide to writing nonfiction* (4th ed.). New York: Harper.

Credits

R.P. Abelson, *Statistics as Principled Argument,* p. 11. Copyright © 1995 by Lawrence Erlbaum Association, Inc. Reprinted with permission.

American Psychological Association, *Publication Manual of the American Psychological Association,* Fifth Edition, 2001, pp. 61 and 196.

Robert Barrass, *Scientists Must Write,* pp. 39 and 56. Copyright © 1978 Robert Barrass. Reprinted by permission of Thomson Publishing Services.

Daryl J. Bem et al., "Writing the Empirical Journal Article," from *The Complete Academic: A Practical Guide for the Beginning Social Scientist,* eds. Anna and Darley, p. 175. Copyright © 1975. Used with permission.

K.S. Berger, *The Developing Person Through the Lifespan,* Second Edition, p. 32. Copyright © 1988. Reprinted by permission from Worth Publishers.

Excerpts. Tonya R. Bergeson and Sandra E. Trehub, "Absolute Pitch and Tempo to Mothers: Songs to Infants," *Psychological Science,* Vol. 13, No. 1, January 2002, p. 72. Copyright © 2002 Blackwell Publishers. Used with permission.

Robert Boice, "Faculty Resistance to Writing Intensive Courses," *Teaching of Psychology,* 1990, pp. 13–17. Copyright © 1990 Lawrence Erlbaum Associations, Inc. Used with permission.

Robert Boice, *How Writers Journey to Comfort and Fluency,* p. 32. Copyright © 1994 by Robert Boice. Reproduced by permission of Greenwood Publishing Group, Inc., Westport, CT.

Excerpt from Wayne C. Booth et al., *The Craft of Research,* Second Edition, pp. 43–44, 82–84. Copyright © 2003. Reprinted by permission from the University of Chicago Press.

Excerpt from Rechele Brooks and Andrew Meltzoff, "The importance of eyes: how infants interpret adult looking behavior" *Developmental Psychology,* 2002, Nov. Vol. 38(6) 958–966. Copyright © 2002 by the American Psychological Association. Reprinted with permission.

Excerpt from D.B. Daniel, "How to Ruin a Perfectly Good Lecture" from Perlman et al., *Voices of Experience: Memorable Talks from The National Institutes on the Teaching of Psychology,* Washington DC, American Psychological Association.

Student paper. Sarah Dougherty, "Unpublished Course Paper." Reprinted by permission.

Index

A *"t"* following a page number indicates a table; an *"f"* following a page number indicates a figure.